EXTINCTION OF TAX AS WE KNOW IT

Nitin Agarwal

Published by Nitin Agarwal
First Edition, 2025
ISBN (Paperback): 978-93-344-2874-2

For permissions and inquiries, contact:
Nitin_agarwalla@hotmail.com
www.nitin-agarwal.com

Dedicated to

My parents – *Vidya Devi Agarwalla* and *Late Basant Kumar Agarwalla* – your blessings continue to guide me toward meaning.

&

My wife, *Jyotika*, and our children – *Ananya* and *Viaan* – for making it all worthwhile, unconditionally.

CONTENTS

FOREWORD

I've been a journalist in the legal sector for nearly a decade now, and in that time, I have received more article pitches than are possible to remember.

What I do remember is that most are immediately irrelevant. Some are at least on-topic but hopelessly bland, while perishingly few present something prescient.

Cue the entry of Nitin Agarwal into my professional life in September 2025 via an inauspicious e-mail.

We then arranged an interview to celebrate his recent distinction of being named International Tax Review's EMEA In-House Indirect Tax Leader of the Year. A reputable accolade, of course, but fairly routine coverage.

But, as it quickly turned out, there was more to Agarwal's story than met the eye. This guy is writing what? A business fiction novel about tax transformation?

Webinars, conferences and thought leadership campaigns, I've seen plenty of those. This, on the other hand (and if you'll excuse the pun), was a novel idea.

But my initial scepticism evaporated once I flicked through *Extinction of Tax as We Know It*'s pages, which seemed to be stained by the tears of Earth's exasperated in-house tax professionals.

In a dramatic and captivating way, it encapsulated the struggle of tax functions, which are often under-resourced, siloed and ill-equipped to deal with the strains of increasingly stringent compliance.

Speaking to the man himself solidified that I was looking at a corporate bible enriched with two decades of experience, a playbook to navigate a profession that had become proliferated with more technology solutions than you could shake an ERP system at.

For aspiring tax leaders, making sense of this modern world is mandatory. According to an April 2025 report from Thomson Reuters, more than four out of five (85%) tax and accountancy firms expect generative AI to become integral to their workflows within five years.

The report also showed that 88% of tax and accounting professionals consider technology as either significant or integral to their overall strategies.

Anyone who has studied the profession at even a surface level in recent years will be unsurprised by these results. Whether it's new e-invoicing mandates, real-time reporting or AI-powered audits, cutting-edge technology is infiltrating every corner of compliance.

What better way, then, to upskill multiple generations of tax professionals than with the power of story?

Because, ultimately, despite what ChatGPT or CoPilot may have you believe, tax is a human business.

It's true that tomorrow's professional will need to fuse tax excellence with technological know-how, but far more fundamental than that is the ability to navigate fragile egos, communicate effectively and rise above office politics.

After all, how exceptional is your expert advice if nobody listens? This book is peppered with such emotional truths, which extend its resonance far beyond tax.

But if you do plan on carving out a career in or around this often-underestimated profession, *Extinction of Tax as We Know It* is required reading.

Students, graduates and early-career professionals – cling to this tome as the most engaging and practical textbook in your repertoire.

External tax advisers – read this and reconsider whether your counsel could be more considerate of commercial realities.

Corporate tax professionals – absorb the career wisdom and best practices on offer, and thank me later.

Tax as we used to know it may well be extinct, but like a phoenix from the ashes, Agarwal's business fable charts its modern reincarnation.

Thomas Baker
Editor, International Tax Review (ITR)

London
26 November 2025

PREFACE

"Nothing is certain except death and taxes."

When Benjamin Franklin wrote those words in 1789, he could not have imagined a world where even taxes — the ancient engine beneath governments and global commerce — might one day face profound reinvention. Yet that is the moment unfolding around us today.

Extinction of Tax as We Know It is written as a contribution to this moment of change. It draws from the collective experiences of professionals across India, the UAE, and beyond — in classrooms, shared service centres, boardrooms, tax departments, and transformation programmes — all confronting the widening gap between the systems we inherited and the world we now inhabit.

This book is not a prescription. It is a lens — a way of seeing the challenges that modern organisations, and the people within them, confront every day.

Across industries and geographies, a quiet shift is underway:

- Chartered accountants closing books under mounting pressure.
- Tax professionals navigating growing regulatory complexity.
- Finance teams relying on legacy tools for modern demands.
- Internal auditors tracing risk across fragmented processes.
- Project and change managers balancing people, politics, and delivery.
- ERP architects and technologists attempting to modernise ageing systems.
- Students preparing for careers reshaped by automation.
- Educationists and parents wondering what skills the future will demand.
- Leaders sensing that traditional models are no longer enough.

A shared tension runs beneath all of it: organisations are evolving faster than their structures, and technology is advancing faster than the people using it.

This book does not offer magic formulas. Instead, it reflects how transformation truly unfolds — through misalignment, resistance, competing priorities, and the persistence required to move forward. It aims to create awareness, challenge assumptions, and spark new thinking about how tax, finance, and technology must evolve.

It also serves a practical purpose: to help professionals understand the tools reshaping the tax and finance landscape — what they solve, where they fit, and how to evaluate return on investment. It outlines the challenges of implementation, the importance of fit-for-purpose design, the discipline of project management, and the expanding role of tax within organisations. In this new world, unlearning outdated assumptions will be as critical as upskilling into new ones.

At its core, the book looks ahead — to a future where careers are hybrid, data and technology sit beside technical expertise, and human alignment becomes the true differentiator. For leaders, it offers a chance to recognise blind spots. For the next generation, it offers a map of possibilities not yet fully defined.

While this book addresses real challenges, I chose to tell them through a story. Fiction has a way of reaching people that reports, frameworks, and presentations rarely can. Stories bypass our defences; they reveal truth without accusation, and they allow us to see ourselves in the journeys of others. The characters of AlphaCorp are fictional, yet the world they inhabit is unmistakably real — drawn from the lived experiences of professionals navigating transformation every day. Their conflicts, fears, blind spots, and breakthroughs reflect patterns we all recognise. In many ways, this is not just their story. It is the story of countless teams, leaders, and organisations across the globe, and it will resonate with anyone who has felt the tension between what work is and what it must become.

Who Should Read This Book

- CFOs and Finance Leaders seeking strategic clarity
- Heads of Tax and Tax Professionals navigating a changing profession
- ERP, Technology, and Transformation Leaders building the next generation of systems
- Internal Auditors tracing risks across platforms and processes
- Project and Change Managers steering complex organisational shifts
- Students and Young Professionals preparing for a very different future
- Educationists and Parents guiding the next wave of talent

AlphaCorp is fictional, but the world it mirrors is not. Its rooms echo the same contradictions found in real organisations. Its teams carry the same pressures felt by professionals everywhere. Its leaders confront the same choices that will define the future of work.

This story is an invitation — to pause, reflect, and imagine what tax and finance can become when people, data, technology, and leadership finally align.

My hope is that this book helps every reader see their own world more clearly, and recognise that extinction is not an ending — but the beginning of reinvention.

— **Nitin Agarwal**

CHAPTER 1

Fort Richard

The Fall

"You don't guard power like that unless there's something underneath."

Maria Mehta sat in the hushed boardroom, in her accustomed place at the side of the conference table. The chair at the head of the table was still warm, its occupant gone — without a farewell speech, after two decades. Without a storm. Just papers stacked neatly, water glasses half-drained, and the faint trace of Richard's cologne lingering.

It had taken less than an hour to dismantle what everyone once called Fort Richard.

The moment came when Julia Williams, AlphaCorp's controller of twenty years, stood before the Ethics and Conduct Committee. Her voice didn't waver. Her hands, folded neatly on the table, trembled only once.

"He isolated me at a Lisbon retreat. Said it was a debrief. It wasn't."

The words cracked like glass.

Maria watched the room shift, like a courtroom after a guilty verdict—everyone pretending they hadn't already known.

Julia's testimony opened the gates. A treasury analyst was coerced out of her role. HR logs coded as "mentorship" were late-night coercion in disguise. Emails buried. Patterns ignored.

Out of years of silence shadows took shape, and formed a record.

The Board acted with unusual speed—less for justice, Maria knew, than for survival: legal exposure, investor panic, headlines. By the end of the session, the verdict was unanimous. Richard would "retire" immediately.

The press release would clothe it in silk—"two decades of service," "transition to mentorship," "continuity of legacy." But everyone here knew.

It wasn't retirement. It was an evacuation.

And word had it, some in the Board still trusted Richard.

Maria sat motionless, her coffee gone cold. Beneath her composure, one thought pressed in:

The tyrant was gone. But what remained of the kingdom?

The Legacy

The chair loomed in her periphery, leather moulded by years of someone else's weight. A fortress doesn't vanish in an afternoon; its shadows linger.

Richard had never ruled with brilliance. He ruled with endurance. An auditor turned insider, he learned to outlast opponents using silence and attrition.

The team Richard had assembled was built on obeisance—carefully curated voices that echoed his own. They were the kind of people who nodded before he finished speaking, who agreed out of reflex, who never challenged, never questioned, never risked falling out of favour. Richard valued the appearance of unity more than the substance of competence. His word was gospel; his team's role was compliance.

And now they surrounded Maria—these polished, compliant loyalists—each one a reminder of the culture he had carved into the bones of the department.

Richard built fog into the system: compliance reports stacked like novels, procedures knotted into mazes, transparency suffocated. The ERP became his fortress wall. In the Enterprise Resource Plan, data were padded, reconciliations delayed, numbers looked clean on the surface but were rotting underneath—garbage in, polished garbage out.

Maria remembered one meeting when a colleague pitched a bold digital overhaul. Richard barely glanced up.

"Low priority," he said.

The idea died in seconds.

Once, he turned to her directly: "You're being too ambitious, Maria."

Richard's words were soft, almost courteous, but the sentence cut with the final, unforgiving drop of a guillotine.

The HVAC hummed overhead. The sterile air still carried his scent—sharp, antiseptic. It dragged her back to childhood nights when authority meant silence, not safety. On days that held difficult meetings with Richard, she'd wake gasping, heart hammering at night.

Richard wasn't just a boss. He was a trigger.

And now, finally, he was gone.

The relief wasn't really a triumph, though. It was a release—the sigh of years held too tightly.

The Throne

The elevator carried her upward, floor numbers blinking like a countdown.

The CFO's corner office opened to London like a stage: floor-to-ceiling glass, dashboards pulsing on one wall, photographs of ribbon cuttings and ministers on another.

At the centre stood the chair: high-backed, leather-stitched, built for domination. Richard's shape still lived in it.

Maria didn't sit right away. She crossed to the glass, watched the city flicker. In her reflection, a shape appeared for half a second—a window cleaner, or a memory rising.

She returned to the desk. Laid her palms on the wood. Not his desk anymore. Hers.

She lowered herself into the chair.

Warm. Hideously warm.

Three breaths later, she stood, phone in hand.

Replace the executive chair—end of the week.

Cosmetic, someone might sneer. She knew better. This wasn't optics. It was an exorcism.

Her phone buzzed. A calendar notification flashed: *Debrief with Julia — 21:00 (Richard).* An artefact, auto-forwarded from a calendar no one had scrubbed. A chill moved through her. She killed the inheritance, watched the name disappear.

On the credenza, a slim folder bore the stamp **BOARD RESOLUTION.** She flipped it open:

...appoint Ms. Maria Mehta as Chief Financial Officer (Interim), effective immediately... subject to review following external audit close.

Not a coronation, really. A countdown to a deadline.

Her gaze moved to the dashboards. Red alerts pulsed like embers: VAT exposures, audit risks. One note read *Holiday Peak Exception—Closed.* She remembered the chaos: misrouted shipments, refunds bleeding out, millions vanished under the label *pilot.*

Her hand tightened on the folder. If another audit slipped, it wouldn't be Richard's name on the filing. It would be hers—signed in black ink, stamped in memory.

The photograph wall drew her next. Davos. Handshakes. History. In the corner of one frame, Maria spotted herself blurred, half-turned, an afterthought at the edge of a legacy.

Her phone buzzed again. Isabel, the CEO:

Congratulations, Maria. Stabilisation plan by Monday. Keep it tight.

She typed back: *You'll have it.*

The office exhaled into silence.

"Why me?" pressed back into her mind. Because she was capable? Because she was convenient? Because institutions don't dismantle fortresses and crown revolutionaries. They appoint caretakers.

Maybe they had underestimated her.

She looked again at the word *Interim.*

If this were a test, it came with terms: earn the title, or be erased by it.

Maria opened a blank document, titled it *Day 0 — Severance and Start,* and began a list:

- Exorcise artefacts
- Untangle reporting lines
- Stabilise optics
- Protect people

The cursor blinked like a metronome.

She drafted her first invite: *AlphaCorp Finance — New Era Sync. 07:30. Agenda attached.* Hovered. Pressed Send.

Seconds later, the screen pulsed.

Reply received: "Looking forward to it. —Richard."

Maria froze.

Outside, London surged. Inside, the system still answered to him.

CHAPTER 2

The Guards Within

"The guards at the fort wore polished armour. But Maria couldn't see the eyes beneath the visors. She hadn't assembled this team—they came with the fortress. Uniformed, polished, and battle-worn—but she had no way of knowing which way they'd fire when orders changed."

Maria stood near the window of the private dining room, glass in hand. The 46th-floor suite whispered luxury, but without comfort—polished oak, heavy linen, lighting that illuminated seating charts more than people. The skyline shimmered beyond the glass like a dream, but inside, every movement was measured.

Silverware clicked in rhythm. Conversations unfolded with rehearsed warmth. Men in tailored suits, women in deliberate simplicity. Not one tie out of place. Even laughter had timing.

Maria approached Michael from Legal near the bar.

"Compliance workstreams holding up?"

Michael offered a dry shrug. "Defined and delayed, as usual. But yes, they're intact."

She nodded. That counted as confirmation here.

It was her welcome dinner—and her formal introduction to the teams she would now lead. She'd met the leads—tax, finance, IT, and compliance. Each handshake was calculated, each exchange was polished. Smiles were professional, interest guarded. Maria noted the cadence: efficient, strategic, never quite sincere.

She met each interaction head-on, clear, calm, and observant. If they wouldn't trust her yet, they would at least understand she was paying attention.

She turned from the table, scanning the room. Gestures had subtext. Welcomes were wrapped in calculation.

The AlphaCorp tower sliced into the London skyline, quietly dominant—glass and steel catching the sunset like it owned the hour. From street level, the building seemed to hover, its sharp edges and mirror finish casting distorted reflections. The entrance was unapologetically grand—gleaming floors, tall glass doors, valets whisking away luxury cars every few minutes. Inside, the air hummed with importance: suits, heels, polished silences. Entering as one of the powerful wasn't just a job—it was a statement. A reward. A conquest. It would satisfy the egos of the best. Maria was no different. She devoured that feeling every morning, chin high, back straight. This was AlphaCorp. A $17.25 billion beast with 61,000 employees across 21 countries. Retail. Logistics. Manufacturing. Mining. It created and reshaped markets.

She remembered getting the offer. Her mother lit a lamp. Her classmates messaged: "You made it."

But once inside the behemoth, she had spent years navigating rooms like this, earning nods but not invitations. She learned how to present without posturing and contribute without offending. She learned to wait.

And now, the wait was over.

She was here.

Maybe this is what arrival felt like.

Her phone buzzed. An anomaly alert. She muted it. Tomorrow.

She raised her glass. Nodded. Played the part.

Later, after most had left, she remained near the head of the table.

Sophia Chan entered, her steps quiet, her posture, as always, composed. She had the kind of presence that drew attention without needing to ask for it. Born in Hong Kong, raised in the UK, and now leading AlphaCorp's tax team from London, Sophia was never merely a type. Her fashion sense alone—tailored, bold, just off the centre of corporate expectations—made her stand out in any room.

She wasn't the stereotype. So she was not overlooked. She knew her impact and used it. Some called it confidence, others arrogance. Maria hadn't decided yet. What she had decided was this: Sophia never walked into a room without knowing what she wanted from it.

"Quite the evening," Sophia said, tone smooth but careful.

Maria turned slightly, her face unreadable. "Yes," she said, watching Sophia out of the corner of her eye. There was something too smooth about her, too precise. Even now, Maria couldn't shake the feeling that every comment had a second edge. She caught Aldo glancing at Sophia, that flicker of appreciation barely hidden. Maria took it in and stored it away. She was still mapping this terrain.

They stood side by side for a moment, saying little.

"I suppose everyone's curious to see what changes you'll bring," Sophia added.

Maria gave a slow nod. "They'll find out."

Sophia glanced across the room. "You built a strong team."

"Still early," Maria replied, keeping her tone neutral.

There was a pause. Sophia stepped in just close enough to suggest camaraderie, but Maria didn't lean in.

Sophia had a reputation: thoughtful, articulate, meticulous—and continuously aligned with whoever held the reins. Her closeness to Richard had raised eyebrows, but she navigated through it untouched, never once questioned. Maria had heard stories. Sophia's tone shifted as the conversation turned to tax compliance.

"We've got filings across 21 jurisdictions running on time," she said, her voice crisp. "Team of eighty. It's tight, but they deliver. I've kept us lean—solid work and discipline without any flashy tech projects. We've stretched where we needed to, and made it work."

Maria nodded slowly.

"Stayed within budget with process, grit, and internal stretch," Sophia added, letting that point linger.

Maria offered a polite smile. Sophia was positioning herself—capable, efficient, aligned. But Maria noted the delivery. Every word was measured, every sentence polished to land just right. Nothing spontaneous. Nothing casual. Did this mean nothing creative?

Maria caught the shift—the slight pause before each claim, the confidence edging toward choreography. Sophia wasn't just speaking. She was taking a position. Maria felt it in the tightening of her posture, the instinctive need to match poise with scrutiny.

Footsteps approached.

"Evening," Aldo said, joining them with a nod. His voice was steady, his expression unreadable.

Sophia turned slightly. "You've seen enough of this place to know how things run."

"Three years in, and some things still surprise me," Aldo replied.

Maria gave him a brief look. "Good. We need eyes that don't glaze over."

She noticed the familiarity between them; it was practised. Sophia and Aldo had worked together. How closely, she couldn't tell. But it registered. The way Aldo's glance lingered half a beat longer on Sophia, the hint of a smile tucked behind restraint, told her enough.

Maria said nothing. She watched.

She was being handed an army. And it was time to learn who among them stood for her, would stand for her.

Aldo cut in. "Been around long enough to see the patterns—and the holes. Still a patchwork. Too many systems, not enough ownership." He glanced briefly at Sophia, then back at Maria.

Maria nodded. "Then let's review and discuss."

Later that night, Maria stepped into her office, shutting the door behind her. The city shimmered through the glass walls, still pulsing with late-night energy. She slipped off her heels and sank into her chair, absently turning her phone in her hand. Her feet ached faintly—an ache that reminded her of long evenings in tight rooms filled with tighter conversations. The faint trace of Sophia's perfume still clung to her jacket, mingling with the dry oakiness of the dining room. Maria exhaled slowly. The politics had begun and the silence felt earned.

The dinner had gone as expected—surface smiles, careful conversations, the usual choreography. Maria had moved between tables and faces, noting who leaned in and who held back. Some wanted to impress, while others wanted to observe. And then there was Sophia—composed, assertive, and unmistakably intentional. Maria leaned back, replaying fragments from the evening—Sophia's crisp delivery, the calculated phrasing, Aldo's dry warning. Nothing jarring. But nothing unguarded either. The pieces were in motion. The intent was clear. The loyalties weren't.

Politics, she could handle. Unclear loyalties—those were the risk.

She reached for her phone, flicking through a few unread messages. Then she paused.

The anomaly alert.

The one she had silenced during dinner.

Still there. Waiting. Persistent.

She didn't open it. But her thumb hovered just long enough to betray hesitation.

Something wasn't right.

She locked the screen, set the phone down, and stared out into the night.

Tomorrow.

CHAPTER 3

The Unguarded Gates

"Everyone was watching the horizon. No one was guarding the gates."

The morning after the welcome dinner, Maria arrived at AlphaCorp's London headquarters just as the city's first light fractured across its skyline. The glass spire of AlphaCorp's tower caught the sun like a blade, slicing through the grey fog. She stepped out of the car, coffee already in hand, the chill biting at her temples. There was no time to pause. The alert she'd seen the night before had refused to leave her thoughts.

Upstairs, she went straight to her office, opened the laptop, and navigated to the Germany VAT anomaly flagged in the system.

She read it, expression unreadable—except for the twitch at the corner of her mouth. A breath caught in her chest, then released in a shallow exhale. Her fingers hovered above the trackpad, just lingering. The anomaly glowed back at her, cool and clinical. She blinked once. Then again, slower. Noted. Logged. Contained, she told herself—but the pulse at her temple said otherwise.

An issue, sure. But in her mind, a contained one. The tax function had its rhythm and guardrails. That's why she had functional heads—to sweat the codes and reconcile the filings. Her role was broader, higher. Strategic.

Germany? She flagged it mentally as 'operational noise'—background static she wasn't ready to tune into.

Her phone buzzed.

It was Sophia. "Noticed the German VAT issue. Started a root-cause trace. Looping in local controller."

Of course, Sophia was already on it. That didn't surprise Maria. But that didn't mean she trusted Sophia's conclusions. She listened now—that was new—but the instinct to verify never left her.

A knock.

Aldo stepped in, tablet tucked under his arm. "Saw the stinger email Sophia shot off to the German tax lead—with the whole world marked on it?"

"Just now."

He swiped open a dashboard. "There've been a few odd mismatches in intercompany tags across EMEA: Europe Middle East Africa. Nothing major, but... something feels off."

Maria looked up. Aldo had a mind for systems—he connected fragments faster than most could spot a pattern. But sometimes, he leapt ahead, diagnosing before the symptoms had even settled. She weighed his instincts against her caution.

"We stay cautious," she said. "But don't jump to conclusions."

A pause.

"Let's have Sophia join us."

Minutes later, Sophia entered briskly, clutching a thick folder.

"Germany's filings don't align with intra-EU requirements," she said, flipping open to a highlighted section. "Spain's corresponding entries are missing. Could be a mismatch somewhere in the intercompany setup—maybe systems integration, maybe data handling."

Maria leaned in slightly. Sophia hadn't been asked for a diagnosis yet, but here she was, floating high-level causes. Maria's eyes narrowed, her grip tightening on the pen she hadn't touched. This wasn't analysis; it felt like evasion: another polished theory, no soil on the boots.

Conveniently, the issue was being shaped into an IT problem.

Maria's thoughts sharpened. Her jaw tightened. If this was systemic, why had it taken a tax authority to discover it? Where was the oversight? Did Sophia's team have a firm grasp of the operational details, or were they merely sending emails upstream and downstream, calling it leadership?

She felt a flicker of unease. Sophia's lens stayed fixed at 30,000 feet—safe, detached. She recited symptoms like summaries. Maria felt irritation crawling in—this wasn't analysis, it was abstraction. It reminded her of a time in Treasury when a forecast dazzled on slides but masked a liquidity gap that nearly derailed a hedge. Big pictures only worked when anchored in pixels you could trace.

Real governance needed both altitude and grip. Currently, Maria was seeing a lot of the former and dangerously little of the latter. And this . . . this exact dissonance reeked of Richard's legacy. Always preaching the big picture, never bothering with the pixels that composed it. He'd made a culture of leaders who could charm a boardroom with a slide, yet couldn't trace a Mispost, a wrongly accounted entry, back to a single vendor account.

At AlphaCorp, zooming out revealed a polished landscape. Zooming in, everything blurred. Maria could feel it now—under the surface gloss, the outlines were melting. She noted how Sophia's explanation danced just far enough from detail to seem informed without ever getting her hands dirty. It was the same template Richard admired. The illusion of control masquerading as vision.

Maria leaned over the desk. "Data entry?"

Sophia shook her head. "Partly," she said, stopping short of elaborating.

She didn't wait for Maria to ask.

"To be clear," Sophia added, her tone clipped, "the COE handles tax strategy. Country teams own tax operations. What happened in Germany—that's operational leakage, not strategic policy."

Maria's brow didn't move, but her silence was sharp.

Sophia flipped the page. "Manual uploads. Mismatched tax codes. Inconsistent definitions."

And just like that, Maria saw it. Sophia wasn't looking for causes—she was assigning boundaries. Protecting scope.

Even before this conversation, Sophia had typed and fired off a sharp email to the German tax manager, CCing half of AlphaCorp's tax and finance leadership. Questions were fired off with the urgency of a checklist, but none aimed inward—as if she were the one investigating, not the one being asked.

In the hallway later, someone muttered to a colleague, "She's done it again—flipping the lens before anyone checks the wiring."

Maria said nothing. She didn't need to.

The structure allowed it. Richard's structure. It thrived on blurred lines—loud about 'strategy', vague about 'execution'. Maria saw it now for what it was: not empowerment, but selective detachment. A system where applause flowed upward and accountability scattered like broken glass. She was inheriting not just the power, but the rot.

In past meetings, Richard would draw lines on whiteboards— 'strategy here, operations there'—as if separation made things cleaner. When systems broke, he'd nod thoughtfully and suggest regional alignment. When they didn't, he'd take credit at the following leadership forum.

No one ever questioned it out loud. The model had survived because it was polished. And it had worked until now.

Maria could almost hear Richard's voice—smooth, firm, convincing: "You see, Maria, we empower our people with freedom."

What he never said out loud: "We hold them alone accountable."

Maria's stomach turned. Her fingers tapped an uneven rhythm on the armrest. It wasn't empowerment—it was abdication dressed in rhetoric. And now she was the one left to sweep up the consequences.

She now felt the hollowness of that doctrine. She was living its echo.

By the end of it, Maria knew—this wasn't a footnote. It would be one of the defining themes of her first hundred days—maybe longer.

And if that was true, she needed to realign her priorities. Fast.

That night, Maria walked into her children's room, kissed Saira and Ishan on their foreheads. They were already asleep, tangled in dreams and soft blankets. She lingered a moment longer before retreating to her room.

She crawled into bed and Arjun's arms, the way she did every night. He instinctively wrapped his arms around her but paused, sensing the stiffness in her shoulders. "Tough day?" he asked gently, more observation than question. She didn't reply. He didn't push. Just held her closer, anchoring her in a calm she couldn't quite feel tonight.

He didn't say anything. He rarely did until she was ready. And tonight, she wasn't.

Not yet.

The silence stretched between them—warm, familiar, and unjudging—a quiet she needed.

But sleep didn't come.

And Maria knew: something had shifted. The tax issue had initially appeared to be a minor leak. It was a crack now.

Tomorrow, she'd call some experts she could trust to discuss.

Tonight, she stared into the darkness, her heart steady, her mind racing.

The spotlight she craved was finally hers.

And it was hotter than she'd imagined. She turned slightly, eyes fixed on the ceiling.

Was she ready to confront the parts of herself she had spent years mastering, managing, and masking? Behind the tailored suits and sharp decisions were softer questions and older scars.

One question pulsed louder than the rest:

Was everything she had built standing on someone else's shaky scaffolding?

The truth was no longer something she could audit from afar.

She was already inside it.

And the walls had started whispering back.

CHAPTER 4

The Making of a Matriarch

"Some questions never leave you. Maria had answered life with grit—but every morning, the old ones whispered back. Some to haunt her. Others to remind her that she was still becoming."

The milk had boiled over.

A soft hiss greeted Maria as she walked into the kitchen, wearing her gym T-shirt and still damp from a hurried shower. The stovetop was a mess—spilt milk curling at the edges of the burner. She cursed under her breath, switched it off, and grabbed a tissue.

The flat was quiet except for the low hum of the radiator. Arjun was sipping his tea and reading the newspaper. He was now running an advisory, having stepped back so Maria could take the driver's seat in her career. The kids were still asleep, school bags stacked by the door, shoes aligned like little sentries. The dining table was half set—two plates out, the box of cereal open, a small note stuck on the fridge in Saira's careful handwriting: "Good luck today, Mumma. Don't forget to eat."

Maria paused, hand resting on the counter.

She was striking in a quiet, commanding way—tall, with sharp cheekbones and expressive eyes that seemed to shift between warmth and resolve. Her skin bore a dusky elegance, and her long, wavy hair framed her face with a timeless grace. She had the kind of walk that turned heads: it wasn't vanity, beauty; it was presence. She didn't dress to impress but always looked like she belonged wherever she stood.

Arjun, on the other hand, had a quiet magnetism—broad-shouldered, with a naturally athletic build that didn't shout for attention but made you turn for a second look. His features were sharp yet grounded—deep-set eyes under thick brows, a strong jaw softened by an easy smile. Salt-flecked stubble now traced the once clean lines of his face, giving him a thoughtful, lived-in look. He carried himself with confidence that didn't need announcing—measured in gait, unhurried in conversation, calm in conflict. He listened deeply, his goal understanding. Even in a crowd, Arjun seemed anchored—his presence quiet but unmistakable.

Maria leaned against the counter, watching him. Arjun glanced up, his eyes meeting hers with a slow, knowing smile. Without a word, he reached for her hand, pulling her closer. She walked into his embrace with the ease of a thousand such mornings. His fingers ran gently through her damp hair as she rested her head on his chest.

"You look tired," he said.

"Just thinking," she murmured.

"You always are."

She looked up and kissed him softly. A familiar, intimate kiss that changed the air in the room. They held each other for a moment longer—grounded, silent, whole.

Their love hadn't dimmed with time. If anything, it had settled into something more profound—anchored in shared struggles, small victories, and the understanding that they were building something, together. Their mornings were often woven with laughter, soft nudges, and gentle chaos around the breakfast table. Ishan's half-zipped bag, Saira's last-minute projects, Arjun's sarcastic jabs, Maria's quick-fire reminders—this was their temple of love, messy and whole. The scent of toast, the echo of mismatched footsteps, the clink of milk glasses—these were sacred sounds in the sanctuary they had built.

But life hadn't always been this generous. Not for Maria. Not in Dibrugarh.

Her career had started far earlier than most. In Year 11, after school, she began working part-time at a local consultancy in Dibrugarh, a small town in the northeastern state of Assam. The family business there, run by her father and elder brother, was teetering on collapse. Money was tight. Hope, tighter. Maria took it upon herself to support the household, even as she pursued her studies full time. Rent, tuition, groceries—she managed it all, juggling spreadsheets by day and textbooks by night.

Her Class 12 Board results quietly put her in the top tier of students statewide, filling those around her with pride. But when her top-ranked counterpart had his achievements splashed across the newspapers and celebrated with a grand party, Maria felt a sting she couldn't shake. Her family couldn't afford the same. She had no headlines or celebration. The comparisons weren't voiced, but they lingered. That silent dismissal shaped her. Recognition and reward weren't indulgences for her—they were rocket fuel. Her perfectionism, her relentless drive, and her intolerance for mediocrity all stemmed from that hunger for excellence . . . and for recognition.

She expected the same of others. This made her fiercely independent, entrepreneurial in mindset, allergic to mediocrity, and fiercely ownership-driven. People who responded well to orders, or expected to give them unquestioningly, were not her kind. That clarity shaped her teams, her peer circle, and even her leaders.

Her first rebellion came in college. A professor, feared by most, had tried to misuse his position to humiliate her. Maria pushed back. She took her case to the authorities. An inquiry followed. The facts spoke, and the professor had to take a step back. It was her first mutiny against authority misused and it stayed with her. Years later, when Richard at AlphaCorp tried to bulldoze dissent and silence voices, she resisted him with the same conviction.

Her move to Guwahati after Dibrugarh was a new chapter—new city, new anonymity, same grit. On rainy days, she'd wrap polythene sheets around her feet and wade through waist-deep water to get to the office. Public transport halted. Streets flooded. But Maria walked the five kilometres, often soaked to the skin. Once, passing a murky puddle, she caught her reflection—blurred, tired, unbowed. She remembered the rusted second-hand cycle leaning against her hostel wall. She looked up and asked herself, "Why me?"

That weight, though heavy, made her. Her family leaned on her. Her team relied on her. Her children looked up to her. And she never shrugged it off. That trust lit something inside her: a sense that she mattered. A quiet flame she carried into every boardroom and steering committee.

Some called it ego and maybe it was. But it was an earned ego, sharpened through years of responsibility.

She didn't ask for space. She earned it.

Space wasn't granted easily to women like her, especially those who didn't conform. But Maria wasn't watching for permission. She watched for patterns.

She had always noticed things. A hesitation in someone's voice. A shift in tone. A missed detail others ignored. Her strength wasn't in declarations—it was in deduction. Quiet. Precise. Reliable.

And that sensitivity could cut both ways. It sharpened her instincts, but it also meant she felt disrespect like a cold draft through a half-closed door. Being taken for granted unsettled her more than any workload ever could. Maria never announced these reactions. She simply adjusted—silently, decisively—and once that inner shift happened, there was no reversing it.

One evening, a message lit up her screen. A request. Technically harmless. The kind she would normally handle without a thought. But something in the tone was different—an abruptness, a quiet assertion of control that didn't match the task itself. A strange urgency around something that had been untouched for days.

Maria sat still for a moment, letting the words settle.

It wasn't the content that struck her—it was the timing.

The way it folded over the small space she had tried to carve out for herself that day.

The way it reminded her, subtly but unmistakably, of who could lay claim to her time.

Later, another small change reached her—a shift in responsibilities, redirected conversations, a role reassigned without explanation.

She didn't question it. Neither did she protest.

She only felt something inside her tilt—quietly, like a door clicking shut.

She stood by the window for a moment, the evening light softening the edges of the room. From the outside, she looked composed, even thoughtful. None of her inner landscape showed on her face.

But within, she felt the faint sting of an arrow she hadn't expected. Not because the work had changed, but because something deeper had—trust, perhaps, or the remnants of respect.

Maria returned to her desk, opened the task again, and moved through the motions with her usual calm precision. Her patience held, her resilience stayed intact.

But somewhere inside her, a line had been crossed quietly.

And once crossed, Maria knew—nothing would return to what it had been.

Maria was also relentless about growth. Staying still, for her, meant irrelevance. She didn't just preach learning—she lived it. That led her to pursue an Executive MBA at INSEAD Business School, in France, after two decades in the corporate world. Many laughed—said it was a foolish spend. Better to buy property, they said. But Maria knew better. The experience was transformational, featuring classmates from over 100 countries, professors at the forefront of global research, and the revitalisation of campus life. She brought Arjun and the kids along during electives, letting them witness her climb anew.

Even now, she was taking an AI fundamentals course. Not for certificates or for show, but because she wanted to understand what was shaping the world her children would inherit. What her teams would rely on. What her leadership demanded.

Trust and respect were her deepest currencies. She gave people what they earned—expected trust and respect without compromise. It was why her teams followed her, not just in the workplace. She genuinely cared. She coached, celebrated, challenged, and protected her people. Success, for her, meant raising leaders. And that's why those who worked with her still spoke of her in reverent tones.

Maria wasn't the textbook perfect leader either, and she knew it. Some mornings, the pause came before the words—the quick, private check she'd learned to make after years of watching how a single sentence could bruise. She noticed things now: shifts in posture, tones that tightened, the way certain managers treated silence like a tool. She kept those memories close. The raised voice. The curt dismissal. The meeting she was expected to understand without ever being invited. They stayed with her more than she admitted.

And Richard—he stayed with her the most.

His office had always been its own strong-gated fort. His loyalists drifted in and out with the unhurried confidence of people who belonged; their conversations dropped into shorthand the moment they crossed the threshold. The rest of the team—Maria included—were left piecing together decisions from fragments of emails and second-hand summaries and chatter.

Even Richard's expressions obeyed the hierarchy. For his loyalists, his whole face loosened—the softened eyes, the easy curve of his mouth, the unguarded warmth that made them feel chosen. He brightened for them, as if their presence alone confirmed his place in the world. But with others, the warmth vanished. It felt less like people belonged with him and more like they belonged to him.

Meetings with him were tests she never got the rules for.

"You know what happened last week, right?"

Her honest "no" always dropped like a mistake.

A sigh. A look.

"You need to be more aware if you want to lead."

Aware of what?

He never said.

And no one explained those fractured communications between the siloed factions in what he proudly called his "team".

There were days Maria would leave Richard's office certain—utterly certain—that she finally had clarity. His instructions sounded firm in the moment: a nod, a direction, a tone that suggested alignment. She would act on it, relieved to have something solid beneath her feet at last.

But the next meeting would come, and Richard would speak as though the earlier conversation had never existed.

"That's not what I said, Maria."

The ease with which he rewrote the past sent a small shock through her every time. For a brief instant, doubt would flicker—had she misheard? Misread? Filled in context she was never given? But the thought always dissolved quickly. The pattern was undeniable.

This was Richard's way.

Strategies didn't shift; they pivoted violently. Priorities flipped without warning. Yesterday's direction became today's contradiction. He called this motion "agility," wore it like a mark of brilliance, never noticing the quiet devastation it caused in the ranks below.

Inside his circle, certainty was a privilege.

His loyalists always seemed to know the backstory—the midnight message, the sudden change of heart, the whispered update in a hallway. They lived in the light.

Everyone else stumbled in the dark.

Maria and the others walked on ground that constantly moved beneath them. Every decision carried the risk of being undone by Richard's next mood or memory. There was no stable truth to rely on—only the version he chose to remember.

The exclusion magnified everything—turned routine work into guesswork, direction into hazard. It wasn't leadership she was navigating; it was volatility disguised as vision.

And yet... she could admit it now.

He shaped her.

Not into the most celebrated leader, perhaps.

But into a better one.

Everything Richard was—she refused to be.

So now, when someone on her team hesitated, she leaned in. She clarified. She offered the context she had never received. She built the transparency he hoarded. She made sure no one on her team ever had to stand outside a circle they didn't even know existed.

She had lived that once.

She would never let anyone under her live it again.

And so, Maria was a celebrity in AlphaCorp now. Junior staff greeted her eagerly. Her presence commanded attention, because she *saw* people like the new intern in the pantry. He fumbled with his ID badge as she nodded. That pause, that eye contact—it lingered. She noticed him. And he knew it.

At home, she noticed just as much. Ishan's fibs. Saira's tension. She adjusted, calibrated, and supported wordlessly.

This morning they left in a hurry. Arjun drove the kids to the bus stop while Maria stood on the balcony, coffee in hand. The kids waved as the bus pulled away. She waved back. The drizzle misted her face, unnoticed.

The coffee had gone cold.

She stood a moment longer than necessary, still looking after the bus. Holding it all was easy. Until one day, it wouldn't be.

From the quiet fog of memory to the live dashboard waiting in her office, something was about to shift. Maria didn't know what. But she could sense it, like the air before a storm.

Somewhere between Dibrugarh's mud roads and AlphaCorp's glass towers, a reckoning had begun—and it was heading her way.

CHAPTER 5

The Map and the Minefield

"Some leaders navigate with certainty. Others, with courage. Maria was learning to do both, with data as her compass."

The morning after her sleepless night, Maria slipped out from beneath the linen sheets, careful not to wake Arjun. The soft gold of dawn framed her silhouette as she moved silently through the room, her silk robe clinging to the quiet tension in her frame.

Arjun stirred, reaching out in half-sleep. "Come back," he murmured, eyes still closed.

She hesitated, standing at the edge of the bed. His voice was warm, familiar. The safe kind of gravity that could pull her back in.

But something else had already taken root.

Maria glanced toward the stack of documents on her desk—redrafted org charts, health check scope notes, the heatmap printouts she hadn't been able to stop rereading.

She pressed a soft kiss to Arjun's shoulder and whispered, "Later."

Moments later, she was dressed in structured navy trousers, a soft cream blouse tucked in neatly, no jewellery except her wedding band. Her hair was pulled back in a low, practical, yet elegant knot. The morning light caught the slight arch of her cheekbone, a quiet authority emanating from her composure. Her eyes, ringed with fatigue, still held a decisive glint.

And when she looked at Arjun, he felt as if she was looking at Ishan on a school day – not expecting him to be in bed still. They were both downstairs in the next 30.

Downstairs, the breakfast table buzzed with quiet chatter and clinking cutlery. Ishan swung his legs beneath the bench, eyes bright with anticipation.

For Maria, the convenience of her instant coffee machine had made her a coffee drinker. However, she still relished Arjun's Masala tea on easier mornings. Today was a coffee morning.

"Mama, can you come to my Year 3 production tomorrow? I'm the narrator!"

Maria paused mid-sip, setting her coffee down slowly. Her silence said more than words ever could. Then, gently, "Ishan, I wish I could. But I've got back-to-back meetings—significant ones."

His face crumpled, just a little. Not a tantrum—he was too used to this by now. But Maria felt the familiar sting creep in under her ribcage.

She turned to Arjun, eyes barely meeting his—a silent ask.

He gave a soft smile, already reaching for his phone. "I'll be there, champ. Front row."

Ishan beamed.

Maria stood, kissed the foreheads of both her children—Ishan and Saira—then turned to Arjun. With the kids' eyes on their cereal bowls, she gave him a quick, playful hug just out of their sight, her lips brushing his ear. A small gesture, but one that brought up a warm smile —something for him to look forward to later.

She walked toward the door with her tote bag slung over her shoulder. Behind her, the morning hummed on. But something in her had pulled tight again—quietly, undeniably.

She stepped into her office with her shoulders squared and jaw set. The horizon had shifted. What she once thought were fragmented symptoms now suggested something more structural. She had never imagined that tax would become the fulcrum of her first year as CFO. And yet, day by day, it demanded more than she could give.

Just as she reached for her chair, a familiar silhouette hovered in the doorway—Sophia, composed but unusually early, a manila folder pressed tight against her side. The folder was a prelude to something unspoken. To Maria, Sophia had begun to feel like a force she couldn't avoid—measured, composed, but draining. Every time they spoke, Maria felt as though she needed to recover afterwards. There was something about the way Sophia carried herself that left little air for others. Her influence wasn't loud—it was steady, pressing, inescapable. It had its own trajectory. And that trajectory, Maria felt, was at cross-purposes to her own. Increasingly, Maria wondered if it had started shaping the decisions around her without her noticing.

"I didn't want to drop this via email," Sophia said, walking in. "The South Africa team flagged a VAT reclaim that was denied. They had supporting documents, but the local authority said the submission didn't align with declared transactions."

Maria blinked. "We're non-compliant in South Africa, too?"

"Possibly. Or it's poor documentation. Either way, we're chasing clarity. But they've been warned that future claims might get blocked."

Maria pinched the bridge of her nose. "How many fires can we put out before we accept we've got a broken pipeline?"

Sophia didn't reply. Her silence was agreement.

Later that day, Maria joined a scheduled steering committee call for finance systems governance. She was supposed to give a strategic update. Instead, she found herself leaning in as the India team mentioned they were still running a side Excel tracker because "our ERP can't handle our indirect tax codes correctly"—a line delivered so casually, it felt like standard procedure.

The voice that delivered it belonged to someone she hadn't met before: Abhishek Iyer, the indirect tax lead based out of India. His tone was crisp, his articulation unhurried. He sounded young but firm, as though he'd done the reading twice and memorised the footnotes.

Maria leaned closer to the screen. "Could you elaborate?" she asked.

Abhishek didn't fumble. "The configuration logic we have doesn't support local jurisdictional overrides for e-way bill mapping. We've built manual reconciliation around it, but the audit risk remains unless we retrofit the logic."

Maria's eyes narrowed in intrigue. His name registered immediately. Amidst the noise, here was clarity.

And in the background of her mind, Maria began moving pieces on a silent chessboard. She said nothing aloud. But a door had quietly opened.

Sophia, in another window, had clocked the moment. She saw the slight shift in Maria's posture, the flicker of attention. It didn't take long. She'd built her career reading the subtleties others missed. And she didn't need the board to move before planning her counter. She was already shaping how she'd portray Abhishek—overcomplicated, too technical, not a team player. It's better to shape the story early than to clean it up later.

Moments later, someone from the UK team laughed, "Our temporary VAT patch is still going strong—four years and counting." Maria's fingers froze on her keyboard. Each remark cracked open a world held together by kludges—improvised workarounds that had long ago fossilised into the company's operational DNA. As singular actions, they might have been tolerable. Together, they revealed something deeply corrosive: a culture of makeshift fixes, with years of marginal gains hiding systemic erosion.

Maria asked one question toward the end. "How many of our tax touchpoints are undocumented but critical to daily compliance?"

The silence that followed said everything.

That evening, she walked down to Sophia's office herself. The day had been long, and Maria's usual calm was thinning at the edges.

Sophia looked up, already sensing something. The flicker of tension in Maria's jawline didn't go unnoticed. She scanned Maria's stance. There was change in the air around her. And Sophia, seasoned in reading rooms, caught the signal. "I can't keep playing whack-a-mole," Maria said, voice tight. "We're reacting to everything. I want a comprehensive tax health check —an audit-like accounting of tax controls, risks and compliances—across all major markets. Not just a tax review. I want to know where we stand, structurally."

Sophia nodded. "That's a big lift."

"I know. But I'd rather lift something heavy now than get buried later."

"Alright. I'll scope it. But we'll need serious alignment—systems, regions, IT, maybe even external help."

"Start with what we have," Maria said. "And show me where we don't."

"This won't just touch tax—it'll rattle accounting, systems, even procurement."

"At minimum, I want clarity on reporting accuracy, system dependencies, and local compliance risks."

"Some regions might see this as an audit in disguise. We'll need to frame it carefully."

"I'll handle the framing."

As Maria walked away, Sophia lingered. A low buzz of unease settled in her gut. A sense that scrutiny was coming, and with it, exposure.

AlphaCorp hadn't run a full-scale tax diagnostic in nearly eight years. Layers of band-aid fixes and legacy shortcuts were about to get pulled back. She didn't know exactly what would emerge, but she had a fair idea.

Sophia turned to her desk and began sketching out what she did know. Japan, Belgium, Singapore—safe ground. India, Brazil, and Poland—wildcards. Maria—unpredictable and increasingly sharp. Aldo—technically brilliant but malleable. If she moved first, maybe she could frame the chaos before it framed her.

Three days into the health check rollout, resistance began to surface in subtle ways. Some countries delayed their responses. Others offered vague summaries. A few sent outdated reports, hoping the alarm would pass.

To Sophia, this was more than process lag—it was personal. Her critics were seizing the moment. In Poland, a local tax lead, silent for weeks, casually declared, "We'll provide full records— without edits. Let the numbers speak."

From Brazil, Maria received an email with just a CSV file and the line: "Better you see this than leave it to someone else to interpret."

The wind was shifting.

Some remained loyal—Japan sent its report early. Singapore escalated their alignment call repeatedly. A regional lead proudly wrote, "As instructed by Sophia, all deviations have been reviewed and resolved." The fine print: the problems were still buried.

Sophia read each submission clinically. She saw who was hedging and who was positioning. And she began building her counter-story, citing inconsistencies from local teams as the problem, not her leadership.

India stood out. No response yet.

In her mind, that was a narrative waiting to be shaped.

Maria reviewed Sophia's consolidated tracker, which covered 21 markets. Six unclear. Three under compliance reviews. India—still silent.

Underneath the numbers, an unofficial story took shape:

"She gets what she asks for. Not a word more." "We follow Sophia because we have to—not because we trust her." "She's sharp, yes. But sharpness without listening? That's just a knife."

And from the loyalists: "She tells us exactly what to deliver." "Clean dashboards mean access to Sophia's inner circle."

Sophia walked into Maria's office. Steady.

"Singapore, Belgium, Japan—on track. India? Radio silence. Frankly, Maria, Abhishek's been difficult. Arrogant. He hides behind nuance and sends five-page rebuttals instead of answers."

Maria absorbed it quietly. She noted Sophia's emphasis.

Sophia had played this game before. Planting impressions. Controlling what stuck.

But what she hadn't shared was Abhishek's actual note:

"The local configuration violates three provisions of the Indian Goods and Services Tax Rules. I cannot sign off on compliance that's knowingly misaligned, even if it's historical. We can't keep managing group reputational risk with silent compliance failures."

Maria read it later. It was precise, responsible, and laced with the kind of integrity that Sophia lacked.

In a hallway chat, Maria stirred her coffee. "You ever notice how some stories walk into the room before their subject does?"

Aldo looked up from his screen. "Sometimes they walk faster than the truth."

That was enough.

Sophia, back at her desk, tossed Abhishek's email aside. To her, compliance was about alignment, not interrogation. Her job was to manage optics at the top, not argue over tax codes.

But she could sense it—India might become her undoing. And if Abhishek wanted to play hero, she'd ensure he walked into his own trap.

The days ahead would reveal more. But one thing was clear: the chessboard had shifted. And everyone was already moving.

CHAPTER 6

Keel of the Ship

"Acceptance had replaced denial. Leadership had forced clarity."

Maria stepped into their apartment just past 8 p.m., the hum of the day still clinging to her shoulders. Arjun was already home, leaning on the kitchen counter, pretending not to glance at the door every thirty seconds. All through the drive home, Maria's mind kept drifting, not to the health check or the open threads of the tax project but to Arjun. She could still feel the playful nip she had left behind his ear that morning. It wasn't just routine affection—it had sparked something. A sense of mischief. A hunger. A craving that had built all day, layered beneath spreadsheets and strategies. She'd imagined his eyes lighting up, the tension in his shoulders easing as he saw her walk in. She imagined the warmth of his breath, the rough texture of his stubble against her cheek, the scent of cardamom still lingering from his morning coffee. By the time she stepped into the apartment, she wasn't walking—she was gliding.

The moment she walked in, his eyes lit up. She tossed her bag down and wrapped her arms around him, pressing a mischievous kiss behind his ear—the same spot she'd targeted that morning before rushing out. He laughed, that familiar laugh that made everything else mute for a second. Then, surprising her, he wrapped his arms tightly around her and lifted her briefly off the floor. "I missed you," he whispered, lips brushing her neck, voice both playful and hungry.

She giggled, letting herself melt into the embrace. "I was hoping you would."

They lingered in that bubble a moment longer—foreheads touching, hearts syncing—before the mundane world crept back in. He led her to the kitchen, where he had already set the pan on the stove, and they fell into a rhythm only they knew.

They cooked together, something unplanned—a quick pan-fry of salmon and leftover quinoa, with just the right amount of lime and precisely the right amount of comfort.

Over dinner, they discussed everything except work: Arjun's new project pitch, a movie they both wanted to watch, and the kids' school updates.

That night, sleep came more easily than Maria had expected. The warmth of Arjun's chest beside her, the quiet safety of a home that felt like hers—these were her fuel, her fortress.

The morning after carried echoes of laughter, the aroma of filter coffee, and the glimmer of something whole. Arjun brewed while humming an old Kishore Kumar tune. The kids tumbled across the living room, their delight unfiltered.

Maria let herself linger in the moment. It was fleeting, but it filled her tank enough to face the grueling course ahead.

She almost wanted to freeze the moment.

By 8:30 a.m., she was back in AlphaCorp mode, jacket pressed, eyes sharp. As the car pulled up outside the office, she took one last glance at a photo of her family on her phone. It grounded her.

Back in the office, Maria stood at the head of the long conference table, arms braced, gaze steady.

She tapped her phone. "Call Aldo in," she said calmly.

As she waited, Maria thought about this unexpected partnership. She had started to count on Aldo. There was something steady about him—unshaken, perceptive. He treated work as work, never playing for points, never veiled in politics. Whoever said Gen Z lacked clarity hadn't met Aldo Maseko. He was fast becoming an ally. Maybe even... a friend.

Aldo entered with his usual relaxed gait, his quiet composure belying his age. Maria gestured for him to sit, her expression softening a fraction.

"Good morning," he said, settling in across from her.

"Morning," Maria replied. She gave him a quick update—this wasn't just a routine report. The tax health check would knit together tax, systems, accounting, and task-level practices, offering a consolidated map of AlphaCorp's hidden fractures.

Aldo nodded, absorbing the information. Then, casually but with genuine curiosity, he asked, "How's the transition been? CFO, are you treating yourself alright?"

Maria smiled. "Ask me on a Friday evening with wine in hand. But yes, it's been... clarifying." She paused. "This office still feels a little too large some days. And a little too lonely on others."

Aldo's eyes didn't flinch. "Comes with the altitude, I guess."

Maria studied him for a second. So young, and yet so grounded. He wasn't playing politics. Just listening—listening.

Something was refreshing about Aldo Maseko. His talent was obvious—but the main draw was his manner: thoughtful, restrained, and yet utterly committed to clarity. Strategic Aldo, his colleagues called him, half-jokingly. But it was more than that. His failure with Smart Receipts, the startup that had crashed before it soared, had given him something rare in someone so young: a humility forged in experience. He had tasted vision, failure, and rebirth—which had given him emotional intelligence that made him invaluable in these fragile transformations.

Unlike the Gen Z caricature, Aldo had chosen depth. He was still finding his edges, still uncertain about how long he'd stay at AlphaCorp—but in every conversation, he brought his full attention. There was innocence in him, but not ignorance. He knew what he didn't know. If this place showed him a purpose and not just problems, he might stay longer than planned.

And Maria? She had started to trust him. What impressed her most was his hunger to learn the functional threads of business and weave them into his technical thinking. Most IT folks just built the car. Aldo wanted to know where it needed to go, why, and how it would run differently in rain versus shine. His brief reference to the Smart Receipts startup, and how it taught him ownership and business fluency beyond coding, stayed with her. He wasn't just a technologist; he was becoming a systems thinker, a strategist.

She saw him as a prototype of the next generation of professionals—those who could straddle technology and function with equal command.

As Maria swivelled her chair slightly, she glanced at the folder in her hand and then back at Aldo. “What do you think of Abhishek Iyer?”

Aldo blinked. “Smart guy. Quietly sharp. Catches patterns fast.”

Maria nodded. “I’ve been watching him. There’s a depth to how he sees tax, not just as compliance, but as a system. He connects the dots between rules, data, and architecture.”

Aldo nodded slowly. “Wouldn’t be surprised. His inputs during the pilot in Brazil were on point.”

Maria smiled slightly, then slid a folder across the table toward Aldo. It was Abhishek Iyer’s file—his resume and peer feedback from HR. A faded yellow Post-it clung to the front: ‘Watch how he sees through systems’ — MM.

“You bring system clarity. He brings tax intuition. Together, you might help AlphaCorp move from panicked patches to unitary precision.” She paused, then added, “And I believe Sophia still brings deep context and ownership to this landscape. If the three of you can align, we may finally have a team that sees the full picture—technology, tax, and transitions.”

Aldo paused and flipped open the folder. The man was a pattern-spotter. Abhishek had worked across both failed and successful tax transformations—Matrix LLC’s collapse and Hybrid LLC’s success. That duality intrigued Aldo. Someone who had seen both sides of the spectrum. Someone who had scars and medals.

“Why wasn’t he pulled in earlier?” Aldo wondered aloud. He glanced again at the list of projects, his brow furrowed in thought. Then he closed the folder gently and looked up at Maria.

“Leave this with me, would you? I want to go through it in more detail,” he said calmly.

Maria nodded. “Of course.”

Aldo stood, offered her a courteous nod, and exited the room quietly.

Later that afternoon, Maria called Sophia and Aldo into the conference room to walk through the preliminary findings from the tax health check.

Across from Maria, Sophia scrolled through her tablet. Her face was composed, but tension stiffened her features. She knew what they were walking into—no, what they had been avoiding. As Maria’s tone grew more abrupt, Sophia’s mind flickered to the cold silence of her first board meeting at Glencore years ago, where she had been dismissed with a smile and sidelined for a quarter. She had learned to survive by not flinching.

"Europe first," Maria began.

Sophia spoke without looking up. "Three countries missed VAT deadlines—intercompany mismatches. Intra-EU services are unaligned. The Netherlands booked IT services to France, but without tax mapping."

Aldo interjected, "Just to be clear—missed filings mean we didn't report the tax we owed?"

Sophia nodded. "Exactly. Like not filing your taxes. Penalties aside, it ruins our standing."

"And the intercompany mismatch?" Aldo pressed.

"Germany ships to Spain. Germany records it as a cross-border sale. Spain logs it as a domestic buy. They don't reconcile, and the tax authorities catch it."

"System glitch?"

"Not entirely. The ERPs are disconnected. Germany's setup isn't synced with Spain's. There's no automated reconciliation. It's like five people playing the same song—but each one has a different sheet of music, and no conductor."

Aldo squinted slightly. "But is it an IT issue, or a process one?"

Sophia hesitated. "Germany flagged the ERP gap last quarter. It wasn't escalated. Spain didn't realise it. The Netherlands bypassed mapping logic to speed things up."

"So," Aldo concluded, "Germany acted. Spain lacked awareness. The Netherlands opted out. This may not be IT. It's a governance blind spot."

Sophia said nothing. She didn't know enough about system prioritisation to argue. Besides, Aldo wasn't cornering her—he was triangulating. And he was right.

"Appreciate the walk-through," Aldo said, turning toward Maria. "Fixing systems without knowing how they failed is like rewiring a house without checking where the fire started."

Maria remained still. "Why wasn't this escalated sooner?"

Sophia exhaled. "I didn't think it was a collapse. More like pressure points. I took calls I thought mattered."

Maria gave no reaction.

Sophia's tone sharpened just a notch. "It's easier to point out what didn't work when you're above the fray. But in the thick of it—it's triage, not apathy."

Maria's eyebrows lifted slightly. Sophia fell silent.

Aldo stepped in. "Let's map it. System by system. Line item by line item. Sophia and I can go through the tax health check—maybe quick wins are hiding in plain sight."

Maria nodded. She welcomed the pivot.

But privately, this confirmed what she had feared: she needed a second set of eyes on tax.

"Asia," Maria said, turning the page.

"GST mismatches in three countries," Sophia replied. "Invoices missing from ledgers. Legacy procurement tools dropped data."

"Meaning?" Maria asked.

"Data entry is manual. Late filings. Duplicate entries. Sometimes invoices disappear. The vendor has already filed on their side, but our records do not match. On paper, we're either double-claiming or not claiming at all."

Aldo blinked, giving a confused look. Sophia clarified, "So the tax we pay vendors is like an advance tax. Sometimes we forget to claim it back. Sometimes we claim it twice. Sometimes, not at all."

Aldo nodded. "And I am sure the authorities don't read it with the same kindness. Inconsistent behaviour creates suspicion. Suspicion becomes certainty."

Maria muttered, "And with real-time e-invoicing in Asia, those types of mismatches get flagged instantly."

Sophia added, "In two countries, we're already non-compliant. The numbers filed to tax portals don't match what we report. It's like changing your story every time they ask. And having no explanation."

Aldo's face darkened. "This isn't about tax alone. It's systemic. The silos are visible."

In his mind, he could trace it: isolated teams, layered systems, inconsistent checkpoints. No shared view of reality.

Maria turned to the last region. "North America."

Sophia hesitated. "Three years of transfer pricing are classified as pass-through. Without mark-ups. Zero margin."

Maria froze. "Industry standard?"

"8 to 15 percent mark-up. We showed none."

Aldo leaned forward. "Break that down for me, please."

Sophia explained, "Imagine you resell coffee beans to a sister company for the exact price you bought them. The taxes in your country are lower than those of the sister company. So, eventually, both of you are together taking the taxman for a ride. The taxman asks—are you adding value or passing gifts?"

Aldo nodded. "Smells like evasion. On a high level, I get it now. But wow—it's complicated."

Maria spoke under her breath. "No one ever talked. There was no centre holding it together."

Silence settled.

"If we clean this now," Maria said, "we pay millions. If we delay, it explodes."

She turned to the window. Her voice was low.

"People think tax is back office," she whispered. "But it's the keel of the ship. Lose it, and everything tips."

Aldo said nothing. But he watched Maria closely. Maybe this wasn't just her ship to steady.

What Maria didn't know yet was that someone else had been watching the same patterns—quietly, from the sidelines. And he was almost ready to step in.

CHAPTER 7

The Manoeuvres of Experience

"Because education does not mean you learn by making mistakes on your own."

The morning after the storm, Aldo arrived early. The war room was still quiet, its glass walls fogged faintly by the chilled hum of air conditioning. But Aldo wasn't looking at the dashboards.

He was reading a file.

It was thick, dog-eared, and annotated in places. The cover read: Iyer, Abhishek. Indirect Tax. There was a yellow Post-it stuck to the last page, almost falling off, but still there, and legible. The handwriting was sharp and familiar: MM.

Maria Mehta.

Aldo flipped through again. This time, not as a CTO scanning for red flags but as a man trying to decipher a potential player on a very broken board.

Abhishek's file was exhaustive—projects delivered, issue logs closed, escalation trails, line-by-line tax reconciliations in excruciating clarity. Even in email, Abhishek had a voice: sharp, analytical, almost surgical.

Aldo scribbled a note in his small notebook: "He doesn't miss. But does he see?"

Because while the data danced beautifully, Aldo wondered if Abhishek lived too deeply in the weeds. There was a difference between being accurate and being strategic. One solved problems. The other prevented them.

He closed the file halfway, letting his thoughts drift.

That's when he heard the soft rhythm of heels on marble.

Sophia.

She entered, framed by the morning light. Her hair was pulled into a loose bun, a few strands rebelliously trailing down her cheek. There was a tension in her eyes, revealing her night of re-analysis, but she moved with that same clipped efficiency he had grown used to. Still, something felt different today. Something was softer.

There was something in the pause between them—a flicker, almost adolescent. The kind of unsaid recognition that hung in high school corridors before anyone dared call it anything. He saw it in her glance, the quick flicker of amusement and surprise. She saw it in the way he hesitated before answering.

Neither of them would speak of it. Neither wanted to. There was too much at stake. They worked too closely, trusted too little. But it lingered, nonetheless. A thread pulled tight but left uncut.

Her gaze landed on the file, then the yellow Post-it. "You're reading his file?"

For a moment, Aldo didn't answer. He was caught.

Not by the file.

By her.

Sophia stepped closer, arms folded now more as armour than comfort. Her eyes lingered on the yellow Post-it for a beat too long.

"Why are you reading his file, Aldo? What's going on? Am I missing something here?"

Aldo looked up slowly, measuring her tone.

"Maria and I spoke last night. She thinks Abhishek could be helpful. He's knee-deep in Indirect Tax and tech delivery—closer to the mess than we are. She wants us to think it through. That's where he could complement us perfectly. We also need someone for the trenches. Do you have the capacity?"

Sophia exhaled, half-curious, half-concerned. "Abhishek's been efficient. Overzealous, even. But he's not a strategist."

"I agree," Aldo said. "But maybe that's why we need him. He spots cracks before they collapse. That's a rare instinct. We've got vision, but someone's got to be elbow-deep in the rubble."

Sophia sighed. "Or someone who follows every crack so far down he forgets to climb back out."

Aldo gave her a look. "You sound like Maria talking about Richard."

Sophia stiffened. Her jaw tightened, just for a second. She knew what was coming, and she wasn't ready to hear it from him.

He tapped the file. "What do you think this means?"

"It means she's testing him. Or us. Or both."

Before Aldo could respond, Maria's voice cut through the air, calm and purposeful.

"We begin with the truth," she said, stepping into view, eyes already scanning both their expressions.

Sophia's gaze flicked to the floor for just a moment. That word—truth—always had weight.

Minutes later, they entered the war room — Sophia still tense from yesterday's long night of note-taking and quiet panic, Aldo with his usual steady gait and a barely visible notebook tucked under his arm—his old-school habit of journaling his days continued into his working life. His world revolved around architecture and integration; tax audit findings were rarely a blip on his radar. But this was different. Aldo saw it clearly: the crisis wasn't just a compliance issue; it was a systemic collapse that had been hiding in plain sight. Staying within IT's traditional boundaries might have been easier, but it was not the right approach. Not when the architecture itself had let it happen. This was his code for debugging, scaling, and fixing.

Maria began not with blame but with a mirror. In her view, everyone bore responsibility. Tax had focused too narrowly on what the COE was entrusted to do. Finance and operations had assumed any problem labelled "tax" would be magically solved by the COE. IT had defaulted to service-provider mode—always reactive, never addressing the whole. No one had stitched the system together. No one walked the extra mile to explore the unknown and understand what was happening at the edges. Master data? Orphaned. Shared services? Detached from tax realities in 21 countries. Tax teams had been shouting for visibility, and no one had listened.

This wasn't just an IT failure. Or a tax failure. It was an AlphaCorp failure. And the cure had to be collective, not siloed.

Reinvention was about more than ways of working. It was about turning dependencies into strategic assets through infrastructure, diverse skill sets, cross-functional collaboration, and top-down resolve. Realistic goals. Clear commitment. And the support to make it all real.

Maria paused, then looked at Aldo. He, she believed, was the right tech leader—not because of his code skills but because of his gift for clarity, and for accurate priorities. He treated technology as a means to elevate business, not the other way around. Sophia, with Aldo and Abhishek, could become a trio bent on resolve and repair.

Once she had their full attention, Maria shifted the lens outward.

She spoke of precedent. The early days of GCC VAT—panic, shortcuts, fear. She had resisted the tide, waited for insight before action. That patience, that hunger to observe first, was her compass again.

"Richard used to scoff at these moments," she said quietly. "'Don't bring me stories, Maria—bring me solutions.' But stories carry truths. And we need them now."

Sophia blinked. "You want case studies?"

"I want the truths behind them," Maria replied. "What broke? What resisted breaking? Who gave up? Who pulled through? And what got them there?"

Aldo nodded. "Abhishek's been on both sides—Matrix LLC and Hybrid LLC."

Maria's eyes gleamed. "Exactly. Start there. Matrix first. Then Hybrid. They were messier than us—but something worked."

Aldo leaned in. "So what do we do next?"

"We study," Maria said. "We learn. And we design better. Why Matrix failed. Why Hybrid succeeded, don't just tell me *what* they did. Tell me *why* it worked—or didn't."

Sophia straightened. "We'll build the framework. But who leads this?"

Maria smiled faintly. "We do. But not alone. Sophia, Aldo—I want you both to lead this with Abhishek Iyer. Form a core team."

They nodded.

But under that nod was something unspoken.

Maria hadn't assigned roles, but Sophia gravitated toward tax, trusting that Aldo would handle IT. Because she had never really understood it.

Aldo saw the shift. Saw the opening. The stars were aligning again.

CHAPTER 8

The Quiet Force

The revolving glass doors of AlphaCorp's London headquarters hissed as Abhishek Iyer stepped inside. He paused for a moment, out of habit. Years of walking into unfamiliar buildings, unnoticed, had taught him to read a room before entering it. The lobby was all brushed metal and matte finishes: it whispered importance without ever raising its voice. Around him, people moved with a certain rhythm — consultants in tailored suits, executives on calls, interns clinging to laptops like life preservers.

Abhishek walked past the reception with a polite nod, his ID badge already clipped to his shirt. Like any other professional arriving for work — or so it seemed.

He took the lift to the 18th floor, watching the numbers climb in silence. When the doors opened, the familiar atmosphere of freshly brewed coffee and static-charged air greeted him. He adjusted the strap on his laptop bag and walked toward the glass-walled conference room where everything was about to begin.

He had arrived in London with two suitcases, a five-year streak of clean audits, and no appetite for office politics. On his first day at the AlphaCorp Global Tax COE, he waited fifteen minutes outside the meeting room because no one had informed him that it had been rescheduled. He didn't complain. He just sent a calm email and used the time to reread the indirect tax policy notes from the ERP migration two years ago: the kind of thing most people had forgotten even existed.

He wasn't flashy. Never had been. In India, he had quietly fixed a blocked GST refund issue that had stalled a quarter's cash flow. No announcement followed. The business assumed that the problem had resolved itself. In London, it was the same. When a vendor mapping error threatened a critical VAT return in Spain, Abhishek didn't escalate. He just stayed back after hours, fixed the logic in the ERP rule set, and sent a clean report the next morning. The CFO's office never knew there was a fire.

Before joining AlphaCorp, Abhishek had worked on tax transformation initiatives with both Matrix LLC and Hybrid LLC. At Matrix, he was part of the indirect tax team during an ERP migration, helping rationalise hundreds of obsolete tax codes and driving the automation of cross-border reporting across five countries. At Hybrid LLC, he contributed to their transition from an Excel-based compliance system to a centralised, workflow-driven VAT platform. At both companies, his logic-building approach within ERPs led to fewer audit exceptions, faster refund cycles, and more predictable compliance timelines. He wasn't the face of transformation, but his fingerprints were on every key success metric.

People liked him. He was polite, always offered to help, and never pushed his way. But they also underestimated him . . . even Sophia. She rarely looped him in for global tax forums or design workshops. He was seen as dependable, not strategic. But those who worked directly with him — especially the country teams — knew better. His inbox was always full. His solutions always worked.

He rarely spoke up in large meetings. But when he did, people usually paused. He wasn't loud; he'd done the work.

The meeting room on the 18th floor overlooked the grey Thames, framed by the dull symmetry of London's financial district. Glass walls, quiet lighting, a wide rectangular table with polished edges. A room that made silence feel permanent.

Abhishek walked in at 9:01 a.m., nodding politely to the two people already seated.

"Morning," he said casually, setting his notepad down. "Looks like I'm the guest at someone else's dinner table. Just tell me where not to sit."

Aldo chuckled. "Anywhere works, man. We're all starving for answers."

Sophia glanced up, expression neutral, but something about the corner of her mouth suggested amusement.

Abhishek chose the middle seat. "Good. That way, I don't get blamed for undercooked ideas."

"Noted," Aldo replied, smiling as he tapped his laptop.

The large screen came alive with the consultants' tax health check summary — colour-coded blocks, flagged risks, red and amber warnings clustered by geography.

"Let's walk through the top-level findings," Aldo began. "We're not solving today. Just identifying patterns."

Abhishek leaned forward slightly. "On item 2B — the Brazil VAT offsets — the consultants missed a key point. The SPED file issue stemmed from a timing mismatch between CT-e upload and local validation."

Aldo raised his hand calmly. "Not today, my friend. We'll get into the wiring later. For now, let's stay high level."

Abhishek nodded, pulled back. He scribbled a note in his pad, eyes briefly scanning Sophia. No reaction. Of course not. She wasn't here for the wiring.

They continued down the list. At item 3C, Abhishek couldn't resist. "The Gulf zero-rating gaps — those stem from misaligned tax codes in procurement. We'll need a master data audit."

"Abhishek," Aldo interrupted gently, "we're not designing solutions right now. Just keep those thoughts noted for the next session."

There was a pause. Abhishek gave a short nod. "Understood."

Inside, he felt it again — that subtle edge of being too early to the problem, too detailed for the room. But he didn't show it. He just wrote down the observation in the margin. You can't build trust with slides, he thought. You make it by knowing how the system works.

Sophia remained silent, eyes on her screen. Not a word of agreement or disagreement. Just a quiet observation.

He knew his place here. For now, he was the outsider. But he also knew something else: when it came time to fix the engine, they'd come back to the one person who knew how to take it apart and put it back together.

CHAPTER 9

Lessons from the Fallen

10:30 AM – AlphaCorp Boardroom

The room was quiet.

Outside, the London skyline was starting to brighten. Inside AlphaCorp's meeting room, no one said a word. Just the low glow of laptops and the tension of what was about to be unpacked.

Maria sat at the head of the table. She didn't need to speak to command attention. Her words from earlier in the week were still fresh:

"Stories carry truths. And we need them now."

Today's story was Matrix LLC.

Abhishek Iyer stood beside the screen. His laptop was open, but he wasn't using it. He held a pen as if it helped him focus. His notes were handwritten, rough, and lived-in. He was here because he had lived this.

Maria had asked him to lead this session. He'd been through two major transformation projects—Matrix, which had failed, and Hybrid, which had found a way forward. They would get to Hybrid later. But today was about what went wrong.

Abishek cleared his throat and waited a beat. Then he began.-

"Matrix LLC launched what they called the Finance Renaissance Program. The goal was to transition from a scattered array of legacy systems to a single integrated ERP. Real-time reporting. Streamlined processes. Shorter close cycles. The CFO promised a 20 percent efficiency gain."

His eyes flashed toward Sophia. Her face was still.

"But they never defined what visibility meant. Or who it was for. Everyone assumed it meant something—but no one clarified what success *looked like* from a reporting, control, or audit perspective."

Aldo leaned forward, turning a pen in his hand. Sophia watched silently.

"The early signs were easy to miss," Abhishek said. "On paper, the program looked fine. Projects completed their sprints. Dashboards were green. Go-live happened on schedule."

He paused.

"But finance and IT were working with completely different assumptions. Finance thought this was a way to improve accounting processes—standardised journal entries, automated reconciliations, and faster close timelines. IT saw it differently— as a tech upgrade—moving infrastructure to the cloud, ensuring system uptime, building integrations."

He looked around the table. "There was no shared blueprint. Finance didn't understand the architectural impact of system decisions. IT didn't understand the downstream consequences of process gaps. Everyone was busy, but nobody was aligned."

Sophia crossed her arms. "Was there no program governance?"

"There was," he said. "On paper. A central PMO. Weekly stand-ups. Design authority boards. But it was governance by documentation. Not governance by consequence. If someone raised a red flag, there was no clear mechanism for escalation or resolution."

He paused again, then added, "I remember a session where the AP team flagged an issue with invoice workflows. The indirect tax field population was inconsistent, and there were timing delays in the integration. IT's answer was: 'It's a downstream reporting issue. Let tax handle it."

He looked at Aldo. "That mindset—'not my job'—became the culture. You had two teams trying to finish a marathon with different finish lines."

Maria nodded. "When did it become visible to leadership?"

"Day one of go-live," Abhishek said. "Journals failed. Tax codes weren't mapped. The interface between purchasing and the tax engine collapsed. Reports didn't reconcile. The go-live felt like a success for about six hours. Then we started seeing panic emails."

He added, "And leadership was caught off guard. Because they only saw what the dashboards told them, which, up until that point, was all green."

He hesitated for a second, glanced away, then shared, "I remember sitting at my desk at 7:45 a.m. that day, and watching the first error logs come in—VAT not applied, tax fields blank, thousands of transactions in suspense. I thought, 'We're going to spend the next six months explaining this to auditors.' That's when I knew we'd lost control."

Abhishek continued. "Another major issue was implementation support. Matrix chose a partner that wasn't built for transformation. The vendor selection decision rated all the competitive bids equally on the technical scale. The logic ? All the vendors are the same when it comes to capabilities. The real differentiator is the price at which they can serve us – that will make us look great in front of the leadership." "

Sophia raised an eyebrow. "Wasn't it a familiar firm?"

"Yes," he said. "They'd done smaller projects for Matrix before. They were good with enhancements, upgrades, patch support—but this was a full-scale ERP rollout. But they underbid for this one. And they didn't push back on unrealistic timelines. Six months in, they realised they were in over their heads and walked."

Maria frowned. "Did anyone validate their ERP track record?"

"Not really," Abhishek said. "The selection was based on price and familiarity. The proposal looked good, but there was no critical review of their capabilities for a global rollout."

Aldo shook his head. "It's a common trap. You assume people you've worked with before can scale with you. But ERP isn't modular plumbing. You need deep design capability. Functional architects. Cutover experience. And governance strength."

He looked at the others. "This isn't a tech project. It's a business transformation. You can't outsource accountability."

Sophia gave a short, dry, involuntary laugh. Aldo glanced at her. She quickly looked away. Maria noticed, but didn't comment.

She leaned forward. "And tax?"

Abhishek didn't hesitate. "Tax wasn't brought in during the blueprint. They were invited into requirement discussions after procurement and order-to-cash flows were already locked."

He continued, "Indirect tax config was done based on static Excel sheets. The logic wasn't validated against actual business scenarios. There was no design walkthrough, nor was there any UAT from a tax control perspective. When issues were raised, the answer was: 'We'll fix it post go-live.'"

He added, "One of the biggest failures was around reverse charge logic. The issue was hardcoded incorrectly in two countries, and we didn't discover it until we saw negative tax balances in the return. The finance team couldn't explain it. The auditors flagged it. We had to restate two periods."

The room fell silent.

Abhishek immediately sensed the shift. "I'm not suggesting AlphaCorp is doing the same. But these are warning signs. They happen quietly. And then suddenly."

Sophia leaned forward. "Close enough to make us uncomfortable?"

Before Abhishek could respond, Aldo stepped in. "Let's not make it about blame. We're here to find the gaps early. That's the point of looking at failure."

Sophia looked at him, her expression unreadable. But her gaze lingered longer than expected.

Aldo noticed and then looked away.

Maria kept watching with quiet focus. She wasn't just listening to content. She was observing behaviour. The alliances forming—or not. The weight of things left unsaid.

Abhishek looked down at his notes. His hand gripped the pen more tightly now. The mood had changed.

Maria broke the silence. "If you had to summarise the root cause?"

He looked up. "People were working hard, but they were isolated. Everyone assumed someone else was handling the parts they didn't understand."

Maria nodded. "That's exactly what we have to avoid."

This time, no one added anything. This quiet wasn't awkward. It was reflective, silence that comes when the story isn't about someone else anymore.

They weren't just studying Matrix.

They were seeing the early outlines of themselves.

1:48 PM – After the Break

The room had emptied briefly. An hour-long early lunch break, Maria had said. Enough time to breathe—but not to forget. When the team reassembled, the lighting felt a little warmer, and the tension slightly diffused. Laptops reopened. Sleeves rolled up.

Someone made a passing comment about the elaborate lunch in Abhishek's lunchbox. Aldo joked that the instant coffee machine was AlphaCorp's absolute transformation failure. Even Sophia smiled. It was a small reset—but a reset nonetheless.

As people settled in, Maria didn't speak right away. She let the informal air linger a moment longer. It was Abhishek who broke the silence, responding to a casual question Aldo had asked as they walked back in.

"How long were you at Matrix again?"

"Just under three years," Abhishek said. "Joined mid-program, stayed through go-live and six months post. Spent more time with IT than my own family that year."

There were chuckles around the table. But Sophia's expression was unreadable.

Maria leaned forward. "And when you left? What was your takeaway?"

Abhishek paused. "That systems don't fail. People fail to align. And by the time someone notices, the damage is already in production."

No one spoke. The room had quietly shifted back into gear.

Abhishek stepped back toward the screen, clicking through to the next slide. "After the partner exited, Matrix didn't replace them. They tried to do it with their own teams."

Maria blinked. "They ran a multi-million-dollar ERP without a partner?"

Abhishek nodded. "The CTO believed they could handle it. Said the knowledge already existed within the org."

Aldo let out a low whistle. "That's either gutsy or suicidal."

"It wasn't about guts," Abhishek said. "It was about pride. They thought external consultants slowed them down. Too many slide decks, too much theory. So they doubled down on execution and believed experience would carry them."

Sophia raised an eyebrow. "And it didn't?"

"No," Abhishek replied. "Because the experience was fragmented. And more importantly, they sidelined key functions. Tax, procurement, and even parts of finance. The people who should've been shaping the design weren't even in the room."

Maria's voice was calm but direct. "So IT took the wheel?"

"Completely," Abhishek said. "They didn't mean to exclude anyone. But once the partner left and business leaders hesitated, IT filled the vacuum. Decisions had to be made. So they made them."

He paused. "The ERP became a system upgrade, not a transformation."

Aldo crossed his arms. "Let me guess—they recreated what they already had?"

"Exactly," Abhishek said. "They rebuilt the old world inside the new tech. Legacy processes, reborn with more visually appealing screens. The logic was: if it worked before, it'll work now."

"But it didn't?" Maria asked.

"No. Matrix had outgrown those workflows. The business was more complex, the reporting expectations were tighter, and the compliance risks were higher. What worked in 2015 couldn't scale in 2022."

Sophia narrowed her gaze. "Were finance and tax consulted at all?"

"They were shown designs," Abhishek said. "But those designs were already done. It wasn't a real consultation. It was a sign-off theatre."

Maria frowned. "And no one pushed back?"

"Some tried," he said. "But the tone was clear. Keep the train moving. Don't raise blockers. IT had timelines to meet and templates to hit. Anyone who challenged that was seen as a risk to delivery."

Aldo muttered, "Box-ticking."

But behind his tone was something more reflective. He could see the dynamic business leaders stepping back, letting IT carry the risk, and then blaming them when things broke. In his mind, IT hadn't seized control. They'd been left holding the bag.

Abhishek, on the other hand, was less forgiving. His silence wasn't agreement—it was indictment. He saw Matrix's IT team as overreaching, mistaking technical scope for strategic clarity.

Neither said it aloud. Not yet.

03:36 PM – The Undercurrent Turns

The team reconvened after a short coffee break. The air had shifted—less caffeine, more reckoning.

Abhishek continued with his Matrix story. "By the time the first wave of user workshops had concluded, the tone had already changed color. What began as cautious optimism slowly morphed into dread. The

Matrix project rooms felt less like a hub of co-creation and more like courtrooms, where business users showed up not to contribute but to defend themselves."

With a laser pointer in hand, his voice was calmer now, more assertive. With every example, he seemed to grow into the room. The earlier restraint in his tone had melted away, replaced by the full tones of assertion.

"Expectations were unclear. Sessions ran long and often overran people's day jobs. Stakeholders were invited but not empowered. Requirements were collected, but rarely revisited."

He glanced at the group, making eye contact with Aldo, then Maria. "Change champions turned into reluctant participants. People no longer saw the ERP as an enabler—it had become a burden. It disrupted workflows, dismissed insights, and slowly eroded confidence."

Maria rubbed her temples. "This sounds like a change management disaster."

Abhishek nodded. "It was. And it was avoidable."

Sophia shifted in her seat. Her earlier dominance in the room was fading. She could feel the attention tilting toward Abhishek—and it unsettled her. Every nod from Maria, every follow-up from Aldo, felt like another inch lost.

"What started as cautious scepticism," Abhishek continued, "turned into quiet resentment. For many, the project became something to endure rather than embrace. Meetings felt more like ambushes than workshops. People stopped bringing ideas; they brought shields."

Sophia broke in, attempting to reclaim space. "You're saying they gave up?"

"They didn't give up," Abhishek replied evenly. "They adapted. They complied, but no longer showed any engagement. Collaboration gave way to survival mode. Just enough to stay under the radar."

He paused, then added, "You know what made it worse? Every time someone raised a problem, they were assigned ownership of it. Raise a broken workflow? Suddenly, it's yours to fix. Highlight a missing control? Congratulations, you're now the lead for that module."

Aldo gave a knowing nod. "Passing the pillow."

Abhishek smiled. "Exactly. It was framed as empowerment, but in reality, it was disguised abdication. People weren't collaborating. They were shielding themselves—carefully passing the risk around like a hot potato."

Sophia leaned back, crossing her arms, but her expression betrayed her. The growing respect Abhishek was earning unnerved her, especially that coming from Aldo.

"And then," Abhishek went on, "when the system went live, the same people who'd been dragged into those sessions—often late, usually underprepared—were suddenly the ones blamed for not understanding it."

Maria's tone sharpened. "Where was tax in all this?"

"Practically invisible," Abhishek said. "When we were finally brought in, the key decisions had already been made. Our concerns—compliance risks, real-time reporting needs, cross-border taxation—were dismissed as 'details that could be figured out later.'"

"Let me guess," Aldo said. "They weren't figured out later."

"Not even close," Abhishek replied. "In the corridors of Matrix, everyone knew what was happening, but no one said it aloud. Tax, finance, operations—they all traded glances in coffee rooms, muttering about how the ERP had become an IT dictatorship."

"I don't get it," he said, mimicking the voice of a tax colleague. "How can they build an ERP without asking us what we need? We're the ones who have to use it!"

Aldo leaned in slightly. "And from an IT perspective, what do you think caused that disconnect?"

Abhishek paused. "Part of it was cultural. The CTO's office believed standardisation equalled efficiency. So, they hardcoded everything into generic workflows, assuming they could retrofit the business later."

Aldo raised a brow. "What about configuration management? Did they have any form of cross-functional validation before transports moved into QA?"

Abhishek hesitated, then shook his head slightly. "Honestly? I don't know. A team ran that part, which I wasn't looped into. I can find out. Or better—maybe we can sit down later and talk it through?"

Aldo nodded slowly, respecting the humility. "I'd like that."

Sophia looked down at her notepad, her thoughts scrambled. She had expected Abhishek to fumble. Instead, he had owned the room with grace and detail—even when admitting what he didn't know.

Abhishek continued. "This quiet discontent was everywhere. But leadership treated it like noise. They assumed it was friction. Normal. Teething issues."

He clicked to the next slide. "But it wasn't teething.

It was haemorrhaging. And no one wanted to say the word."

Maria exhaled. "Alright. Tell me about the moment it all fell apart."

05:12 PM – The Filing Day Debacle

Abhishek stood by the screen again, the next slide already queued. He didn't raise his voice—he didn't need to. The gravity of what he was about to share settled the room into silence.

"Tax filing day. That was the moment it all came crashing down."

Aldo leaned forward. "You mean that literally?"

Abhishek nodded slowly. "Seven days before the statutory deadline, we finally got the tax reports from the system. They were a disaster. Transactional gaps. Intercompany mismatches. Missing customs data. And no audit trail to trace the problems back."

Maria's brow furrowed. "No one caught it earlier?"

"People tried," Abhishek said. "But every escalation turned into a spreadsheet trail. Nothing was centralised. Nothing traceable. The system hadn't been configured to produce validated tax outputs—it was built around order-to-cash, procure-to-pay, and left tax hanging on the side."

Sophia stirred slightly but said nothing.

Aldo glanced at the slide. "And IT?"

"Couldn't help," Abhishek replied. "They didn't know what went wrong because tax logic had never been scoped. They didn't design the output. There was no mapping or reconciliation layer. Just flat files and frustration."

Sophia shifted again. Her arms crossed, then uncrossed. Her pen tapped, then stopped.

Maria's voice was steel. "What happened next?"

"We tried to fix it," Abhishek said. "Worked around the clock. Seven straight days. Rebuilding reports, reconciling manually. But the numbers wouldn't align. We filed late. Inaccurate returns. The penalties ran into millions."

He paused. "But worse than the money, we lost trust. The regulators stopped believing us. Leadership panicked. The tax team fractured."

Sophia exhaled sharply but didn't speak.

Maria tilted her head. "What about governance? Who was running this show?"

"There wasn't any," Abhishek said flatly. "The Finance Head was technically the sponsor but was barely involved. IT took control by default."

Aldo's voice was quieter now. "And they focused on speed over stability."

Abhishek gave a single nod. "Exactly. Everything was about meeting the go-live date. Fit the template. Push the volume. Compliance? Documentation? Cross-functional testing? Later, later, later."

Maria's hands were clasped now, knuckles tight. "And of course, 'later' never came."

"Not in time," Abhishek said. "By the time we fixed even 30 percent of the issues, the reputational damage was irreversible."

Sophia tried to interject, but Aldo cut in before she could. "Was there any change after that? Any remediation plan at all?"

"There was talk," Abhishek said. "But mostly damage control. The COO attempted to launch Phase 2, but it lacked substance. People were burnt out. Distrust was everywhere."

Sophia's voice finally returned, clipped. "They didn't have the right change agent."

Abhishek looked at her. "No. They didn't have alignment. Or humility. Or cross-functional trust."

Sophia blinked.

Maria let the silence stretch for a beat, then spoke. "Let's make sure AlphaCorp learns from that. I would like to have a governance framework by next week. Risk controls. Compliance checkpoints. And tax isn't optional—it's central."

Abhishek turned, eyes scanning the room. He stepped to his seat and took it. Sophia didn't meet his gaze.

Aldo finally broke the silence. "And this time, we build the house with the lights on."

07:57 PM – When Testing Became Theatre

Abhishek remained at the front of the room, more grounded now, more certain. He wasn't embellishing. Just laying out the facts, one shard at a time.

He clicked to the next slide. A diagram labelled "UAT Scope vs. Real Coverage."

"Now we come to testing," he said, voice steady. "Or what they called testing."

Aldo raised an eyebrow. "You're saying UAT didn't happen?"

"It happened," Abhishek said. "But only in name. What we had was a theatrical production. A tick-the-box performance under deadline pressure."

He paused. "Matrix leadership locked a go-live date early. Non-negotiable. Everyone was working backwards from it. By the time testing began, there was no time left for realism."

Sophia shifted in her seat. Not with boredom—with agitation. Her eyes darted briefly toward Aldo. A glance held a beat too long. Then she scribbled something furiously in her notepad. But Abhishek continued, undeterred.

"The business users were exhausted," he said. "Finance was closing Quarter-3. Procurement was deep in year-end renegotiations. Tax? We were mid-audit."

Maria nodded slowly. "And yet they were handed test scripts?"

"No, Maria," Abhishek said. "They were handed PowerPoints. Massive decks. Screenshots – without any walkthroughs or sandbox time. Just: 'Here's your scope, sign here when done.'"

Sophia let out a sharp sigh, as if exasperated by the memory—or the way Abhishek was framing it. Her pen now rested on her lower lip. Her gaze floated sideways toward Aldo again.

Aldo ignored it. He was focused. "And the test cases?"

"Happy path," Abhishek said. "The cleanest scenarios. They shied away from edge cases and known complexity. 'Click here, get green tick, next.'"

Maria's voice was laced with disbelief. "And tax?"

"Looped into five test cases," Abhishek said. "All post-fact. Our flows were tied to finance. We weren't even listed in the critical path."

Sophia sat back now, arms folded. Her expression was neutral, almost too neutral, like a mask.

Aldo tilted his head, watching Abhishek closely. "Okay. But let me test you on something. Was there any form of test data obfuscation? Masking? Or was production data used raw?"

Abhishek thought for a second. "Mostly raw. Some vendor data was masked. But a lot of it was inconsistent. I wouldn't call it controlled."

Aldo nodded, impressed.

Then another question. "What about data reconciliation tools? Did they have anything to track variances between system and report outputs?"

Abhishek paused. "That's one I can't answer with confidence," he said. "I think there was a tool implemented, but it wasn't being used properly. I'm happy to unpack that with you later."

Aldo smiled slightly. It wasn't mockery. It was respect. "Appreciate the honesty."

Maria looked between the two of them, quietly observing the emerging chemistry. Sophia's gaze tightened. She shifted again, one hand now resting on the table, fingers drumming faintly.

Abhishek returned to the room. "Bottom line: testing was a mirage. Executives saw green checkmarks. Users saw screenshots. But no one saw the gaps."

Maria exhaled, calm but cold. "And the system went live with those gaps."

Abhishek nodded. "Right over the cliff."

09:43 PM – Post-Go-Live Fallout

Abhishek didn't need a slide for this part. He rose but stood away from the screen now, closer to the room, the story still fresh in his bones.

"The system went live."

He let the words linger. Everyone already knew what was coming.

"Day one was quiet—but not the good kind. People were hesitant, clicking through unfamiliar screens, trying to map their muscle memory from the old system onto something alien. Some were hopeful. Most were just... confused."

He glanced at Maria. "By day two, hope turned to panic. Invoices disappeared mid-process. Tax codes misfired across jurisdictions. Revenues miscalculated. Intercompany reconciliations broke across legal entities. And within a week, the realisation hit: key compliance reports were missing."

Maria closed her eyes. "Month-end must've been a bloodbath."

Abhishek nodded. "The tax team hadn't been in the loop. Now, they were expected to perform surgery during an earthquake. Users turned on the system. What was meant to empower them... became the villain."

Silence took hold—the kind that follows not from disbelief, but recognition.

Abhishek continued, his voice quieter now. "Every team that had been sidelined—tax, finance, compliance, procurement—they were now asked to fix problems they never signed off on. Root causes couldn't be identified. The system became a fortress of bad decisions, locked behind a wall of poor documentation."

Maria's gaze was steady now, forged by clarity. She looked around the room—at Abhishek, resolute but scarred; at Sophia, intense, perhaps too much so; and at Aldo, calm but calculating.

"We begin," she said, "by rewriting the script. This is not about one function getting it right. It's about all of us getting it right—together."

Yet even as she outlined the future, Maria sensed the subtle current in the room. The Matrix case had done more than surface tactical lessons. It had cracked open the team dynamic. And she could sense some of that unease in that room as well.

Sophia, while engaged, was becoming sharper in tone, her focus narrowing to the attention that Abhishek was able to garner with the showcasing of his in-depth clarity on the Matrix case. She no longer wanted to be in the room. She was no longer paying attention to what Maria was saying. She was trying to conclude the long day, just waiting for everyone to leave.

She didn't know if she wanted comfort or control. Maybe both.

Aldo, watching from across the table, wasn't sure who Sophia wanted to distract—him, or herself.

As the room emptied, Sophia lingered behind. Her voice barely rose above a whisper.

"Walk me to the elevator?" she asked. The smile didn't reach her eyes. It never had.

Aldo hesitated, just for a beat, then followed.

The hallway lights flickered. Somewhere between silence and misstep, the line between insight and impulse quietly dissolved.

Maria remained seated, staring at the whiteboard. Her voice, low but resolute, carried only to herself:

"This isn't a solo act anymore. From now on, we build in harmony—or we don't build at all."

As she walked out of the boardroom, she felt the currents moving. The shadows of failed implementations no longer loomed so large. In their place was a shared sense of resolve—rooted not just in fear of repeating history, but in the belief that they could write a different one.

For the first time in weeks, Maria felt the tight knot of dread in her chest loosen.

In its place bloomed something unexpected.

Hope.

CHAPTER 10

What Success Looks Like

"Sometimes, the future hides not in the new, but in what the old dared to do right."
Most people assumed Matrix was the only transformation I'd been part of. They were wrong.
Before I ever set foot in that chaos, I had lived through something else—something rare. I had seen a transformation work.
Hybrid LLC wasn't perfect. No company is. But they did something extraordinary. They turned VAT compliance—yes, compliance—into a strategic muscle. Not through magic. Not through expensive tools. But through alignment.
And yet, even with that memory etched into my muscle, my thinking, my principles—I failed to recreate it at Matrix. That part of the story would come later.
Today wasn't about me: It was about the **system** *that had worked, about a group of people who rehearsed, aligned, and executed like a symphony.*
About Hybrid.

—Abhishek Iyer

9.30 AM, Monday - AlphaCorp Boardroom

It was a Monday morning that didn't quite feel like a Monday morning.

The boardroom carried the scent of freshly brewed Ethiopian roast—Maria's favourite—and the faint echo of the cleaning staff's jazz playlist from down the corridor. The weekend had come and gone like a soft reset. Even the city outside AlphaCorp's glass façade seemed slower, quieter, as if waiting for something to start.

Sunlight sliced through the tall windows, painting long shadows across the matte oak table. A half-full fruit bowl sat untouched, next to a tray of almond croissants no one had reached for. The smartboard behind the presenters' screen blinked softly, a patient bystander to the silence in the room.

The meeting had resumed, but no one had spoken for a while—not really.

Maria sat with her back straight, but her elbows slightly tucked inward, a posture she used when holding back emotion. Her dark green blouse matched the seriousness in her eyes. She was listening—but also waiting and calculating where to step next.

To her left, Sophia scrolled through her phone, her thumb moving in smooth, controlled arcs. Her face was unreadable. She hadn't challenged anyone yet, but her silence wasn't surrender—it was observation. There was a reason she never reached for coffee in the first fifteen minutes of a meeting. She wanted to see who broke the quiet first.

Aldo leaned back in his chair, half-turned toward the window as if drawing energy from the city skyline. He tapped a pen rhythmically against his notebook, not taking notes but keeping track of the tempo. His body language was relaxed, but his eyes—whenever they flicked back to the room—were sharp, calculating. Something had moved in him since Friday.

And then there was Abhishek.

He stood by the whiteboard, an erasable marker in hand, but not yet writing. The corners of his lips twitched in restraint—he didn't smile easily in moments like this. Instead, he breathed through the silence, as if trying to match the rhythm of the room before stepping into it.

His fingers brushed against the edge of the whiteboard.

Maria gave a slight nod, the kind that could mean anything.

"Let's shift to Hybrid," she said. "You were there. Show us what orchestration looks like when it works."

Abhishek leaned forward, his gaze steady. "Hybrid LLC," he began. "They turned VAT compliance into a strategic accelerator. Everything we wish Matrix had done—they did. And what truly made it work was the partnership among business, finance, tax and IT—seamless, strong, and intentional."

He clicked the remote, projecting the first slide. "They didn't treat VAT like an IT problem. They treated it as a catalyst for business transformation. And it paid off."

Maria folded her arms, her tone brisk but hopeful. "Alright. What set them apart?"

1. Lead Before the Legislation

Abhishek uncapped the pen and drew a long horizontal line across the whiteboard.

"Hybrid started eighteen months before the law came out," he said. "We worked off drafts. Structured the unknown."

Maria glanced up. "That early?"

He nodded. "We treated it like a supply chain problem. Dependencies, flows, blockers. Every week, we tested assumptions across various functions, including Finance, IT, Tax, and Legal. We didn't wait for the rules to arrive. We built muscle first."

No one interrupted. The room felt charged. Sophia was a silent listener during the Matrix debrief, and in this one.

"We assumed 80% global alignment," Abhishek continued. "Got the structure right. Dealt with the exceptions once the law matured."

He marked points on the timeline as he spoke. Draft guidance. Simulation cycles. System walkthroughs.

"We flagged high-risk areas early—intercompany, partial exemption, delivery terms, pricing mismatches. IT mapped them into the system design. Controls weren't bolted on later—they were part of the build."

Aldo folded his arms, watching. "So nothing reactive."

Abhishek shook his head. "Testing was validation there."

Maria leaned back, her expression unreadable. "Matrix waited," she said. "Hybrid moved."

Sophia didn't speak. But the resistance in her shoulders was gone. What remained was quiet calculation.

Abhishek looked around once more, then stepped away from the board.

"Preparation gave them confidence," he said. "And confidence gave them credibility."

No one disagreed.

2. Build the Dream Team

Abhishek switched to the next slide. It was a simple table: roles, names, outcomes. "Hybrid paired each expert with someone grounded in a business context. Skill met familiarity. That's what made it work. Every expert came paired with someone who knew the business inside out."

He paused at the second row. His name was listed as Project Lead—no title inflation—just someone who knew the business, the data, and the people who made things work.

"They pulled me in from Internal Audit to lead the program. There was no tax function then. Finance and IT were stretched. However, we were familiar with the business, the data, and the dependencies. I had the global trust, and we had Big 4 consultants to guide the technical edge."

Sophia tilted her head, watching him with curiosity.

Maria leaned forward. "So, how did the tech side stay aligned?"

Before Abhishek could respond, Aldo picked it up, almost like they'd rehearsed. "We were there from the start. IT joined every workshop — to shape, design, and anchor the system to real business needs."

Abhishek nodded. "And tax didn't sit in a silo. Because it didn't exist, we built it from scratch—anchored to business flows. The controls came from how transactions behaved and not just from theory."

Sophia spoke slowly. "So execution and policy grew together."

Aldo smiled slightly. "That was orchestration. No one led alone. Each part adjusted to the others. What emerged was a system that played in time."

Maria looked across the room. Abhishek, measured and clear. Aldo, quick but grounded. Sophia, absorbing more than she questioned. The tempo was ramping up. This was no longer a debate; it was a rehearsal for something bigger.

She made a note. Three names. One direction.

3. Own the Process, Share the Load

Abhishek stood by the chart, the Hybrid governance model projected behind him. "The Group CFO didn't just sponsor the program. He chaired the steering committee. Weekly. Without fail."

Aldo leaned back, arms crossed. "Decisions weren't parked. Issues moved. Everyone knew who was on point. If something slipped, it wasn't invisible."

Sophia followed through, eyes still on the screen. "Conflicts didn't fester. They escalated fast and got resolved faster."

Abhishek nodded. "Because roles were clear. Accountability wasn't just a slide—it was lived. And every team knew why they were there."

Aldo added, "When tax explained the 'why,' the build found its shape. That's how IT delivered clean."

Maria turned toward the fading Matrix Gaps chart. "Matrix had no compass. Hybrid had a coordinated crew."

Sophia didn't look up. "That's why it didn't break under pressure."

4. Business First, System Second

"We mapped how the business worked," Abhishek said. "Not how it looked on the org chart. We didn't start with requirements, we started with reality. Who touched what? Where value changed hands. When the VAT trigger happened. What documents were moved? We walked through the process like auditors."

Aldo joined in. "IT captured the flow. Tax decoded the meaning. And together, they found the friction points. Then they redesigned around that."

Maria leaned forward. "So when VAT finally landed, it didn't shake the system?"

Abhishek shook his head. "It just ... fit. We had already taught the system how to behave. VAT wasn't layered on. It was part of the logic."

Sophia, quietly now, said, "They didn't digitise chaos. They structured order."

Maria sat back. The difference was clear now. Hybrid didn't react to situations, but it was prepared to respond with precision. They reimagined the business in the new reality. And AlphaCorp could, too — if they chose to.

5. Design Together, Decide Together

Abhishek paused before shifting the next slide into view. It was a web of names — of real people. "At Hybrid, every function nominated VAT champions. People who others listened to."

He let the silence hang just long enough.

"They weren't figureheads. They were translators. When an issue showed up in procurement, pricing, or returns, these champions didn't escalate — they engaged. IT worked with them directly. Problems were solved before they took root."

Sophia's eyes narrowed. The kind that comes when someone realises the old playbook might no longer serve. "How did you get them to take ownership without making it ... extra work?"

Abhishek nodded slightly, welcoming the question. "We didn't ask them to carry the tax. We asked them to defend their processes. Once they understood how tax shaped system behaviour, they saw the ripple effect. They stopped delegating compliance and started owning design."

Aldo added, "And we designed with them, not for them. Nothing went live that they hadn't touched."

Maria spoke softly, almost to herself. "That's how trust forms. And that's how culture gets built."

At Hybrid, the tax hadn't been shouted for a seat. It had earned one by making itself impossible to ignore. Policy came early. Interpretation was stable. People trusted it because it was usable and practical.

Maria leaned back, satisfied. This wasn't just alignment. This was awareness ripening into belief.

Abhishek glanced once at the screen, then at the group. For the first time, it didn't feel like he was presenting a case. It felt like they were building one together.

6. Train to Test, Not Just Use

Abhishek moved to the next slide — a heatmap of testing outcomes across geographies. "At Hybrid, training wasn't designed for usage. It was built for breakage."

Maria raised a brow.

Abhishek clarified, "We didn't walk users through manuals. We asked them to challenge every scenario, find what wouldn't work. Provoke errors before the system has a chance to."

Sophia leaned in. "So you trained them to test, not follow?"

Abhishek smiled. "Exactly. We called them 'power users,' but they were architects in disguise. The more they tested, the more they owned.

And when they found gaps, IT didn't defend the code. They rewrote it — fast."

Aldo added, "And tax wasn't on the sidelines. Every test cycle had legal logic embedded within it. Not just 'Did it work?' but 'Did it comply?' There was no room for assumption."

Maria glanced around the room. "That's real simulation."

Sophia was quiet for a moment, the memory of Matrix's silent implosion flickering behind her eyes. This wasn't admiration. Not yet. But it was the first time she'd heard a plan that didn't sound like hope dressed up as strategy. Then, with a softened voice, she added, "I remember how, at Matrix, they handed out training decks like fire blankets. But the system burned anyway. People nodded through the sessions, followed the steps, and still couldn't explain what the system meant. It looked like readiness on paper. But it was imitation."

Abhishek listened, but didn't interrupt. Sophia was no longer reacting to Hybrid.

She continued, more slowly now. "What struck me most is... at Hybrid, training gave people awareness. They didn't just follow paths — they saw intersections. Impacts. The why beneath the click. That sight made them collaborators."

Aldo nodded. "And once you collaborate, you stop needing escalation. You fix things where they start."

Abhishek added, "Every defect logged during training told a story — of failures and insights. We built a knowledge base from those lessons. By go-live, most users already believed the system could work — because they had shaped it."

Sophia looked up, quiet but resolute. "That's why it didn't collapse. It wasn't luck. It was understanding, distributed across a hundred small decisions."

Maria leaned back in her chair, the silence almost reverent. She saw it now — the output and the intention behind it. And AlphaCorp could choose that same intention, if they dared to test before trusting.

7. A Pre-Mortem, Not a Post-Mortem

Abhishek flipped to a blank black slide. Four bold words appeared: What could go wrong?

He let the room sit with the question.

"One month before go-live, we imagined every possible reason for project failure. We ran a pre-mortem analysis — to prevent and prepare for every risk that could lead us to failure."

Sophia leaned in. "You logged the risks?"

"Yes. But not as a formality. These were real scenarios — human error, interface gaps, regulatory changes, and system lags. And each had a clear owner from both Tax and IT."

Abhishek smiled faintly. "We even kicked off the session by watching *Back to the Future*. That set the context beautifully. And then the pre-mortem made so much more sense."

Maria's pen stilled. "Now that's what I call visionary project planning and maturity."

Abhishek nodded. "Most teams learn after wounds. We learned before them — on paper, with courage."

He scanned the table.

Maria spoke softly. "This is what AlphaCorp needs. A team willing to imagine risk — and walk and work toward it together."

8. Train to Embed, Not Just Explain

"Twenty thousand trained in eight weeks," Abhishek said. "With thorough walkthroughs and peer-led sessions."

Aldo continued, "Tax made it real. IT made it repeatable. Trainers became coaches, and users became advocates."

"One of the surprises was a store supervisor, Ahmed, in Saudi Arabia. Initially sceptical, Ahmed became the team's most vocal trainer — even building his cheat sheets in Tamil to help others understand the new VAT workflows."

But Maria didn't nod — not immediately. Her mind was processing the more profound truth beneath the numbers.

This wasn't just training. It was immersion — a strategic act of shaping knowledge and mindset. VAT wasn't a footnote on policy manuals — it touched every system, every process, every employee, and every customer. There was no room for blind spots. None.

And Hybrid's leadership knew it. They approached training as enablement, as alignment. Each session was more than instruction — it was an invitation to understand why every detail mattered. Why a missed configuration could ripple into customer dissatisfaction, financial risk, or regulatory penalties. And why ownership couldn't stay with just a few — it had to be shared by everyone.

"If they hadn't trained this way," Maria finally said, "they wouldn't have made it past go-live. This wasn't just about UAT (User Acceptance Tests) success in the test environment — it was about post-go-live consistency. Matrix passed tests but collapsed in execution. Hybrid trained for compliance and also for continuity."

Sophia nodded. "It was as if Hybrid had taken the ghost of Matrix as a silent advisor — every misstep, every delay, turned into foresight."

Aldo added, "They didn't follow a template. They created a new one. They turned each risk into a requirement, each unknown into a deliberate design choice. That's mastering context."

Maria's expression was serious now, but impressed. She felt the weight of what this meant for AlphaCorp.

Awareness breeds insight. Insight breeds ownership. Ownership enables transformation, she thought. This isn't just about learning how. It's about understanding why. And we'll only succeed if that 'why' runs in everyone's blood by the time we go live.

9. A Go-Live Worth Remembering

"New Year's Eve, 2017," Abhishek said. "A thousand five hundred sites. Not one incident. A multi-country VAT rollout with zero disruption."

Aldo leaned back, visibly moved.

"Even the tax authority was impressed. They didn't see a deployment. They witnessed something rare — a living, breathing ecosystem functioning in perfect rhythm," Abhishek added.

For a moment, none of them spoke—the weight of what they had just walked through, though secondhand, felt deeply personal.

Maria finally broke the silence, her voice soft but glowing. "That's the dream."

But this time, it wasn't just a line. There was reverence in her tone, as if honouring something sacred. She turned to Sophia and Aldo, and they met her gaze, eyes reflecting the same quiet awe.

They hadn't implemented Hybrid's project. But in this moment, through every insight they had unpacked, every failure they had translated into foresight, every leadership principle they had internalised — it felt as if they had.

Aldo smiled, almost unexpectedly. "If we can carry even half of what they did, we won't just succeed. We'll inspire."

Maria nodded. "This wasn't a case study. It was a blueprint for how teams transform — when they trust."

She then looked out the window.

It starts here, she thought. With strategy, with tech and shared belief. And maybe — just maybe—we're finally there.

10. Cultural Anatomy of a Transformation

By the time they had finished Abhishek's presentation, it was nearly 9 p.m. The sun had long disappeared behind the skyline, leaving the AlphaCorp floor bathed in a quiet, amber glow from the emergency lights and cleaning crew overhead. Coffee cups sat half-drunk, whiteboards layered in scrawled arrows and Post-it echoes of tension turned into trust.

"Abhishek," Maria asked, "was Hybrid's rollout really that perfect? No cracks? No challenges at all? That's not reality."

Abhishek gave a half-smile. "No, Maria. It wasn't flawless. There were cracks. But every one of them was addressed. The residual risks were all addressed after the pre-mortem."

He took a deep breath, remembering. "There were tensions with the consultants — we often disagreed on how VAT would apply in real business scenarios. I felt they didn't understand the business. They thought I didn't get the tax nuance. Eventually, we brought in a second set of consultants to mediate the situation. That helped reset things."

He continued, "Early on, we had friction with IT, too, much like Matrix. They tried to patch things their way. But our Group CFO stepped in and reinforced the role of Design Authority. That realignment was critical."

Sophia interjected. "Design Authority — can you clarify what that means?"

Abhishek nodded. "It's like a legislative body in a government. A Design Authority is a governance structure that reviews and approves any changes to the systems, processes, or data structures that deviate from the agreed project architecture. Just as a law must go through Parliament for approval, a design change must pass through the Design Authority. It prevents individual functions, such as IT or Tax, from making isolated decisions that could impact the entire ecosystem. It ensures alignment, cross-functional input, and sustainability."

Sophia gave a thoughtful nod.

"And what about data?" Maria asked, her tone casual — almost too casual. "What about the quality of data? We often assume technology can clean up everything. But at Matrix — and I suspect even at Hybrid — was that the case ?"

Abhishek exhaled sharply, then nodded. "You're right. At Hybrid, we ran into that wall early. Everyone wanted automation to fix everything, but you can't create magic out of garbage. GIGO — Garbage In, Garbage Out — wasn't just a warning. It was a guarantee."

He continued, his voice firmer. "Our initial test runs failed. Reports were misaligned, tax codes were misapplied, and test filings were inconsistent. Why? Because master data was broken — outdated vendor records, missing tax classifications, duplicate customer entries."

He looked around the room. "That's when we took a detour. We couldn't move forward without rebuilding the foundation. We established a master data governance framework, brought in specialists, and validated every input at the source. Only then could the automation work."

Sophia nodded slowly, understanding dawning. "So the tool wasn't the problem — the data was."

"Exactly," Abhishek said. "You can buy the best car in the world — but if you fuel it with dirty petrol, don't blame the engine when it breaks down."

Sophia leaned forward again. "What exactly did Hybrid do about MDM, master data management? We've never had a real MDM team at AlphaCorp — and frankly, it's always felt abstract to me."

Abhishek smiled. "Think of it this way — imagine trying to find someone in a city where no one has a name or address. How would you even start? Or imagine delivering a package to a building with no street name, no number, no postcode. That's what operating without master data feels like. You can't identify, track, or differentiate anything reliably."

He continued, "Master data gives everything its identity — vendors, products, customers, tax codes. Without clean, consistent data, your tax engine and compliance process are like couriers driving with no GPS. At Hybrid, we were late to realise that. However, over time, we hired the right experts, defined tax-relevant data fields, and established a robust governance structure. That foundation enabled every other layer to function."

Aldo leaned in. "What tax technology suite did Hybrid choose apart from their ERP? How did it perform? Were you happy with it in hindsight, or would you have chosen differently?"

Abhishek didn't hesitate. "As far as the tax technology suite is concerned, I wasn't happy with the choices Hybrid made — in hindsight. For a business of their size, with a remote shared service centre supporting multiple geographies, I would've preferred a tax determination tool and a compliance engine. Instead, they relied on the ERP tax module, customising it for each country. That created redundancy. Shared service teams needed regional tax experts to maintain compliance and accounting integrity. A proper tax engine could've removed much of that complexity."

Sophia frowned slightly, still unsure. "Sorry, maybe a silly question — but does technology impact tax that deeply? I mean, isn't tax about rules and reporting?"

Abhishek turned to her with a gentle seriousness. "It's not a silly question. It's the right one. Think of a call centre — say, for a multinational bank. Its customers are spread across the globe — in New York, Tokyo, London, and São Paulo — but its call centres are located in places such as Taiwan, the Philippines, Serbia, Egypt, and India.

Now, for standard queries like 'What's my account balance?' or 'Can I reset my password?' — would the bank want to hire multilingual staff in every location to handle every language and nuance? Or would it prefer to build a system-driven language translation and menu-routing functionality that answers 80% of those questions instantly, accurately, and at scale?

"Coding and customising your ERP to handle every tax rule in every country is like hiring multilingual agents everywhere. It's inefficient, hard to update, and expensive to maintain. But using tax technology is like automating the language selection, auto-response flows, and intelligent routing for edge cases — it's scalable, innovative, and adaptable.

"In both cases, the human still matters for complex queries, complaints, or judgment calls. But the machine takes the load off the system, so the human effort is focused where it matters most."

Sophia nodded slowly. "Okay. That... makes sense now."

Maria looked at him with admiration. She was now getting curious and reaching conclusions. "Why do you think Hybrid succeeded while

Matrix failed? Both had a budget. Both had top-tier technology. You led both, but the outcomes were opposite."

Abhishek was quiet for a moment. Then he answered with calm precision.

"Because in my opinion, both the transformations were not about the tools. It's about the people who used them. Matrix had strategy, funding, and systems. But there was no alignment. No shared vision. No accountability or ownership. No one felt responsible — and no one was empowered to care."

He paused. "Hybrid wasn't perfect. But it had something Matrix never did — clarity of purpose and a culture that showed up for the transformation every day. Leadership was visible. Cross-functional teams were genuinely collaborative. We didn't outsource ownership; we embedded it."

"We defined objectives. Identified impact points. Designed collaboratively. Built iteratively with constant feedback. Tested like it was a crash simulation. Deployed with care. Hypercare wasn't support — it was stewardship."

"There was one more difference," he added. "Matrix was implementing ERP, led by IT, with Tax as a component. Hybrid was implementing Tax, and Tax was in the driver's seat. But more than function, it was the way the project was led. With intent, rhythm, and shared ownership."

He looked up, steady now. "Yes, there were roadblocks. Plenty. But leadership was invested. The governance worked. And that made all the difference."

"And when the tax authority chose to audit Hybrid one year after implementation — and that audit lasted three years — there was nothing material in the findings. Compare that with Matrix. You have the answers now, I guess."

Maria studied him for a moment, then nodded slowly — but this time, her expression softened with a flicker of satisfaction. As if Abhishek had finally articulated what she had always known deep down — that transformation was not born from tools, but from orchestration. She didn't need to say it. He had arrived there on his own. "Thank you," she said. "That's what I needed to hear."

Aldo also nodded slowly, this time with respect.

They didn't notice Sophia's reaction.

And that, too, was telling.

Maria stayed behind, alone in the room. Her gaze swept across the empty chairs, the fading agenda still glowing on the projector screen.

Next week, she would stand before the board.

Tonight, she had what she needed.

A pitch deck, yes. But far more - a coalition. A reason to believe.

CHAPTER 11

The First Strike

"Often, getting your foot inside the door is all that matters. The rest follows."

Setting the Stage

The late afternoon light cast long rectangles across the oak table. The boardroom was quieter than usual — no assistants, no screens, no formal agenda. Just four people, each holding different pieces of the same unsolved puzzle.

Maria leaned forward, elbows resting on the table, sleeves rolled, notepad closed. "Let's set aside politics and platform demos for a moment," she said. "What should AlphaCorp do next?"

Her voice was even. Unforced. But no one mistook the weight behind the question.

Aldo glanced at his tablet, then turned it face down, "We stop pretending we know," he said. "The global tax function looks like a patchwork quilt. Every country stitched in with a different thread. If we don't understand what's underneath, we'll automate confusion."

Sophia clicked her pen. Once. Then again. She didn't raise her voice. "But this isn't just about tax anymore. It never really was. Accounting, IT, operations—all of them feed into what tax becomes. The output reflects the integrity of everything upstream. Some countries already operate with considerable discipline. Take Germany. Under Karsten, they haven't had a single compliance issue in over a decade. That's not about clean charts. It's about how the teams show up—aligned, consistent, cross-functional. That's the orchestration Maria kept coming back to— functional excellence and how the notes harmonised across departments. Tax was where the discord became visible. So we should also study what's working there, not just replicate Hybrid blindly."

"That wheel runs on Karsten's spreadsheets and goodwill," Aldo replied, still not looking at her. "We copy that, we inherit the cracks."

Maria let the exchange land and fade. She turned to Abhishek.

He didn't look ready to speak. But when he did, it was with the calm of someone who'd seen both sides of the story. "At Hybrid," he said, "we had rituals. Weekly syncs. Shared language. Everyone could read the tax logic, not just the tax team. We didn't need more tools. We needed alignment." He glanced down briefly, as if recalling something precise. "I remember one Friday in Kuala Lumpur—our last week before go-live. The finance lead, the IT analyst, even the warehouse ops guy—they all sat together arguing over a single tax rule. Not because they had to. Because they wanted to get it right. That's when I knew it was working."

He paused.

"Matrix had budget, software, and consultants. Still failed because no one trusted the process. Or each other. We never even defined who owned what. Everything was everyone's job—or no one's."

Sophia shifted in her seat. Maria caught the motion but didn't comment. "So what's your recommendation?" she asked.

"Start by mapping how work gets done," Abhishek said. "The real workflow. The informal approvals. The duct tape solutions people rely on. Until we see that, anything we design is just theatre."

Maria sat back, pen uncapped but idle. Her eyes scanned the table—listening and registering everything. Sophia's restraint. Aldo's quiet provocation. Abhishek's hard-won clarity. She looked at each of them in turn.

"Sense-making first," she said, nodding toward Aldo. "Stabilise on what's working," toward Sophia. "And map the true operating model," toward Abhishek.

"Then we begin there. Function by function. Country by country - with people. Because until people are aligned, systems replicate the chaos faster."

—

That night, Maria stayed in her office long after the lights outside had dimmed into a soft blur. The hum of the air-conditioning was the only sound. Her coffee had gone cold hours ago. She flipped her notebook shut and walked to the window. The city glowed below, steady, unaware. The silence gave her room to think—about both what was said and what was meant.

She flipped through her notes and paused for a moment.

This wasn't a tax problem. It was a systems problem. A finance transformation problem. The kind that needed the full engine—accounting, reporting, master data, technology, tax—to move as one.

Richard, for all his flaws, had left behind something helpful: a line item in this year's budget labelled "Finance Innovation – Strategic Allocation." It was classic Richard—obsessed with buzzword projects more for headlines than outcomes. But this time, he'd left behind a loaded weapon she could now wield. Enough funding to build something real. Budget wouldn't be the bottleneck. Alignment would.

Maria stood and paced slowly, then opened her drawer and pulled out a single sheet of paper. A hand-sketched matrix. Board members. Influence lines. Allies. Detractors. Those who followed Richard. Those who distrusted her. Those who played both sides. One in particular—Becker from Operations—still carried the sting of Maria's first cost-control proposal, the one that slashed half of Becker's team. That memory would colour the vote, whether it was spoken or not.

She knew this proposal—if framed right—could define her tenure. Or fracture it.

She listed her generals next:

Aldo: The idealist-technologist. Young, sharp, and allergic to bureaucracy. He thrived on building what didn't exist. But could he operate under pressure? Yes—but only if he believed in the mandate.

Abhishek: Disciplined. Reflective. Grounded in failure and success. He wouldn't lead with volume, but his frameworks were gold. Maria saw him as the internal compass—slow to speak, impossible to ignore.

Sophia: The most unpredictable piece. Brilliant, guarded, and politically fluent. She would align only if she could steer it—or if she feared being left behind. Maria knew she'd need to handle Sophia carefully: offer her ownership without threatening her control.

She underlined one word beside each name: Leverage. And yet, the word tasted metallic tonight. To leverage someone meant to calculate their angle, not just trust their worth. It was necessary—but it came at a cost. Every time she turned insight into influence, she wondered if she was still leading or merely orchestrating. Still building a team—or bending one.

Then she picked up her phone.

"Get me Mark Healy."

Healy was more than a consultant. He was a fixer. An expert in business transformations who understood the mechanics and the boardroom theatre. London-based. Boutique firm. Trusted by legacy and growth leaders alike. He'd worked with Maria before. And more importantly, had allies on the Board.

When he answered, Maria didn't waste time. "I need you in the AlphaCorp office tomorrow. I'll send the brief. We're proposing an end-to-end finance transformation. It needs to land right."

The following week moved like a metronome. Sharp. Coordinated. Maria drove the strategy. Mark's team shaped the story. Aldo and Sophia stitched together data and architecture. Abhishek diagrammed the operational model, illustrating the difference between actual and perceived values.

And just before the weekend, they finished.

A single deck. Forty pages. Titled: AlphaCorp Finance Transformation – Unifying Vision and Execution.

Maria skimmed the title slide and closed her laptop. Her reflection stared back at the black screen.

Wall of fame. Or torn-out chapter.

Either way, the boardroom lights would be on again on Monday.

—

The AlphaCorp boardroom had the stillness of a courtroom before testimony. Morning light filtered through the floor-to-ceiling glass, cutting geometric shadows across the table's brushed steel. Eight seats were occupied—four men, three women, and AlphaCorp's CEO, Isabel Hartmann. All seasoned. All familiar. Isabel rarely intervened in these sessions unless it mattered. Today, she sat with her tablet closed, eyes scanning the room. The faint hum of the air conditioning was the only sound.

They wore the quiet power of old money and polished influence—tailored suits, understated brooches, wool-blend blazers in cool greys and navy blues. Nothing flashy. Just expensive. Elena's pearl earrings caught the light as she turned her head. Mikhail's Italian cut was pristine. Becker looked ready for a tribunal in his triple-stitched pinstripe. Even Jill, in her muted olive pantsuit, exuded composure laced with alertness.

Then Maria and Aldo entered.

Maria wore a charcoal suit—clean lines, precisely tailored—with a soft ivory blouse that glowed against her skin. Her hair was tied back in a low, elegant bun. Her eyes were calm but alert, like someone used to pressure but not immune to its weight. There was a quiet defiance in her walk, resolve. She inhaled, almost imperceptibly, remembering the sting of a failed budget defence years ago—before Richard, before AlphaCorp. She held that failure in her spine, where it had become posture. She looked at Becker and recalled the first meeting after Richard's exit—how he had glanced past her, as if Finance had no future without its patriarch. That slight had stayed with her, quiet and unresolved. Today, she had earned his attention, if not yet his approval.

Beside her, Aldo moved with quiet authority. He wore a navy blue Nehru-style jacket, crisply cut, paired with slim black trousers and polished oxfords. The high collar suited his posture—upright, balanced, unfazed. His eyes scanned the room. Focused, observant, prepared to engage. Where Maria's calm came from internal steel, Aldo's came from systems logic— precise, tuned to every variable.

Today, they weren't just representing their functions. They were co-pilots of a new idea. Aldo was the architect behind AlphaCorp's evolving digital infrastructure, and his presence signalled that this wasn't just a finance problem—it was a systems challenge. Mark Healy trailed slightly behind, tie loosened, unfazed. He had a way of making even his entrance look like a part of the context.

This Board meeting was Maria and Aldo's battle to win. Sophia and Abhishek had wished them well.

Maria opened the meeting with quiet confidence.

"Thank you for your time. We're here to present a critical recommendation—one that addresses the full structure of how AlphaCorp manages its financial systems, including tax, accounting, reporting, and underlying governance."

She clicked forward.

What's the challenge?

She paced slowly, eyes steady. "AlphaCorp has outgrown its legacy processes. What worked in eight markets doesn't hold across twenty-one. The tax health check revealed surface-level symptoms—late filings, mismatched reconciliations, and rising penalties. But those are outputs."

What brought us here?

Maria looked at Aldo. He stood.

"Inputs are the issue," Aldo said, stepping forward. "We've built layer upon layer of local customisation—workarounds, quick fixes, spreadsheets duct-taped into legacy systems."

He gestured to the slide. "Every region has its logic. Finance says one thing, IT another. Tax waits for both. This isn't misalignment—it's fragmentation by design. Until we unify our data architecture and process ownership, transformation will remain surface-level."

Becker interrupted. "Isn't this your job to manage? Why escalate it to a transformation?"

Maria nodded. "It definitely is, Tom. And we've done it—case by case. But when every fire comes from the same faulty wiring, you don't keep changing the smoke alarm. You rebuild the circuit."

Aldo added, "And to be clear, we've mapped the source codes, charted process drift, and triangulated user feedback. The problem isn't invisible. It's ignored. Patching systems without fixing the underlying architecture is like painting over rust; it's like paving over potholes without checking the roadbed. You'll look smooth until the next monsoon."

Mark glanced briefly at Becker, catching the resistance behind the question. His eyes lingered for a second—just long enough to register judgment—then flicked back to the slides.

A few heads nodded. Jill scribbled notes.

Maria continued, "What brought us here isn't going to take us forward. AlphaCorp is still running on muscle memory—structures, approvals, decision styles that don't reflect the speed or culture of the next generation."

She looked around the table.

"We're not ready for the kind of people we say we want to hire. They walk in with ideas and leave with resignation letters. This transformation isn't just about fixing tax or finance. It's about reconditioning how we operate—our expectations, our language, our leadership norms. In the same way that we need to upgrade our systems, we also need to upgrade the culture that guides our business practices. If we don't, we'll keep losing the very talent we're trying to attract."

She paused, then added: "Culture isn't changed by policy—it's changed by what we reward, who we promote, and what we tolerate."

Isabel leaned forward slightly.

"I agree with Maria," she said, her voice firm. "What got us here won't get us there. We've been patching symptoms. But the AlphaCorp of tomorrow—leaner, faster, digital-first—can't be built on the habits of yesterday. We need to change the tech, and the tone. Not just the platform, but the people who power it."

There was silence—and then slow, quiet acknowledgement.

What has been the consequence?

"Beyond penalties, we've had three restatements in 18 months. We have incurred $1.2 million in tax penalties in the last half-year alone and suffered a significant reputational impact in the US. Close calls in India and Saudi Arabia. Audit findings are rising. Our ability to forecast is becoming guesswork."

Christine raised her hand. "How do we know this isn't just noise from local teams?"

Aldo responded before Mark could. "Because the same noise is coming from too many places. And in my world, when signals repeat across systems, it's failure logic. The data tells the same story in India, France, and Mexico."

He added silently to himself: If this worked, it wouldn't just change AlphaCorp. It would prove that systems thinkers could lead and fix.

Mark followed seamlessly. "We validated the findings across five geographies. Same patterns. Governance fatigue. Exceptions are the norm. We're not fixing problems—we're firefighting them. At scale."

Mikhail spoke up next. "What's your ask?"

Maria didn't flinch. She moved on to the next slide in her presentation.

"We propose a full-scale finance and tax transformation. The groundwork is in the current year's strategic allocation."

Silence.

Then Raghav smirked. "Bold ask."

Maria let the jab land. Then answered.

"I joined AlphaCorp to fix what was left undone. If this proposal feels ambitious, it's because we've ignored complexity for too long. This isn't about me. It's about giving our teams a system they can rely on."

It wasn't lost on Maria that some Board members, Becker chief among them, still saw her as Richard's compliant successor—the safe pair of hands, not the reformer. She had been chosen, some believed, to maintain stability. And yet here she was, presenting one of the boldest transformation proposals AlphaCorp had seen in decades. That incongruity didn't sit well with everyone at the table, and Becker's stiff posture reflected more than policy scepticism. It was a challenge to her right to reshape the rules.

Becker folded his arms. "We're not signing off on a full transformation. Not yet."

Aldo didn't hesitate. "With respect, Tom, if we only treat the symptoms, we're locking ourselves into a cycle of repair. The world is evolving. Our peers are evolving. If AlphaCorp doesn't get ahead of this now, we'll be reacting to crises instead of leading with capability."

Mark Healy chimed in, voice steady. "This isn't just a systems overhaul. It's a reputational decision. Stakeholders—from regulators to investors—are watching how AlphaCorp responds. A partial fix sends the wrong signal. A structured, measurable approach demonstrates intent."

Across the table, Raghav leaned back, expression unreadable. He'd seen Mark in action before—deft, polished, persuasive. Part of him admired it. Another part? Cynical.

Jill looked up from her notes.

"You're proposing culture change," she said. "That doesn't come with a six-month metric."

What Maria and Aldo had just demonstrated—through data, poise, and resistance to being cornered—wasn't merely competence. It was will. This meeting was a test of character as well as strategy. The Board wasn't evaluating feasibility alone—they were evaluating backbone.

Anwar leaned forward. The room had tightened posture, tone, and patience. He noticed it. The tension wasn't just ideological now; it was institutional.

"We're circling," he said. "Let me offer an alternative."

He glanced at Isabel, then back at the room. "What if we greenlight the initial implementation—starting with tax automation—and revisit scope after six months? We de-risk the start, but show serious intent."

Heads nodded. Mikhail offered, "If tangible progress is shown, we revisit the rest."

There was a brief pause. Maria's shoulders lifted, then steadied. Disappointment flickered—visible but controlled. After a breath, she nodded.

"Agreed."

Her voice was even, measured, just as it needed to be. This was the AlphaCorp Boardroom—professional, direct, sharp on challenge but respectful in tone. Here, restraint was a currency. But inside, Maria felt the friction—the cost of leverage. Every strategic ask came with invisible interest. Political capital spent, reputational risk wagered. Her hands were steady, but her gut knew the price.

Aldo remained composed beside her, fingers loosely interlocked, but his eyes had narrowed just slightly. He understood the subtext: the approval was strategic, but conditional. Still, he offered nothing but affirmation. And for the first time that morning, he let out a slow breath, longer than usual. The kind that comes after holding something in too long.

They both knew what this meant. The door wasn't wide open, but it wasn't shut either. What they had now was a platform. A foothold. And in rooms like this, that was the key.

Some Board members exchanged glances. Inwardly, they recognised the rhythm—this was less about content and more about conviction. No executive team could be handed a transformation mandate. Not without proving they were ready to fight for it. Behind the nods and British courtesy, the Board was hedging its bets. Testing. Giving them a shot—but only one. Deliver, and the full scope would follow. Fumble, and this window would close faster than it opened.

The vote was informal but clear. They had secured a phased entry—defined, bounded, and real.

The room emptied slowly. Mark gave Maria a nod—part pride, part warning. Aldo exhaled, shoulders square, the weight of restraint still on his frame. His smile was brief but resolved—already recalculating what six months needed to look like.

Outside, as they packed up, Maria looked at Aldo.

"This wasn't the outcome we wanted."

Aldo adjusted his sleeve, then said, "No. But we have a foothold. That's more than we had yesterday."

From the far end of the hallway, one Board member lingered—Raghav—watching the team leave. He turned to Elena with a whisper.

"Healy always shows up when there's a big invoice to follow."

Elena didn't reply. But as she watched Maria and Aldo walk away, she made a note to herself.

The tone of the boardroom had changed in the past year. Conversations were sharper. Assumptions were being challenged. Once, tech had waited outside the room. Now, it sat beside Finance. And for the first time in a long time, the dialogue didn't feel like a formality. It felt like leadership.

She glanced again at the table, where the shadows had begun to shift, darker now as the sun set. The light had changed.

She opened her notebook and underlined a word beside Maria's name. **Steady.**

Then another beside Aldo's. **Emerging.**

She closed her book. The door clicked & shut behind her.

In six months, the proof would come — from real delivery.

Maria paused by the glass wall, watching the elevator descend. They hadn't won the war. But today, the battlefield had evolved.

CHAPTER 12

The Search for a Partner

6:48 PM – 27th Floor, AlphaCorp Tower

The elevator doors slid open with a quiet sigh, releasing Aldo and Maria onto the near-empty 27th floor—the one earmarked for the future Transformation War Room. For now, it still smelled of fresh paint: a new atmosphere fighting the old, stale smell of a space long closed.

Outside the glass walls, London blushed in twilight. Canary Wharf glowed like circuitry in the distance, and the Thames shimmered, its curves like question marks asking what came next.

Maria stepped out first, loosening the grip on her notebook.

"Well," she said, half to herself, "we didn't walk out with the prize, but we're not out of the race either."

Aldo followed, his shoulder bag slung carelessly, but his mind was still pacing that boardroom.

"They gave us the runway," he said. "We just have to build the plane while we're taxiing."

Maria cracked a smile. "That's exactly the problem. Tax never gets the plane. We get a scooter and a one-way ticket to nowhere."

"Not this time," Aldo said, voice low but steady. "You cracked something in that room."

They walked down the hallway, past vacant meeting rooms and a coffee station that still hadn't been stocked.

"We kick off the RFP for our project consultant this week," Maria said. "No delays. No games. And no 'partner' with a recycled slide deck from 2019."

Aldo nodded. "We'll need a consultant who can sit between tech and function," he said. "We're not hiring a vendor. We're hiring a mirror—someone who reflects what we refuse to see."

"And one who doesn't just echo but someone who'll challenge you too," he continued. "Even if it's uncomfortable."

She exhaled slowly. "Fair."

They reached the corner office that would soon become the project's nerve centre. She paused there, looking out.

"This is where it begins, isn't it?" she said.

"No," Aldo replied. "This is where we stop pretending it never began."

She gave him a look—a mix of gratitude and exhaustion—then checked her watch.

"And Maria?"

She turned halfway.

"You held the room today," Aldo said. "You earned it."

She didn't answer. Just a nod. Then she was gone.

8:10 PM – Outside a Low-Key Bar in Shoreditch

Aldo leaned against the exposed brick wall, texting with one hand and watching people spill out of a fintech launch party next door. London nights in spring still held a bite.

His phone buzzed.

Sophia: "You better not have invited me here just to gloat."

He grinned and texted back:

Aldo: "Absolutely not. Gloating's more fun with drinks."

Moments later, she appeared—sharp black blazer, silver hoops, hair tied high, expression unreadable.

"I hope this is worth a train ride," she said, brushing past him into the bar.

Inside, the lighting was dim, the music ambient, and the whiskey menu far too long. They took a corner booth.

"So?" she said, raising a brow. "You here to sell me hope?"

"No," Aldo replied, flagging the bartender. "I'm here to share it. Big difference."

She ordered a mezcal. He stuck with an old-fashioned.

"Maria thinks the RFP will magically fix alignment?" she asked.

"She thinks it'll reveal who's willing to align. Subtle difference."

Sophia swirled her drink. "Still feels like window dressing to me," she said, then added more quietly, "I've seen what happens when tax lets someone else write the brief. We end up chasing compliance with someone else's metrics."

"True," Aldo said. "But tonight's not for cynicism. It's for strategy. And this"—he raised his glass— "is for not quitting when things move slow."

Her eyes lingered on him. "You're optimistic for someone who usually predicts failure first."

"I'm adaptable," he replied. "And I know talent when I see it."

She didn't smile, but her posture softened. "Flattery or manipulation?" Her fingers tapped lightly on the side of her glass. "This used to be my Friday ritual. Before... never mind."

"Whatever gets you to help me draft the RFP this week."

Her phone buzzed. She glanced at it.

"Abhishek says thanks but no thanks," she said, reading the message. "Says he's knee-deep in the draft already. Added footnotes. Of course he did. He's home with the kids."

Aldo nodded. "Of course he is."

"Predictable."

"No. Anchored," Aldo said. "There's a difference. He's already reading the scope with a cup of chai in one hand and a toddler on the other."

Sophia snorted. "You're building a strange little army, Aldo."

"Only the best kind," he said. "One that doesn't need to raise its voice to change the system."

They clinked glasses.

She didn't pull away immediately. His hand brushed against hers—lightly, maybe accidentally. Or maybe not.

The music shifted. Her laugh came softer now, half-earnest and half-curious. A question danced in the silence between them, unspoken and unacknowledged.

When they stepped out into the night air, the street was quieter. A cab rolled past, empty.

She looked at him. "One more somewhere quieter?"

He didn't answer.

But he didn't say no.

Somewhere in the distance, a night bus groaned past, and the city exhaled into its Friday night rhythm.

Tuesday, 9:02 AM – 27th Floor War Room, AlphaCorp Tower

The glass-walled war room smelled of fresh starts—dry-erase ink, warm coffee—and vibrated with the hum of too many devices coming online at once. Screens blinked to life on three sides of the room, each logged into a different system: one displayed legacy ERP reports, another showed a blank RFP template, and the third scrolled through internal tax pain points like a slow-burning slideshow.

Aldo stood at the far end, laptop open, already deep into the architecture of the scope document. He hadn't said much since stepping in. He didn't need to.

Abhishek was seated across the table, neat and trim, notebook angled, pen ready, eyes alert but serene. He was dressed as always: crisp but unpretentious. His coffee was black. His focus was sharper.

And then there was Sophia.

She walked in like she owned the floor. Which, in some unspoken way, this morning, she believed she did.

There was a gleam in her posture—confidence in her control. As if she'd woken up having won a private battle no one else had seen. In a city that rewarded masks, hers was flawless.

Her heels tapped out a rhythm that was neither rushed nor uncertain. A hint of a smile played at the corner of her lips—the kind of smile that said a lot, yet nothing.

She took the seat to Aldo's left. Left of Aldo—close enough to signal alignment, far enough to keep mystery alive.

Aldo glanced at her just once. An unreadable flicker—respect, calculation, maybe even restraint.

Abhishek, always the observer, took it all in. Said nothing.

The room was quiet but humming. Something had taken another step.

Aldo broke the silence. "Alright. Let's draft a scope no one can misinterpret."

Sophia leaned in, though her voice lacked its usual edge. "Then we start by defining what we're not hiring," she said, pausing too long.

Aldo glanced at her—subtly, sharply. The hesitation didn't sit right. He said nothing, but the flicker in his eyes had dimmed.

Abhishek smiled gently. "And not someone who thinks tax is just a line item."

Aldo nodded. The war room came to life.

What they were building now was more than a document. It was a manifesto. And each sentence would carry the weight of past failures and future commitments.

Sophia stood and walked to the whiteboard. She picked up a green marker and wrote one word in bold strokes: Credibility.

"We cannot afford a Matrix repeat," she said.

Aldo nodded, already pulling up comparative case studies on the screen. "Matrix collapsed because IT took over and tax was sidelined."

Abhishek flipped open a notebook but didn't speak immediately. He drew a clean line across the page, then placed six dots beneath it—one for each selection criterion.

"When we chose a vendor at Hybrid," he said finally, "we treated it less like hiring a builder and more like hiring a surgeon. You don't just look for credentials. You look at what they do under pressure—what happens when a cut bleeds more than expected."

He gestured lightly toward the board. "The ones who failed at Matrix? They had the right lingo. But they froze when the bleeding started."

Sophia raised an eyebrow.

Abhishek didn't elaborate. He just turned another page and kept writing.

Later, as the conversation turned to jurisdictional presence, he added, "A tax partner who's never sat across from a Gulf customs officer or argued with a mid-tier EU VAT inspector can't help us. We don't need Google Maps—we need someone who's driven the roads."

His voice never rose. But each word landed like a well-placed file note—a quiet witness to things that had gone wrong before.

They began building the selection grid together.

Sophia clicked open her laptop, projecting the six-point partner framework:

1. Proven Track Record in Large, Complex Environments

2. Deep Tax-Tech Expertise with ERP Integration
3. On-the-Ground Presence in Key Jurisdictions
4. End-to-End Capability: Strategy to Support
5. Credible Relationships with Major Tax Tech Vendors
6. Collaborative, Business-First Approach

"We don't want theory-only players," Sophia added. "We want scars. They need to have survived failure—and fixed it."

"No IT-led consultants either," Aldo said. "We need partners who understand line-item tax logic in any ERP that we use—not just process flows, but how compliance breaks at the config level."

"And no guessing from Geneva," Abhishek added. "We need local knowledge in every VAT and e-invoicing country we operate in. Someone who knows how finance teams work."

"Not a relay race," Sophia said, then faltered. "At least, that's the theory."

Aldo looked up, brow tightening. "Is that hesitation, or is there something you're not saying?"

She waved it off with a half-smile. "Just realism."

But Aldo didn't return the smile. Something about her tone—it wasn't grounded caution. It was deflection. And it was starting to wear thin.

Aldo looked up. "And no resellers pushing biased solutions. We want someone who knows the vendors inside out, but doesn't worship at their altar."

Sophia grinned. "Neutral. But not naive."

They paused. Then Maria walked in.

She hesitated for just a beat, long enough for Abhishek to notice. This wasn't just about vendor fit. It was about her credibility.

Her eyes scanned the board. She took the marker from Sophia, circled **Credibility**, and turned to face them.

"This RFP isn't about hiring a firm," she said. "It's about choosing how AlphaCorp will function for the next decade."

Everyone nodded.

The war room buzzed to life again.

Wednesday – Midday

Markers squeaked. Screens filled. Coffee cups multiplied. The debate over wording, qualifiers, scoring logic, and deal-breakers developed its rhythm. Maria brought in Procurement to cross-check the scoring rubric. Abhishek cross-referenced previous RFPs from his time at Hybrid. The team huddled deep into Thursday.

They weren't just building a document—they were engineering a decision framework that could survive executive scrutiny and internal politics.

Tuesday – The week after

Three shortlisted candidates emerged after lengthy sessions and exhaustive internal reviews. The mood was slower now—fatigue had crept in—but so had conviction.

A global Big Consulting brand—credible, structured, but slow and rigid. Their decks were flawless, but their delivery record in emerging markets was suspect.

A multinational IT giant—technically sound, with implementation muscle, but hollow on tax nuance and strategy. They could build, but not guide.

And then there was Grayson & Holt Consulting.

They weren't the cheapest. They didn't come in with glossy brochures or celebrity partners. But what they did bring was clarity.

Their proposal was lean, their team led by former in-house tax leads, and their questions during the evaluation had cut straight through the fluff. Instead of pitching tools, they asked about governance. Instead of showcasing frameworks, they spoke about cultural bottlenecks and cross-functional breakdowns.

AlphaCorp's procurement team ran a complete evaluation cycle. RFP responses were standardised, commercial terms were negotiated, and cross-functional scorecards were assessed behind closed doors.

Maria and her team weren't part of the final procurement decision, but when the result was announced, they weren't surprised.

The procurement email came in at 11:03 AM.

Subject: Final RFP Outcome – Consultant Selection

Selected Partner: Grayson & Holt Consulting

The rationale was concise:

Proven success in rescuing failed e-invoicing rollouts in Southeast Asia.

A multidisciplinary team with deep tax, ERP, and analytics capability.

High score for "challenger mindset"—constructive pushback with solutions.

Strong alignment to AlphaCorp's culture of reform without rebellion.

Maria read the note twice. Then, she forwarded it to Aldo and Abhishek with a single line: "It's on."

By noon, the War Room was alive again.

Aldo was reviewing vendor onboarding timelines.

Sophia walked in late, holding a black coffee she would never drink. She placed it on the table, forgot about it, and then reached to adjust her wristwatch—only to realise it had stopped ticking. She frowned and turned the crown slowly, then gave up.

She hovered by the glass wall longer than usual.

When Aldo updated the group on Grayson & Holt's onboarding cadence, Sophia started to interject, questioning whether it was too fast, but Aldo's jaw tightened mid-sentence. He almost cut her off—nearly—but caught himself just in time.

The silence that followed wasn't awkward. It was instructive.

She sat down.

Aldo didn't look at her again for the rest of the meeting.

Maria stood at the head of the War Room, eyes scanning the final draft of the onboarding brief.

"Send them the final draft," she said to Abhishek.

He nodded.

She turned to Aldo.

"And brief Daniel. We start Monday."

Friday, 6:30 PM

By week's end, Grayson & Holt were on board. Contracts signed. Kick-off calls scheduled.

Sophia watched it all unfold—each step sealed, each decision finalised. And slowly, something inside her began to contract.

She had started the month as the conductor of her unspoken symphony. But now, the tempo had changed, and the baton felt foreign in her hand.

This was the brutality of fragility. It had slipped in quietly, when her control was too soon assumed.

Abhishek was gaining ground. Aldo was pulling away. And she—she was still at the table, but not quite in the circle.

The thin end of the wedge had landed.

Everything after this would widen the crack—or drive the stake home.

CHAPTER 13

Garbage In, Ghosts Out

10:32 AM – AlphaCorp Tower, Executive Lounge

The man by the window didn't move when they entered. He stood like a study in stillness, a dark silhouette against the London skyline, as if the city itself had hushed its breath for him.

Daniel Grayson led with gravity. And even in silence, the air in the room seemed to adjust around him, charged with an unspoken expectation.

Maria saw him first. No handshake, just a look that passed between them—a recognition that carried the weight of past battles. "Grayson," she said, the name a soft echo of a promise or a warning.

He turned, his eyes calm, almost preternaturally knowing. "Maria Mehta. Still walking into boardrooms with storms in your pocket?"

She offered a small, wry smile. "Only when the sky needs clearing." Inside, though, a familiar dread began to coil. This was the man. The one who always found the hidden wiring. The one she'd pinned so much on. If he couldn't find a path through this labyrinth, then what?

Behind her, Sophia and Abhishek exchanged glances, a shared understanding passing between them. They'd all heard the whispers: Daniel Grayson, senior partner at Grayson & Holt Consulting. A man with no public footprint, yet his global reputation was whispered among the elite. He'd reshaped entire industries, transcended borders, and navigated generational shifts. Now, in his early fifties, AlphaCorp was rumoured to be his final assignment before retirement—his last, monumental score.

Daniel stood with a quiet authority that transcended his tall, broad-shouldered frame. Salt-and-pepper hair, trimmed close; a neatly groomed beard. Matte black glasses framed sharp, absorbing eyes—eyes that seemed to take everything in. He was, more than anything, an observer. His navy suit was precise, stripped of pretence. But it was the stillness that marked him, not the suit: The profound self-possession of a man who had spent three decades in rooms where decisions outlived people. He wasn't rushed by noise or intimidated by status. Wisdom was etched into the fine lines at the corners of his eyes and mouth. And yet, behind that composed exterior, Maria sensed something else. A quiet finality. Like a conductor raising his baton for the last symphony, knowing this performance would echo long after his name faded.

Daniel Grayson never led from the front. Things fell into place once he entered, as if he commanded them to. He asked the questions others feared to voice. He brought perspective instead of PowerPoint. His gift wasn't execution; it was orchestration.

The glass-walled room was silent, charged with anticipation. The chilled, sterile conference space, where secrets often got buried under budget decks, now hummed. This wasn't a status meeting; it was a reset of roles and expectations. They had worked with Daniel Grayson before, but today was different. He wasn't just returning as an advisor; he was stepping into a far more engaged role. While he wouldn't be embedded in the trenches himself, his team would now work hand-in-glove with AlphaCorp to deliver the transformation on the ground.

Maria folded her arms - to hold something in place—a deep-seated fatigue that strategy alone couldn't fix.

Aldo stepped in then, his presence calm but deliberate, the collar of his navy jacket slightly askew—as if he'd just jogged over from another crisis. "Daniel, good to see you again," he said, walking in with a half-smile that didn't quite conceal his intrigue. "In a very different capacity this time."

Just then, the door nudged open again, and the hospitality assistant stepped in quietly, balancing a tray with cups and a notepad.

"Coffee, ma'am? Sir?" she asked politely, glancing first at Maria.

"Black, no sugar," Maria replied, the brief interaction a small anchor in the swirling unease of the room.

"Flat white, please," Aldo said, barely looking up from his tablet.

"Cappuccino," Sophia said crisply, her voice betraying the least hint of her internal calculations concerning this new dynamic.

Then the assistant turned to Abhishek, who offered a warm, almost apologetic smile. "Tea, please. With milk and a little sugar." It wasn't common in this temple of cold brew, but it was his small, consistent rebellion.

She nodded and disappeared for a few moments, returning with their choices. One by one, she placed the drinks gently before each of them. The quiet clink of porcelain against wood grounded the room in something human, the soft aroma of coffee and cardamom tea filling the sterile air. It felt less like a boardroom and more like a team truly coming together.

Daniel accepted his long black coffee with a brief nod. "Thank you." He liked his long black—hot water crowned with a double shot of espresso, the crema swirling like molten gold on the surface. It smelled of quiet strength. Allowing the scent of possibility to permeate the space, already charged with familiar aromas, softly but firmly, he asked:

"Before we start, I want to know, what's the real fear here?"

The question landed with surgical precision.

Sophia crossed her arms, her usual composure momentarily disturbed as she considered.

Maria didn't answer. Not yet. But the quiet truth rose unbidden in her mind: she was terrified this would become another polished project, looking brilliant on paper but collapsing under the immense weight of its legacy, drowning her along with it. She couldn't afford another public failure, especially not after the last, painful attempt to reform the old guard.

Aldo leaned forward, resting his forearms on the table. "That we'll automate noise. That we'll solve the wrong problem beautifully." Daniel's eyes met his. He nodded slowly.

Abhishek, thoughtful as ever, finally spoke, his voice tinged with the bitterness of lived experience. "That we'll underestimate the glue. The invisible things—handovers, accountability, trust." He paused, choosing his words carefully. "And that we'll assume the technology will do the heavy lifting. At Matrix, we rushed the 'as-is' study. What should've taken two months was squeezed into three weeks. The results? Rework, noise, and mismatched assumptions. We were flying blind." He rubbed the back of his neck, the memory a physical ache.

Daniel turned slightly toward him, his gaze sharp. "You've lived that, haven't you?"

Abhishek nodded, a deep sigh escaping him. "At both ends. At Hybrid, we spent almost fifteen to twenty percent of the total time just understanding what already existed. That made everything else faster and cleaner. But at Matrix, the tech arrived before the truth. People struggled with the interface—the inputs weren't intuitive, and no one knew how to answer the tool's questions. It's user-friendly on paper, but reality is messy. You'll need to train teams carefully, or you risk GIGO—garbage in, garbage out." The quiet admission hung in the air, a testament to his earnestness and a plea for a different outcome this time.

Daniel studied him for a long moment, then made a mental note in his unmoving mind. This was a man who understood the trenches.

Maria broke the moment, sensing the shift in the room's energy. "We need your team to stitch together the operational picture—the process gaps, system issues, and regional realities that haven't made it to the surface. It's the only way we stand a chance of moving forward." Her voice held a desperate urgency, a plea for the foundation she knew was crumbling beneath her.

Daniel nodded, pulling out a chair. "Exactly. I'll work with you to steer the overall architecture and direction, and my team will drive the detailed execution. Let's start by aligning fully on how AlphaCorp operates at the ground level."

Sophia leaned forward, her eyes on the blank screen. "We've done some of that legwork. Risk mapping, major systems, process summaries. But we're hoping you'll help us connect it all correctly and comprehensively." Her voice was composed, but Daniel could sense the undercurrent—an eagerness to be reassured, to be seen, to get this right finally.

Daniel opened his notebook and tried to connect his laptop to the room's screen. The computer refused to connect. He raised an eyebrow, a flicker of something almost like amusement in his eyes, but said nothing.

A young service desk technician was summoned, his face flushed with the pressure of executive eyes. While cables were swapped and network settings re-tuned, Daniel pulled back his chair slowly and turned to the team. "Well, since the machine's still booting up, I might as well talk you through the engine before letting it show itself off." He offered a small, almost imperceptible smile.

Maria nodded, a glimmer of relief in her eyes. "Let's hear it. You know this team values substance over flash."

He nodded toward Aldo and Abhishek. "That's obvious. I read your blueprint. There's more signal than noise here." He folded his hands loosely on the table.

"Our AI Diagnostic Engine is built on a curated, anonymised dataset of over 700 transformation journeys across 47 multinational groups. What makes it different isn't just the volume—it's the pattern recognition. The model doesn't just say what went wrong; it predicts why it likely went wrong. Organisational design. Data landscape. Change fatigue. Missing executive sponsorship. Governance model debt."

Aldo leaned forward, visibly intrigued. "So it's not just taxonomy-level triggers? It reads behavioural risk?"

"Exactly. And then proposes solution pathways, benchmarked in context. We don't expect anyone to follow its advice unthinkingly, but it dramatically shortens the decision loop. What would take a consulting team six weeks to map, surfaces here in three minutes."

The technician smiled nervously as the diagnostic tool finally appeared on screen, only to blink, buffer, and reload twice more.

Sophia raised an eyebrow, a wry smile touching her lips. "It seems this engine isn't quite ready for AlphaCorp yet?" Her scepticism, honed by years of glittering but hollow promises, was barely concealed.

Daniel let out a dry laugh. "Touché, Sophia. Perhaps the old days of offline PowerPoint weren't so bad after all. Intelligence has gone artificial. But the art of intelligence—" he paused, looking directly at her, then at the flickering screen, "—may be turning superficial."

Maria smirked, the image of their struggling AI a surprisingly poignant metaphor. "It's poetic, in a way. We teach machines to think, but forget to teach ourselves how to reflect."

Abhishek, almost imperceptibly raising his hand as if in a classroom, added softly, "In India, we say buddhi—intelligence—isn't just sharpness. It's timing. Appropriateness. Wisdom. Sometimes what's not said matters more than what is. Matrix implementing tech before understanding context was a classic example of that, Daniel." His gaze lingered on the still-flickering screen, a silent prayer for a different outcome here.

Daniel nodded, his tone warming. "You get it. Most systems still don't."

Aldo, however, wasn't entirely convinced. He swirled his coffee and leaned back, a glint of the future in his eyes. "But isn't that just a matter of time? AI is advancing so rapidly that it's now mapping medical diagnostics more effectively than human experts. I wouldn't be surprised if in five years, context is just another data point it understands better than we do."

Daniel raised an eyebrow. "Now that's the future-of-work optimism I expected from a CTO."

Maria raised her cup slightly. "Let's just hope it doesn't automate our coffee preferences before it learns to handle nuance." While she acted normal on the outside, in the pit of her stomach, a different metric ticked louder: trust. If this failed, if this entire exercise unravelled, it wouldn't be Daniel or Aldo who took the fall. It would be her again. The woman who dared replace the old guard and bet on something radically different.

Even Sophia cracked a smile. "Unless it starts judging our flat whites." Then, unrelenting, she pressed further. "But first impressions do matter, don't they, Daniel? Aren't we just wrapping fragile tools in buzzwords and calling them game-changers?"

Daniel leaned back, a rueful smile playing on his lips. "Because imperfect tools still provoke perfect conversations. That's the paradox. The engine's not here to give answers—it's here to spark better questions."

Just then, the technician interrupted, his face breaking into a relieved grin as he gave a nervous thumbs-up. The tool had finally stabilised.

"Showtime," Daniel said, tapping the keyboard. The screen pulsed to life.

"This is not just a heatmap. It's a diagnosis. A full-body scan of AlphaCorp's tax function, as it exists today."

The dashboard was minimalist and sleek. But behind its simplicity was something surgical, something profound. Aldo squinted at the interface, a thought forming in his mind: Were they still solving tax problems—or just levelling up in a game no one remembered designing? "You built this? How does it work?"

"I adapted it," Daniel corrected. "The orchestration tool maps six dimensions of 'as-is' maturity. Each domain is linked to specific pain points you've raised in earlier sessions. We've structured the tool to collect inputs through short self-assessments, which are cross-validated by workflow analysis and ERP field mapping."

Daniel gestured to the screen as a circular chart bloomed, resembling a radar, but with pulsing, colored layers. He began to narrate, walking them through the core dimensions, each explained as a living part of AlphaCorp's reality:

"First, Business Operations & Revenue Streams: How AlphaCorp truly makes money across retail, real estate, and services. Where we spend and invest. We identify income types that are complex or sensitive from a tax perspective. It's about mapping the flow of the organism."

"Next, your Geographical Footprint & Entity Mapping: A living map of all AlphaCorp's companies worldwide. We match each to its actual business role and tax registration, flagging discrepancies where the legal setup doesn't align with real-world operations. No more paper tigers."

"Third, Current Tax Mappings & Compliance Challenges: Transaction mapping that draws out revenue and expense under each country's tax laws. We map applicable taxes to those streams and gather real stories from regions—delays, mistakes, audits. This ranks which problems are biggest and most common, giving you actual ground truth."

"Then, your ERP and IT System Landscape: A clear list of all major ERPs and systems used, you name it. We create swim lanes of data and information flowing through your IT, identifying where systems don't communicate effectively with each other. We highlight manual workarounds and the data issues that cause bottlenecks."

"Fifth, Data Governance & Reporting: We look at how tax master data is entered, stored, and reported. We verify the accuracy, completeness, and consistency of critical master data, such as customer types and product tax codes. This identifies weak spots and control lapses in the data journey that lead to tax errors."

"Finally, Tax Team Structures & Responsibilities: Who's doing what across global, regional, and local tax teams? We spot unclear handovers or duplicated work. Then we suggest a cleaner setup for roles, escalation, and documentation. It's about ensuring every player knows their position."

Aldo grinned, a genuine, unforced expression. "Honestly, Daniel, it's like running a multiplayer game on bad Wi-Fi. Everyone thinks they're doing the right thing, but the delay creates chaos. This tool? It syncs the server."

Maria almost smiled at that. Daniel hadn't even opened a spreadsheet, yet somehow he'd surfaced what most consultants missed after weeks of interviews. He'd gone straight for the nervous system.

Sophia spoke, her voice laced with the very scepticism Daniel had just addressed. "This assumes teams will give accurate inputs. That's optimistic." She glanced sideways at Abhishek, who was still staring at the dashboard, his brow furrowed. She knew that look—the one of a man seeing both salvation and peril.

Abhishek finally looked up, a ripple of unease crossing his face. "It's intuitive—for someone like Daniel. But I've seen seasoned tax analysts freeze at the sight of a dropdown menu labelled 'GL Source Object.' The teams aren't ready. This tool might feel too clinical. They'll need handholding, training, and even translation. Otherwise, we risk irrelevant input. Rework." His gaze returned to the dashboard, particularly the "To Be Mapped" rows, which were glowing red. At Matrix, they never even saw the rot until it was too late. Here, he had a chance to help catch it early—to build something clean, honest. But if this tool collapsed under false inputs, if people lied or didn't know...

then it would be Hybrid to Matrix all over again. Only this time, it would all be on him. The weight of that responsibility settled heavily on his shoulders.

Daniel agreed. He met Abhishek's gaze, understanding. "Then let's plan for handholding. But don't dilute the questions. We owe them clarity."

As the meeting wrapped up, the team didn't rush to leave. The air had shifted, thick with a new understanding, a new sense of purpose. This wasn't just about deploying a tool; it was about recalibrating how they worked, how they saw themselves.

Daniel watched them closely as they left—Aldo scribbling thoughts in the margin of a systems map, Abhishek still reflecting on interdependencies, and Sophia quiet, a new mix of admiration and uncertainty in her eyes. Each, in their way, had been affected.

He turned to Maria as the door closed behind them. "You've got pieces of something powerful," he said quietly, his gaze piercing through her. "Aldo sees the system. Abhishek sees the glue. Sophia... sees the frame. The real AlphaCorp is in how they move together. That's where we'll start."

Maria looked at him, surprised by the chilling precision of his read, as if he'd seen the fault lines running through her team. A small exhale escaped her lips, a weight she hadn't realised she was carrying lifting, if only for a moment. She wasn't afraid of starting. She was scared of what they'd uncover. She admitted, her voice a low murmur, "If we don't get this diagnosis right, every future investment—from ERP upgrades to shared services—sits on sand."

She glanced back at the screen, now dark behind them. So much structure, so much promise. But in her gut, she knew: structure doesn't expose shadows. People do.

Daniel slipped his notebook into his coat pocket and walked toward the hallway, coat folded neatly over his arm — clearing space for others to lead, to step into the difficult light of what was to come.

CHAPTER 14

The Turning Point – Conversations that Changed Everything

"We've talked about the problems long enough," Maria said aloud, her voice cutting clean through the quiet. "Now, let's talk about the solutions."

Daniel smiled, stepping forward from the corner where he'd been observing. "That's exactly what's next. I've invited some of the best minds in tax technology to walk us through the tools that can help AlphaCorp bridge these gaps. We're not just talking dashboards and data warehouses. These are platforms that understand the transaction, automate the decision-making process, and ensure compliance from day one. They won't just show us what exists—they'll help us imagine what's possible."

Aldo, who had been leaning forward, alert and quiet, nodded. "So, we're finally moving from diagnosis to prescription."

"Exactly," Daniel replied. "We've mapped the pain points. Now, it's time to explore how technology can turn these vulnerabilities into strengths."

Aldo leaned back slightly, arms crossed, a rare flicker of satisfaction crossing his features. "We've cracked open the real issues—without pushback, without drama." He resisted the urge to smile. Too soon to celebrate.

As the meeting adjourned, a quiet current of anticipation ran beneath the shuffle of laptops closing and the refilling of coffee cups. The next phase was no longer theoretical. It was here. The question was no longer whether AlphaCorp needed transformation—it was how to design it right.

Daniel lingered near the doorway, watching the room slowly empty. Every project had its inflexion point. This feels like one of them, he thought. The real challenge now? Keeping the momentum alive when the shiny demos give way to the messy middle.

Sometimes, all it takes is one honest conversation to change everything.

Reframe the Future

The room was buzzing again—but this time, it wasn't tension. It was adrenaline. The first Show & Tell had laid bare their systems, processes, and pain. AlphaCorp's tax teams had seen their challenges dissected with empathy and data. Now, for the first time, they weren't just spectators. They were co-architects.

Daniel returned to the front of the room, this time flanked by his crew from Grayson & Holt. They didn't look like typical consultants. One wore sneakers and a smartwatch. Another had a sleeve tattoo peeking out of her blazer. These weren't salespeople—they were former in-house leads, ERP wizards, and architects who'd lived the grind.

"Let's talk about where we go from here," Daniel began. "In today's regulatory climate, tax technology is no longer optional—it's survival. But the real question isn't whether we should automate. It's how to do it right."

A few heads nodded. Maria didn't speak, but her arms were loosely folded—the CFO's version of an open door. She noticed Sophia hadn't taken a single note. Just two glances at her phone. Was she distracted, or deliberately distant? Maria's gaze drifted to Aldo, who sat beside Sophia, his posture mirroring hers in a way Maria hadn't fully processed before. A thought, unbidden, surfaced: Those two. There's always been something there, hasn't there? A shared wavelength, an unspoken understanding... A flicker of curiosity, tinged with suspicion, sparked within Maria. She knew office romances, even fleeting ones, could complicate everything.

Sophia glanced sideways at Aldo, tension flickering across her brow. This session mattered. Aldo met her gaze, a micro-expression of their shared history passing between them – a flicker of that high-school-like attraction, that undeniable, volatile pull that had led to a blurring of lines, and the subsequent subtle fight and love moments that had tangled. It was a wordless communication of absolute trust, forged in a crucible of passion and friction, earned in ways Maria could never comprehend.

Daniel clicked the presentation remote. A minimalist slide lit up behind him. No logos. Just five words: "From Friction to Flow: Tax Reimagined."

"Before we dive in," Daniel said, his voice even, "let me ask you something."

He paused. "What is tax technology?"

A few tax managers stiffened. One coughed. Another adjusted her glasses. No one answered.

Daniel smiled. "It's not just software. It's a strategic enabler. It's how businesses stop firefighting and start being proactive. It's how tax becomes predictive."

Sophia listened, jaw tight. She'd seen tools like these promise the moon and collapse under the weight of insufficient data, of human resistance. Transformation was never truly about the tool—it was about who held the remote, who believed enough to see it through.

She finally spoke, her voice precise. "Right now, most of our work is manual. We pull data from seven disparate systems, painstakingly clean it, verify tax codes, reconcile inconsistencies—that's seventy per cent of our time gone before any actual strategic review happens."

A tax lead from India added, his frustration resonating with many in the room. "And even then, errors relentlessly creep in. Missed reconciliations. Mismatched GL codes. One mistake, one minor oversight, and we're back to firefighting again, wasting weeks."

Daniel advanced to the next slide. A bold statement filled the screen: "The future of tax is digital. But digital alone isn't enough. Smart technology + strategy = transformation."

"Tax technology," he continued, his voice gaining momentum, "reaches from basic robotic process automation to advanced, AI-driven compliance tools. It eliminates the repetitive, soul-crushing work, dramatically reduces compliance risk, and, crucially, gives our brilliant teams the time to think, to strategise, to truly innovate."

Aldo raised an eyebrow, cutting through the optimism with his signature pragmatism. "But tax teams have dealt with complexity forever. Why now? What's changed that makes this so critical at this very moment?"

Daniel nodded. He'd expected that.

Click.

A vibrant world map appeared, with dots highlighting regions across the globe that were rolling out real-time e-invoicing, stringent digital reporting mandates, QR code validation, and even government-issued pre-filled returns.

"Governments have changed," he said, letting the profound weight of that statement hang in the air. "We're moving toward a world where tax isn't just filed quarterly or annually. It's validated at the source. Real-time. Always on. No room for last-minute cleanups. And the only way to survive that? Centralised, trusted data. Integrated logic. And comprehensive automation."

Sophia folded her arms, a dawning realisation in her eyes. "And that's where these specialised tools come in?"

Daniel nodded. "Exactly. Let's look at the toolkit."

Click.

The Tax Technology Toolkit

The screen displayed a structured, intuitive visual. "Think of it as The Tax Technology Toolkit," Daniel began, then described each component, weaving it into a seamless explanation: "First, we have Tax Determination Engines. These are the brains that automate complex tax logic across numerous jurisdictions, virtually eliminating the need for risky manual overrides and hardcoding rates. Then there are Compliance Reporting Platforms, which enable centralised, often real-time, submission of all your tax returns and statutory reports globally. Next, we find Analytics & Dashboards, providing unparalleled visibility into risk patterns, anomalies, and, crucially, new planning opportunities. Moving into the cutting edge, we utilise AI & Machine Learning Applications—these are designed to detect errors proactively, automate complex reconciliations, and even intelligently support documentation, such as Transfer Pricing reports. And finally, essential for any modern operation, are Cloud-Based Archiving & Workflow Tools, ensuring secure record storage, robust audit readiness, and seamless collaborative approvals across distributed teams."

A beat passed.

Daniel glanced around the room. He caught Sophia's eye. She gave a subtle nod, almost against her will, a quiet acknowledgement of the solution's elegance. Aldo tapped his pen once on the table—his uncharacteristic signal that something significant was landing.

Abhishek leaned forward, his expression thoughtful. "Daniel, I agree—tech is powerful. However, only if we first fix the inputs. Otherwise, it's just lipstick on a spreadsheet." A few chuckles rippled through the room. Daniel nodded. "That's exactly the point. Technology can amplify excellence, but it can't fix fundamental misalignment or a lack of trust in the underlying data."

In the back, a junior tax executive was scribbling furiously into a notepad, headphones still half-on. Daniel smiled. That's the moment, he thought, when someone starts seeing the future in their own handwriting.

But he also knew the road ahead wouldn't be slick with dashboards and instant ROI graphs. There would be pushback. Budget fights. Legacy systems stubbornly refusing to cooperate. People are afraid to let go of the old, familiar ways, even the painful ones.

He steadied himself.

The hard part isn't just showing what's possible. It's convincing people they can get there—and staying with them, guiding them, when it inevitably gets harder before it gets better.

The spark had been lit. Now came the real test: Would AlphaCorp carry the fire, or let it flicker out in the maze of politics, entrenched systems, and human resistance?

For now, at least, the room was wide awake.

Flashpoint

Much later that afternoon, in a quiet meeting room with city lights streaming through the glass walls, Maria, Sophia, Aldo, and Abhishek sat to debrief. Coffee cups in hand, a soft hum of the building's ventilation masked the weight in the air.

They had momentum. But Maria knew momentum was a fragile, volatile thing, easily sabotaged.

Sophia's phone, which had been facedown moments earlier, was now flipped over on the table as she skimmed notes on her tablet.

Then it happened.

A vibration. A screen flash. A name.

"Richard AlphaCorp"

The room froze.

Maria saw it first. Her breath hitched. Her heart skipped.

Richard. Calling Sophia?

The man who had embodied everything Maria fought against was the architect of the very bureaucratic inertia she was now dismantling. The ghost of her predecessor, the man who had blocked every actual transformation effort, forcing Maria to quietly replace his influence, brick by painstaking brick, without ever naming him aloud. Why now? And why Sophia, of all people? A bitter thought formed: And what about Aldo? Does he know? Or is Sophia caught between old loyalties and new promises?

Sophia didn't flinch. She reached for the phone as though it were any other call, silencing it with a practised swipe.

But Maria's gaze didn't move from the silent, inert screen. Her fingers tightened around her coffee mug, the ceramic suddenly cold against her skin. What does he want? And what does Sophia know? What don't I see?

Sophia casually turned the phone face down again. But it was too late. The signal had been seen. The implications, unsaid, vibrated in the air.

Aldo's eyes flicked between them, his posture shifting—curious, cautious. His attention, usually laser-focused on systems, was now entirely on the unfolding human drama. He caught Sophia's quick, almost imperceptible glance towards him—a silent plea for understanding, perhaps, or a warning. He felt the familiar, complicated pull of their history, even here, now.

Abhishek's pen paused mid-sentence, hovering over his notepad. He glanced at Maria, then Sophia, then back again, his expression unreadable. Something had fractured, even if it hadn't yet been named.

Maria cleared her throat, forcing composure into her voice. "Let's continue. We still have vendor evaluations to align on."

But her mind was already elsewhere, replaying the flashing name, dissecting Sophia's non-reaction, and now, critically, re-evaluating the subtle connection between Sophia and Aldo.

Something, she realised with a cold certainty, had just cracked open. And it wasn't just about data anymore.

CHAPTER 15

The Power of Tax Determination Engines

Daniel let the room settle. It was barely 9 a.m., the kind of hour when soft sunlight still clung to the carpet and people warmed their hands on takeaway cups. Jackets hung over mesh-backed chairs, ID lanyards twisted from hurried mornings. The scent of floor cleaner lingered faintly, fighting with the steam rising from fresh brews. AlphaCorp's tax teams looked eager, yes, but also weary. Years of manual workarounds had etched lines of scepticism around their eyes; they trusted their battered expertise more than any promise of automation.

Carlos, a tax manager from Mexico, leaned forward, cutting through the quiet. "I understand automation for reporting, but how can a system replace human judgment in tax determination? There are too many edge cases—complex transactions where tax treatment isn't straightforward."

Daniel gave a slight nod. He'd lived that question. "That's a great point, Carlos. Think of a tax determination engine not as a simple calculator, but as a specialist doctor. It doesn't just apply static rules. It performs a rapid, in-depth scan of factors—jurisdiction, product type, transaction details, and exemptions. It diagnoses the correct tax treatment every single time."

Abhishek, ever calm, unruffled, spoke up. "We tried a similar engine at Matrix a few years back. The engine itself was robust, truly state-of-the-art. However, our upstream data was a disaster. Garbage in, garbage out. We spent more time on cleansing data than on tax work. The project stalled. It proved how crucial clean, consistent data is—even for the smartest systems."

Sophia chimed in, her voice smooth, almost too calm. "Abhishek raises a critical point. Currently, our tax codes are manually selected in the ERP by finance teams. If they misclassify or leave a field blank, we only catch the error at reconciliation. It's like waiting for the autopsy report to confirm the cause of death."

A tax lead from Indonesia muttered, "*Sialan* . . . or during an audit." A few chuckled, the humour brittle.

"Exactly," Daniel affirmed. "And by then, it's too late. A tax determination engine prevents the disease at the source. It integrates directly with your ERP, procurement, and point-of-sale systems, calculating and applying the correct tax in real time." He paused. "Of course, such deep integration is like surgery. Complex, precise, demanding, and sometimes painful."

Sophia's eyes flickered to her phone. Maria caught it, unease prickling low in her gut.

Daniel remembered dismissing such tools once, until an Indian audit nearly collapsed a JV with retrospective tax claims. That was the day he stopped romanticising manual controls. The day he saw the real cost of human error, written in red ink across a multi-million-dollar penalty.

Tax Determination Engines: The Game Changer

Aldo pulled up a slide showing a simplified transaction flow integrated with a tax engine.

"Imagine AlphaCorp operating globally," Daniel explained. "Every country has its VAT, GST, or sales tax rules—plus exemptions, thresholds, special treatments. Manually tracking that for every transaction? It's a nightmare. Impossible to scale."

Karsten from Germany asked, "So the system automatically applies the right rate?"

"Yes," Daniel said. "But smarter. It determines taxability. Sell digital services to an EU customer—the engine instantly pulls customer type, location, invoice details, and applies the correct VAT treatment. No human intervention needed."

Indu from India asked, "What about exemptions? Many goods or services are zero-rated."

"Engines rely on constantly updated legal databases," Daniel replied. "If a product qualifies for exemption, it applies it automatically. No more hours spent looking up obscure laws."

As Daniel spoke, Sophia absorbed every detail. Richard was right. This was a formidable beast. Every vulnerability Daniel highlighted, every integration point—she catalogued it. She was listening but more: she was learning a language to own later.

Aldo finally broke his silence. "I get how it works conceptually. But why AlphaCorp now? What's the burning platform?"

Sophia exhaled. "We can't scale tax compliance the way we're doing it today. Manual effort, reconciliation challenges, inconsistencies. Our biggest risks—VAT/GST and customs compliance—carry our highest volumes and audit exposure. It's not just a ticking time bomb, Aldo. It's already bleeding money and reputation."

Mohamed from Saudi Arabia added, "We've had penalties. Big ones. Just because transactions were misclassified."

Daniel's smile was grim. "Exactly. Automation isn't about replacing expertise—it's about eliminating unnecessary, costly risks. Tax professionals should focus on advisory and strategy beyond chasing missing codes or playing clean-up."

Gabriel from Brazil looked sceptical. "We've manually reviewed transactions for years. How do we know the system won't make mistakes?"

Daniel spread his hands. "Fair concern. But how often do human errors happen in manual processes?"

Silence. Heavy.

"More often than we'd like," Sophia said quietly, her gaze briefly meeting Maria's. Consistency, yes—but also control. If she mastered this, leverage would follow.

Daniel nodded. "The key advantage is consistency. Engines don't tire. They don't err after long days. They apply rules systematically, across every transaction, ensuring compliance at scale."

Aldo chimed in, "Think of it like an air traffic controller—it guides every transaction to a safe landing, regardless of complexity."

Daniel let that sink in. "This is just the first tool. We'll cover compliance automation, analytics, and e-invoicing. By the end, you'll see how each fits into AlphaCorp's transformation."

Aldo folded his arms. "Fine. But which tool is right for us?"

Maria finally spoke, her CFO voice, competent and calm, breaking the rhythm. "Let's not lose sight of the bigger picture. Engines and ERPs aren't just tools—they're part of a governance model. If this is surgery, then someone needs to own their recovery. That's what the board will ask me."

A hush followed—reminding the room that strategy lived beyond the technical detail.

Daniel grinned. "Let's go through the full session. Clarity will come."

ERP Tax Modules vs. Specialised Tax Technology (Reframed as Debate)

Karsten leaned forward. "Our ERP already has a tax module. It handles domestic sales. Why not just enhance it instead of layering on additional tools?"

Daniel's eyes narrowed thoughtfully. "Good question. ERP modules are strong for domestic transactions. They're like general practitioners—they treat common conditions well."

Abhishek leaned in, voice steady. "At Hybrid, we thought the same. ERP modules seemed safer and cheaper. But as we expanded across countries, the complexities crushed us. We ended up back in manual overrides and messy workarounds. It looked clean on paper, but it was duct tape in reality."

Aldo interjected, "So ERP handled the basics, but when complexity hit, it collapsed. Sounds less like a doctor, more like a first-aid kit. Useful until you need surgery."

Daniel nodded. "Exactly. And AlphaCorp isn't dealing with colds anymore—we're in the ICU. Multiple ERPs, legacy platforms, and changing tax laws across 21 countries. Your GP doesn't cut it here."

Yuxin from China jumped in. "Our ERP works for domestic, but the moment we do cross-border trade, we're fixing everything manually."

Indu added sharply, "And every tax rate change takes weeks to update. We sit in limbo, adjusting by hand."

Claire from France cut in next. "We've had similar issues—our ERP logic collapsed during a VAT rate change in 2023. We had to override half our sales transactions manually for weeks."

Daniel turned back to Karsten. "That's the risk. ERP tax modules are rigid. They can't keep pace with dynamic, multi-jurisdictional rules."

Sophia folded her arms, her gaze flicking sideways to Aldo. "Which is why we override transactions manually. A fever spike every time."

"Exactly," Daniel said. "Every override means inconsistency. Different teams are applying different logic. Auditors love that kind of chaos—it gives them so much work!"

Mohamed cut in. "We use three versions of the same ERP and another legacy system. They don't talk to each other. ERP modules can't bridge the gap."

Abhishek added, his tone measured. "That's where specialised tax engines shine. They're built to integrate across ERPs, connect to legacy, and apply tax rules consistently—no matter the source."

Aldo leaned forward, summing it up. "So, ERP modules are good for the flu. But AlphaCorp? We need a surgical team."

Daniel smiled. "Exactly. The right strategy is a hybrid approach: using ERP modules for simple cases and specialised engines for complex ones. Piece by piece, we build resilience."

Sophia's smile was subtle, glancing at Aldo. "Then we evaluate which tools fill the gaps. And which ones can be... understood, then controlled."

Daniel grinned.

The room shifted. They weren't defending the past anymore. They were sketching the outline of a different future.

But Maria, watching Sophia's flicker of calculation, felt a chill. Richard's protégés always asked the right questions—then emerged holding the reins. The system might be ready for transformation. But Maria knew: Sophia wasn't building AlphaCorp's future—she was scripting her own.

CHAPTER 16

Closing the Loop with Tax Compliance Tools

Sophia tapped her pen on the table, her gaze sweeping the room. A subtle flicker in her eyes, of careful cataloguing—each point a potential lever. "So, if I'm summarising this correctly, Daniel, our ERP tax modules handle the basics, but they buckle under complexity. Third-party tax engines step in to manage multi-jurisdictional chaos. And for our simpler subsidiaries, cloud-based tax solutions could be a neat fit?"

Daniel's smile was genuine. "Exactly, Sophia." The resistance in the room was softening into understanding.

Aldo leaned forward, his voice low. "So what's next? What's the next layer of this... transformation?"

Daniel clicked the remote. A stark word flashed on the screen: **Automation**.

"Because tax transformation," Daniel's voice sharpened, "isn't just about calculating tax correctly. It's about filing without breakdowns, reconciling without weeks of torture, and seeing every penny, every risk, across your global operation."

Sophia nodded slowly, her expression unreadable but her mind buzzing. More pieces of the puzzle. "Let's keep going."

The Audit Storm

Gabriel leaned forward, weariness in his eyes. "We understand how determination engines help us calculate. But what happens after? Filing returns is where the chaos begins. Every month feels like a war."

Daniel met his gaze. "That's where Tax Compliance Tools come in. They don't calculate. They ensure every piece of tax-relevant data—from every transaction, every country—is aggregated, reconciled, and reported perfectly."

Sophia's tone was crisp. "So, they can handle corporate tax, withholding tax, too? Total visibility—end-to-end control."

Heads nodded. Curiosity was replacing resistance.

Navigating the Data Minefield

Indu raised a hand, voice tight with years of frustration. "Our biggest pain is data. Extracting it, consolidating it from multiple ERPs, accounting software, spreadsheets... we spend weeks preparing returns. Every month. And still, mismatched numbers."

Daniel nodded sympathetically. "That's the wound compliance tools heal. They pull data from disparate sources, normalise formats, and ensure consistency. Automated validation rules flag discrepancies before submission."

Abhishek leaned in. "At Matrix, even before the engine failed, we saw the time savings from this aggregation. Manual wrangling is the silent killer of efficiency."

Aldo let out a breath. "So, no more compiling endless reports across twenty-one countries? That alone feels revolutionary."

Maria finally cut in, in her CFO voice. "Our filings aren't just numbers. They are signals—to regulators, to investors, to the board. If a tool provides me with a single dashboard, I can view exposures before anyone else does. That's more than efficiency—it's control of our narrative."

The room stilled at her words, the strategic weight clear.

The Pre-Audit Shield

Karsten frowned. "What about audits? Authorities flag inconsistencies even when we follow our process. It feels like a roll of the dice."

Daniel clicked to a slide. "That's where pre-filing validations come in. Compliance tools check data against government requirements *before* you submit. Completeness, transaction-level matching, regulatory checks—it's your pre-audit shield."

Carlos grimaced. "That would have saved us last year. We missed a minor VAT update. It cost us dearly."

Sophia added coolly, "Many of our compliance errors come from manual overrides in ERP. A tool that flags them before they reach auditors would save us disputes—and protect us from exposing deeper weaknesses."

The Automated Lifeline

Mohamed raised a hand. "Every country has different formats. XML, PDFs, even physical filings. It's a logistical nightmare."

Daniel nodded. "Compliance tools automate filings in required formats—CSV, XML, JSON, PDF. They handle multi-format reporting, scheduling, and direct submission. No more manual uploads."

Carlos groaned. "We still manually log into portals, re-upload files, and pray they're accepted. If not, we start over."

"Exactly what these tools solve," Daniel affirmed. "Pre-configured validations, native integration with portals, real-time confirmations. One dashboard, one timeline, full visibility."

Aldo chuckled. "No more chasing confirmations across time zones."

Daniel leaned in, voice low. "And no more surprises."

The Forensic Trail

A tax analyst from China spoke up, voice tinged with fatigue. "Audits paralyse us for weeks. We dig through old spreadsheets, emails, praying we find what authorities demand."

Daniel pulled up an example. "Compliance tools build a forensic trail. Digital audit logs, automated reconciliations, and dashboards highlighting risks in real time. You can pre-empt issues instead of reacting."

Yuxin sighed. "That would've saved us our last penalty. We couldn't prove why a tax adjustment was made—the data was gone."

Sophia smiled faintly, her eyes sharp. "Which means less firefighting, more time for strategic planning."

Daniel noticed her tone. Empowered. She was starting to see the system as a means of leverage.

The Surgical Integration

Leo from Paris raised a hand. "Can these tools integrate with our ERPs? We can't afford a full overhaul."

Daniel reassured him. "That's their design. Bolt-on solutions. They integrate with ERPs, legacy systems, and cloud platforms. They work alongside determination engines, linking directly to e-invoicing and tax portals. Most use API or middleware connectors, so the integration layer is seamless rather than disruptive."

Aldo nodded. "That's crucial. A full overhaul would be a non-starter."

Maria added, "Enhancement, not replacement—that's the only pitch the board will accept."

Daniel smiled. "Exactly. This isn't new plumbing—it's a vital upgrade."

The Unseen Engagement

As the meeting ended, chairs scraped against the floor. Gabriel groaned, staring at his tablet. "Still no update on Italy's tax data. And the UK VAT document was emailed to the wrong lead. It sat unread for a week."

The dysfunction Daniel promised to cure was still alive, reminding Maria of the stakes.

Aldo approached Sophia with a hopeful smile. "Drinks tonight?"

Sophia's smile was sweet, her refusal softer than her eyes. "Packed week. Back-to-back. Perhaps another time." Inside, she thought, Aldo's offer was human. She had no time for human. Richard's call mattered more. Power mattered more.

Maria caught the instant shift—the smile vanishing, replaced by a glint of control.

Abhishek noticed too. He'd seen it before: different company, same script. The danger wasn't in tools or processes. It was in who got to narrate the story.

As Sophia stepped into the hallway, phone pressed to her ear, Maria and Abhishek exchanged a silent look. The transformation wasn't just about systems anymore. It was about power—and who would wield it.

Maria's thought lingered as the corridor buzzed back to life: *The real risk wasn't missed filings. It was a missed intent.*

CHAPTER 17

Automating with Robots

The next morning, the aroma of freshly brewed coffee filled the breakroom. Maria found Abhishek, Sophia, and Aldo by the machine, their mugs already full.

"Morning," she said, measured and casual. "How are you all finding the post-meeting buzz?"

Sophia poured a dash of milk into her coffee, stirring slowly. "It's certainly energising," she said, her voice light. But inside, her thoughts coiled. Richard would have loved this fixation on Matrix stories—history masquerading as wisdom. Was Abhishek repeating the past to impress Maria? To her, it felt like déjà vu all over again.

Maria sipped her espresso. The coffee was bitter, but not as bitter as the certainty that Richard's ghost still lingered—in strategy decks, in momentum, in Sophia's smile. Was Sophia blinded by the same force Maria once had been, or was she consciously playing into it?

Abhishek spoke quietly, tea in hand. "Automation has its merits in terms of speed and efficiency. But also its risks—especially in a global context."

His eyes flickered with memory. At Matrix, decentralisation had been gospel—sold as empowerment, lived as chaos. Country teams bore the brunt, juggling compliance with fragmented systems. It had looked like an orchestra without a conductor. Beautiful in theory, dissonant in reality. Until it all collapsed.

Sophia stirred harder. *Here he goes again—Matrix this, Hybrid that.* She resisted rolling her eyes. *This isn't Hybrid. This isn't Matrix. This is AlphaCorp.*

Maria, however, nodded. In Abhishek's stillness, she saw truth. He was someone she could lean on. Sophia noticed the nod and bristled. The approval felt like Maria was waiting for Abhishek to propose, only to say *yes* every time.

Aldo swirled his mug, his tone firm. "Tech discussions are fine. But if we ignore people in the change, it's like building a cathedral on sand. Magnificent outside, but one tremor and it crumbles."

Silence followed—shared memories of past failures, systems that promised clarity but delivered chaos.

Footsteps echoed outside. Daniel was on his way.

Abhishek murmured, half to himself, "Let's see what the robots have to say."

Technology Roundtable: RPA in Action

Daniel entered, his facade calm though tension was pressing on his chest. This was his final act. One misstep, and his legacy collapsed. His eyes found Maria. Their gaze locked—shared stakes, unspoken. *Shall we?* he asked with a nod.

Aldo leaned forward. "Yesterday, you showed us engines and compliance tools. But what about the grunt work—the soul-draining reconciliations, the monthly madness? Won't we add another tool on top of legacy systems?"

Daniel smiled, recognising the pain. "Exactly why we're zooming in on RPA, robotic process automation, today. It might be our only shot at scaling sanity."

The lights dimmed. On-screen, a tax analyst explained: *At 11 PM, the bots wake up. They log into the ERP, extract sales tax reports, match ledgers, flag discrepancies, and store findings before I've even made tea and three hours of work is reduced to ten minutes and ten thousand hours saved annually.*

Polite applause. The magic trick kind—sincere, but wary.

Abhishek broke the silence. "RPA is fragile. It works if your data is clean and the instructions are precise. Surprises? It buckles."

Daniel nodded. "True. But when done right, it's a strategic enabler."

He revealed a stark slide:

- 60–70% of tax effort: extracting, validating, reconciling
- 20–30%: compliance

- 10–15%: advisory and firefighting

"Unless we solve fragmented data, no transformation will stick."

Sophia cut in. "Our diagnostic showed how fragmented AlphaCorp's tax data is."

"Even ERP tax codes vary," Karsten added. "It's a nightmare."

Daniel nodded. "New engines don't fix this. Without validation, you're always behind. Bots don't guess—they plug into ERPs via secure APIs."

Maria's voice was sharp. "But if processes are broken, won't bots just automate chaos faster?"

Daniel paused, then conceded. "An excellent point. RPA alone isn't enough. It must pair with process re-engineering."

Intelligent RPA

Daniel shifted slides. "Basic RPA moves your hands faster. Intelligent RPA gives your hands a brain."

Aldo stepped in with an example. At his previous firm, basic bots had blindly posted mismatched currency invoices—errors cascaded. Six months later, with ML-powered bots, anomalies were flagged, halted, and predicted downstream. "That's the difference," he said. "One repeats mistakes faster. The other prevents them."

Daniel played a clip: a bot verifying 4,200 intercompany invoices, matching transfer pricing rules, simulating tax impacts in minutes.

Carlos, from Mexico, leaned forward. "So this isn't just automation. Is it decision intelligence?"

"Exactly," Daniel replied. "Bots that forecast ETR impacts, suggest strategies, and enforce compliance guardrails. All repeatable."

Implementation Challenges

Maria pressed. "And the price? Complexity? Risk? Return on investment?"

Aldo exhaled. "It's not plug-and-play. Rush it, and it fails. One pilot I led triggered penalties. Bad process plus good bot equals faster failure."

Daniel underlined the line on the screen. "Bots must be governed like employees—monitored, retrained, audited."

Jean-Luc raised an eyebrow. "In Paris, our RPA froze on exceptions. We wrote it off."

Daniel countered by showing ROI numbers, but instead of narrating them, he let Jean-Luc scoff first. "These numbers look like fantasy." Then Daniel defended: "8-month payback, 2.6x ROI year one, 4.1x year two. Real pilots. Real savings. But only when governance and alignment exist."

Abhishek added calmly, "RPA reflects what we feed it. It can't replace judgment. But it can accelerate insight."

Sophia slipped in smoothly. "That's why co-creation matters. Build with country teams, not above them."

Daniel nodded. "This isn't a tech-only journey. It's human transformation, too."

Maria leaned back. "Then we pilot with clarity."

The room settled. Thoughtful, cautious—but awake.

At the back, a young analyst scribbled five words: *No bot can fix chaos.*

Sophia's Dinner

7:12 PM – Kensington, London

Sophia stood by the window, city lights reflected in the glass. Her phone buzzed.

Richard.

"Dinner. Scott's. Nine." His tone was too smooth, too practised.

She didn't ask why. She never had. "One hour," she said.

Later, dressed in navy and ivory, she slid into the Mayfair restaurant's opulence. Richard sat smirking, Oban in hand.

"Maria's sprinting through a minefield," he said after small talk. "You're caged. Come with me. Feed me their roadmap. Slow them down. I'll make you the transformation lead at the new firm."

Her breath caught. Years ago, he'd promised legacy. He had broken that promise. But AlphaCorp was suffocating. Maria's fire. Abhishek's scars. Aldo's steady watch. Ghosts everywhere.

Better to act first. On her terms.

She met his eyes. "I don't play small."

He smiled. "That's why I chose you."

When he left, pride and dread wrestled within her. No one saw the strings tightening—because she shrouded them in the language of progress.

Closing Beat

Maria left the conference room last, Daniel's warning still circling: *No bot can fix chaos.* She thought of Richard—how chaos always wore a suit and spoke with conviction. Now, bots threatened to do the same. She tightened her grip on her folder. If AlphaCorp was to survive, automation had to be more than a trick. It had to be discipline. And discipline started with her.

CHAPTER 18

Data Is the Fuel

7:42 AM – AlphaCorp Tower, Level 27 – Transformation War Room

The Canary Wharf skyline bled pale light into the glass-walled room. Flipcharts leaned in one corner, Post-its clinging like exhausted soldiers from last night's skirmishes. The air still smelled faintly of marker ink and burnt coffee.

Sophia arrived first. She flipped her laptop open, screen glow washing her face. Daniel's file blinked on the screen—tax data frameworks, Pillar Two inputs, e-invoicing prep, RPA candidates, master data. Half of it she already knew. The rest she would mimic until she did.

Richard's words whispered back: *You lead from the shadows. Let others do the heavy lifting.*

She traced the phrase "master data alignment" with her fingertip, lips curving faintly. If this circus collapsed, she'd carry the vocabulary elsewhere and claim the stage as her own.

The door sighed open on its hydraulic hinge. Maria entered first, Daniel, Abhishek, and Aldo close behind. The conference room roused itself—the dull scrape of metal chair legs against the worn blue carpet, the soft whir of vents pushing out over-chilled air, laptop lids snapping open like nervous tics. Someone's citrus-sharp perfume drifted across the table. Sophia's face went perfectly still, as though smoothing away the shadows clinging to her from the night before.

9:45 AM – War Room

Daniel tapped the projector awake. "Let's loosen up. Quick poll."

A Kahoot popped onto the screen:

- Fit-for-purpose tax data
- Fragmented IT systems
- Lack of tax awareness
- Complex legislation

Within seconds, colored bars climbed. "Data" surged to the top—56%. No one looked surprised.

Daniel nodded. "Exactly. Let's talk about the fuel that powers—or stalls—everything."

Sophia raised a brow, voice laced with irony. "Back to poor hygiene?"

"Not just hygiene," Daniel said evenly. "Ownership. Governance. Without it, master data, transaction data, contextual data—they all rot. Miss them, and the whole house falls."

Abhishek leaned forward, his tone deliberate. "Master data first. Legal entities, vendor IDs, tax registrations. Get those wrong, everything downstream fractures."

Maria nodded. "And transaction data?"

"Journal entries, invoice lines, tax codes," Sophia replied smoothly, reclaiming space. "Map them wrong, reconciliations spiral."

"Contextual data?" Karsten asked.

Abhishek answered, steady. "The why. Contracts, system notes, rationales. Why 0% VAT here? Why that GL code? Without context, you're just guessing."

Daniel added, "Pillar Two alone needs 150+ data points—legal structures, income flows. Same with transfer pricing docs. It's Lego, but half the bricks are mislabeled."

Maria's tone cut sharper. "Even clean numbers need a story. Regulators want the *why*, not just the *what*."

A ripple of chuckles followed. Sophia didn't join. Her phone buzzed once—an old number she didn't need to check. She stilled her expression. *Always watching and always waiting.*

Daniel capped his marker. "Who owns the fix? Tax? Finance? IT?"

Karsten muttered, "Good question."

"No," Daniel replied. "Wrong starting point. It's not about who fixes—it's about who owns, every day. That's governance. Master data management isn't spring cleaning. It's river management. You can't clean it once. You build dams, filters, checkpoints—then monitor the flow."

Aldo leaned forward, finally speaking. His voice carried calm precision. "Think of application programming interfaces, APIs. If they pass dirty payloads, every downstream system chokes. Clean interfaces need clean data. Otherwise, all you've done is automate garbage."

The room stilled. His metaphor landed. Even Sophia tilted her head, conceding the clarity.

Maria broke in. "Then should tax own governance? We're the ones who bleed when it fails."

Daniel shook his head. "Not quite. Governance is a discipline, like finance or HR. Tax must define requirements, flag risks, and collaborate on controls to ensure effective management and control. But ownership sits with those who manage data as a craft."

Abhishek added quietly, "Otherwise, we're forever fixing leaks in pipes we didn't build."

Maria absorbed that, her pen tapping softly.

Daniel pressed on. "One client bought a state-of-the-art tax engine. But their master data was a scrapyard. Result? Months of chaos. Clean tools, dirty fuel."

Sophia interjected, her tone cool. "So the problem isn't systems. It's us, failing to control the inputs."

Abhishek's gaze flicked toward her. "Not us failing. We're not being allowed to. Data is treated like plumbing—someone else's problem until the pipes burst."

For the first time, Maria caught Sophia's jaw tightening.

Daniel pivoted. "Governments have seen it. That's why we face real-time reporting, live uploads, and e-invoicing. It's early intervention. They're forcing us to clean the river by changing the dam itself."

Silence.

Maria leaned forward. "You're saying mandates aren't burdens—they're opportunities."

Daniel's eyes gleamed. "Yes. Governments hand us a reason to fix what we ignored. Everyone has to change. Resistance dies. That's the gift."

Sophia exhaled softly, masking calculation as indifference. She noted every word.

The projector hummed. Coffee cooled. The team sat in the quiet aftershock of Daniel's framing.

Maria's voice finally broke it, low but firm. "We've been treating data as dirt. Something to sweep up after the mess. But it's fuel. And AlphaCorp has been running on fumes."

She closed her notebook with a deliberate snap. "That ends here."

The words hung heavy. Even Sophia didn't respond.

But her mind was already rewriting the script.

The war room emptied slowly, the echo of Daniel's words still clinging to the glass. Post-its drooped under the air-con draft, coffee cups sat abandoned, and the projector hummed into silence.

Maria remained seated, her palm pressed flat against the table. *Data is fuel,* she thought. *And AlphaCorp has been coasting on fumes.*

Out of the corner of her eye, she caught Sophia slipping out, phone already at her ear. Too quick, too poised. Aldo lingered by the door, tapping his pen against his notebook, watching but saying nothing. Abhishek stayed seated, scribbling notes with the calm focus of someone who knew this wasn't theory—it was survival.

Maria exhaled. The mandates Daniel had called a "gift" hovered in her mind. Real-time reporting. Digital invoices. Governments are forcing the future into the present. For years, she had cursed them as burdens. Tonight, for the first time, she saw them differently.

She straightened, closing her notebook with a quiet snap. Tomorrow, they would return to confront the reality of real-time. And AlphaCorp would either see it as punishment ... or as the opportunity of a lifetime.

CHAPTER 19

Real Time, Real Opportunity

The lights dimmed. No one expected Daniel to start this way.

The screen flickered with grainy footage from the late 1980s. A boy sat cross-legged in front of a bulky CRT television, thumbs hammering at a clunky controller. Pixelated spaceships dodged asteroids. The boy's laughter filled the silence—pure, absorbed, unbreakable.

The scene faded. A new video began.

Now, a child stood in a minimalist living room, sleek VR headset strapped across his face. With every swipe and jump, an AI-rendered universe bent instantly to his movement. Real-time physics. Predictive AI. Cloud rendering. Without any lag. Pure immersion.

The video ended on a single line against black:

If this is play, what will work look like?

The lights returned. Daniel stood by the screen, arms folded, smiling. "That's me in the first clip—Space Invaders. I thought nothing could top it. The second kid—that's my nephew. His game runs on real-time physics, AI, and cloud computing. An undeniable example of life and code in perfect sync."

He let the silence breathe. "That's where society is heading. Instant shopping. Instant banking. Instant everything." He paused, eyes steady. "And guess what? Tax authorities are no different."

A ripple of laughter broke the tension.

Three phrases blazed onto the next slide:

Real-Time Reporting. Blockchain. Artificial Intelligence.

Daniel's tone deepened. "We've all heard these terms. But how many of us have *lived* them? Governments want visibility at the source—transaction by transaction. Periodic returns are becoming relics."

He gestured at the AlphaCorp dashboard. "Across our 21 countries, 14 already mandate e-invoicing. More are coming. This isn't a trend. It's the standard."

The Scars of E-Invoicing

Carlos leaned forward, his voice tight. "Our ERP couldn't handle the XML schema. Extensible Markup Language was too demanding. Hundreds of invoices failed clearance. We built middleware and ran 5,000 simulations. Rejections dropped from 18% to 1%. But every ERP patch sends us back to Excel. We fear updates more than audits."

The room chuckled nervously.

Fahad shook his head. "Half our suppliers weren't digital in phase one. Some sent e-invoices, others paper, some both. AP was chaos. We paid penalties for mismatches we couldn't even trace. Even now, reconciliations are manual nightmares."

The air thickened with memory—screens blinking red, coffee-fueled nights, Excel files crashing under their own weight.

Daniel nodded slowly. "I hear the pain. But what if e-invoicing isn't just a disruption? What if it's our biggest opportunity?"

Clash of Lenses

Sophia's voice cut through. Low. Controlled. "Daniel, every e-invoicing mandate feels like implementing a new ERP. Brazil, Mexico, Italy—each schema different, each deadline shifting. Exhausting. Across our countries, every vendor has its own protocol. Fragmentation is the rule, more than the exception."

Her fingers tapped against the table, drumming scepticism.

Daniel didn't flinch. "You're right. Fragmentation exists. But 80% of requirements are common. The real failure is in how companies implement. Different vendors per country? That's like running 20 ERPs with no integration. Without central governance, it collapses."

Sophia frowned but said nothing.

Daniel pressed on. "Mandates look like burdens. They're actually blueprints. Over 110 countries are moving toward real-time controls. This is our chance to refine master data, rebuild processes, and create leverage. If tax authorities can spot anomalies with AI, why can't we?"

Sophia opened her mouth, then stopped. Her eyes narrowed, calculating. The flicker was there: reluctant recognition.

Aldo leaned in, his words calm, deliberate. "We treat invoices like paper ghosts. Real-time reporting forces us to see them as living data—breathing, moving through systems. The choice is whether we orchestrate them, or let governments do it for us."

He glanced at Sophia. "And fragmentation isn't destiny. Middleware can harmonise streams. Imperfect, but better than islands."

Then Aldo added, more slowly: "In my last firm, we survived mandates only because we invested in reconciliation discipline. We built an RPA tool that cross-checked ERP records, e-invoicing clearances, and the tax portal every single day. Thousands of records reconciled overnight. It saved the tax team hundreds of hours monthly—and more importantly, gave leadership confidence that the numbers matched across all streams. Without that daily orchestration, trust in the data would have evaporated."

Lessons From Failure

Abhishek's voice joined, steady. "At Matrix, we let vendors enrich data outside our systems. Easier in the short term, but without a backbone or governance. Different vendors, different models. When the weight grew, it collapsed. Compliance-only thinking doesn't scale."

He leaned forward, his words deliberate. "In some African countries, audits uncovered unexplained differences between e-invoicing data and financial statements. Regulators didn't buy our explanations. The penalties were severe—millions in adjustments and fines. And tax was left to absorb the blame."

He paused. "To cope, we built middleware after the fact, layering patches to meet mandates. But we never redesigned the backbone. That was the fatal mistake. Compliance-only thinking collapses when the pressure builds."

He added, more quietly, "And e-invoicing isn't just tax. It isn't just IT. Like ERP, it fails when left to one function. Success requires collaboration among tax, finance, IT, and governance to move as a unified team. Every reconciliation error is a clue—a chance to fix root causes. But only if tax owns the conversation."

The words landed heavy, like a warning.

From Burden to Backbone

Maria leaned in, voice calm but pointed. "Daniel, you've convinced us e-invoicing can be an opportunity. But how? Fourteen countries. Fourteen different headaches. What are the best practices?"

Daniel softened. "I'll show you."

Slides flashed: a consumer goods client.

- **87% reduction in rejections**
- **60% touchless AP processing**
- **Invoice-to-payment cycle cut from 11 to 2.3 days**
- **Returns filed within 5 days, not midnight scrambles**

"They standardised architecture, validated data at procurement, built vendor trust. Efficiency unlocked working capital and vendor loyalty. Compliance turned into leverage."

He faced the room. "Now imagine AlphaCorp. Twenty-one countries. Cleaner data. Real-time analytics. Unified backbone. With blockchain and AI, we don't just comply—we predict, prevent, lead. Tomorrow's tax leader isn't a form-filler. They're a data translator."

The silence was thick. The words had landed.

The Question

Daniel's eyes scanned the table. Maria—steady. Sophia—guarded. Aldo—measured. Abhishek—watchful.

"For too long," he said, "we've reacted to mandates. This is our blueprint moment. The question is: are we brave enough to redesign AlphaCorp—before the mandates redesign us?"

The room held still.

Maria's gaze lingered on the slide, then on the faces around her. Outwardly calm, inwardly resolved. The question had already shifted in her mind.

Not *if.* Not *when.*

Who would be standing when the mandates arrived?

CHAPTER 20

Workflow Management Tools – Bringing Order to Tax Chaos

Daniel didn't begin with a slide this time.

Instead, he stepped forward, eyes scanning the room as if he were about to reveal something half-remembered from another age.

"Let me tell you a story," he said. His voice, quiet, drew everyone closer. "One that's older than spreadsheets, dashboards—or even tax."

The room quieted.

"We've just spoken about e-invoicing, AI, and real-time compliance. But before we dream of those frontiers," Daniel said, "we need to make sure we can even walk in rhythm. And that starts with governance—the backbone that holds everything together."

He told the tale of Virellum, a hilltop city-state that thrived on trade and prosperity but fell in a single day. Its magistrates worked in silos, uncoordinated and contradictory. By the time danger arrived, the treasury was drained, the armies scattered, and the walls unguarded.

Daniel paused, letting silence thicken. Then he clicked to a cluttered screenshot: sticky notes piled on sticky notes, overdue reminders, missed deadlines. The room chuckled uneasily.

"This," he said softly, "is our Virellum."

Aldo grinned. "So instead of us chasing deadlines, the system chases us?"

Daniel's smile curved. "Exactly—except you define the rules. Approvals can't be skipped. Deadlines can't vanish into inboxes. If one part slips, the entire system shows it. Everyone sees everything that's at stake, not just their own corner."

The screen shifted to a clean dashboard. Calendar blocks snapped into place, reminders glowed in orderly rows, and approvals ticked across a timeline. It was discipline made visible.

Maria leaned forward. "And what happens when ownership fractures? Who does the system expose first?"

Daniel held her gaze. "Everyone. That's its power—and its risk."

Sophia's voice cut in, sharp but measured. "Or it's overkill. Let's be honest—half the time, teams crawl back to Excel anyway. Do we really want to sink millions into another shelfware experiment?"

She swept her eyes across the table, knowing the cost of pain was shared. Indu gave a wry smile. "In Delhi, our tax calendar is longer than our constitution. Multiply that across twenty-one countries? It's a war map."

Fahad added dryly, "We once lost three weeks just hunting down old audit logs. Weeks. A system trail would've been worth its weight in gold."

Carlos leaned forward. "So no more spreadsheets flying across time zones?"

"Exactly," Daniel replied. "Live dashboards, one version of truth. LATAM prepares a filing, while Europe reviews it, and the US sleeps. Notes, approvals, revisions—all in one record. And because the tools link to the ERP, an invoice post can trigger a workflow, and a failed reconciliation alerts the right team before it becomes a crisis."

Sophia crossed her legs, calm and deliberate. "And regulators don't care about dashboards. They care about filings on time. Maybe we're solving problems that don't exist."

Daniel's tone sharpened. "The better tools do more. They flag anomalies early, log every action for audit trails, and plug into regulatory databases to catch when thresholds shift. They don't prevent dysfunction, but they reveal it instantly. Garbage in, garbage out—but now everyone sees it."

Maria tapped her pen. "Governance is never about the framework. It's about the fractures. Let's remember that before we congratulate ourselves on blueprints."

Abhishek broke the silence. "Then let's make it real. Should AlphaCorp explore this seriously?"

Daniel looked at him directly. "Your call. Ready to bring structure into the chaos?"

Abhishek nodded slowly. "Yes. If governance stays at the centre — it could change everything."

Sophia tilted her head, feigning concession. "Alright. Explore, yes. But carefully. Small pilots. Controlled steps. No boiling the ocean."

Maria noticed the subtle narrowing of ambition, wrapped in caution. Outwardly, Sophia looked aligned. Inwardly, Maria suspected otherwise.

The meeting closed with uneasy laughter. But as relief rippled through the room, Sophia discreetly raised her phone and snapped a photo of Daniel's polished dashboard slide. This time, she added a caption before sending it off:

Clean dashboards, clean lies.

Outwardly, she was aligned.

Inwardly, she was already drafting another map.

CHAPTER 21

Blockchain, AI and the Future of Tax

Daniel stood at the front of the room, the projector humming behind him. A glowing image of a digital ledger filled with cryptographic hashes stretched across the screen—neat, futuristic, and intimidating.

But his opening words weren't what anyone expected.

"Before we dive in—let's be clear. AlphaCorp isn't ready to implement blockchain or AI tomorrow. Not in the next budget cycle, maybe, perhaps not even the one after that. But the world is moving in that direction. My suggestion is simple: understand the possibilities. Put them on your radar. Nothing more."

The room fell into a thoughtful silence.

Maria's pen, poised to write, paused midair. That single sentence enhanced her perception of him. So many consultants she'd sat through had come armed with shiny slides and exaggerated urgency—pitching solutions AlphaCorp couldn't afford, didn't need, or wasn't ready for. Daniel wasn't selling. He was guiding. In that moment, she felt a rare thing in the world of advisory services: trust.

Across the table, Aldo leaned back, a flicker of admiration in his eyes. He'd seen too many technology evangelists leap straight into a sales pitch, blind to context. Daniel's restraint—anchoring the conversation in readiness rather than hype—marked him as something different. Aldo thought of his own failed startup, how much he could have used someone with Daniel's balance back then.

Maria exhaled, almost with relief. "Good. Keep it that way—brief and concise. We're already wrestling with e-invoicing, workflow governance, and data chaos. We don't need shiny toys distracting the board."

Sophia's lips curved, the faintest spark in her eyes. "It's true the corporate world is buzzing about AI," she said lightly, her tone probing but careful. "CEOs are dropping it in earnings calls, and regulators are running pilots. Shouldn't AlphaCorp at least think about how we position ourselves in that wider conversation?"

Aldo leaned forward, fingers steepled. "I wouldn't dismiss it so quickly. I've seen entire industries blindsided because they thought something was just hype. I had a startup once—it failed, yes—but I learned that sometimes the use cases you dismiss as fringe are the ones that change everything. Blockchain in tax sounds obscure, but it's a real-world space nobody's cracked yet."

Daniel nodded, flipping to the next slide—a simple ledger showing immutable tax transactions. He let his gaze sweep briefly over Aldo and Sophia, both visibly intrigued. "I can see the excitement," he said with a small smile. "But this is about whether AlphaCorp is prepared. It's a huge leap, and when the time comes, it will have to be phased. That's why it belongs on the roadmap, not on tomorrow's agenda."

Maria leaned forward, her CFO instincts sharpening. "Daniel, give us real-world examples. Where has blockchain or AI actually delivered in tax? And how are companies dealing with the obvious data privacy issues?"

The following slide revealed an animated flow: a contract that executed itself. "Smart contracts," Daniel explained. "Self-executing agreements on blockchain. Once conditions are met, they run automatically."

Aldo leaned back. "Give us an example. Something beyond marketing gloss."

Daniel spread his hands. "Say AlphaCorp signs a vendor agreement stored on blockchain. The smart contract could auto-calculate VAT and withholding based on product and jurisdiction, deduct tax before releasing payment, and file the transaction with tax authorities instantly."

Aldo frowned. "Transparency is fine for fraud. But if everyone sees everything? Sensitive data, supplier margins? That's dangerous."

Daniel clicked on a balancing scale. "And that's the paradox. Blockchain's permanence is both its strength and its flaw. You can't erase mistakes. IDs can be traced. General Data Protection Regulation, GDPR, requires the right to be forgotten, but blockchain never forgets."

Sophia exhaled. "So, we kill fraud but break privacy law. Perfect."

Abhishek asked, "So how do companies deal with that contradiction?"

"Permissioned blockchains," Daniel said. "Access limited to tax authorities and key stakeholders. And zero-knowledge proofs—cryptography that proves a transaction without revealing details. Governments are already testing these ideas."

Maria tilted her head. "Testing where?"

"China, for one," Daniel replied. "They're using blockchain for e-invoicing to prevent fraud. It's not theory—it's live."

Abhishek remained cautious. "Maybe. But many of these pilots look better in white papers than in practice."

Daniel nodded and advanced the slide. The blockchain ledger dissolved into an image of a robotic assistant poring over tax files. "Which brings us to AI. Same principle."

He spread his hands. "Think of AI as a co-pilot—never stealing the wheel, but giving you sharper eyes. And it's not science fiction. HMRC already uses AI to catch carousel fraud, tracing VAT chains in real time."

Aldo whistled. "So the system itself raises alarms before auditors even knock?"

"Precisely," Daniel said. "The IRS is piloting models that sift millions of returns to flag audit triggers automatically."

Maria raised a brow. "If the IRS can find needles in haystacks that size, imagine what we could do with our own data before regulators get to it."

"Exactly," Daniel agreed. "Brazil's Receita Federal does the same—AI monitoring electronic invoices and flagging suspicious patterns. If regulators can do it, businesses can too—proactively, before being caught off guard."

Maria pressed further. "But if we already have automation—our VAT tools calculate, our compliance engines file—what makes AI different from a souped-up Excel macro?"

"Traditional tools are rule-based," Daniel said. "They struggle with three things: changing laws, unstructured data, and foresight. They report history. They can't predict tomorrow."

He clicked again. On one side of the slide, a messy scanned invoice; on the other, a neatly structured tax entry. "This is Natural Language Processing. AI reads the invoice, extracts vendor, jurisdiction, VAT rate, exemptions—everything. Ninety-five per cent accuracy, straight into ERP. Humans only review the exceptions."

Abhishek cut in. "And yet too many firms wasted money on invoice-scanning AI, when clean e-invoicing data could have solved it more cheaply and sustainably. Novelty doesn't equal value."

"I agree," Daniel said. "But when paired with e-invoicing, AI has cut invoice processing times by sixty percent. Transactions flow straight into the ERP. Humans add value, not keystrokes."

Aldo tilted his head. "What about beyond invoices? Forecasting, simulation, predicting audit risks?"

Daniel clicked to the next slide: AI for Tax Planning & Forecasting. "That's where strategy lives. AI doesn't just process—it simulates. During an EMEA sourcing review at a client, an AI modelled customs duties, VAT recovery, and incentives simulation, revealing that relocating a procurement hub from Country A to Country B would result in millions of dollars in savings over five years. A spreadsheet could never juggle that complexity."

Carlos leaned forward. "So instead of reacting, we could use AI to plan."

Daniel smiled. "Exactly. And scan transfer pricing comparables in hours instead of weeks. In audits, AI can flag potential issues and identify red flags long before authorities do. Again—not a pitch for adoption today, but literacy for tomorrow."

Sophia, arms crossed, broke in. "And judgment calls? Court rulings? Complex interpretations? AI doesn't argue with tax authorities. Humans do."

"True," Daniel said. "AI isn't a lawyer. But it's a researcher who never sleeps. It scans rulings, case law, and regulatory memos. Drafts SOPs, suggests policy updates, and builds training material. Instead of weeks on a new rule, your team gets a concise brief overnight. Think of it as Spotify for tax knowledge—it curates what matters before you even search."

Aldo shook his head, smiling. "Sounds neat. But if it's so good, why isn't everyone rolling it out? And practically, tax wouldn't adopt this alone. It must tie into ERP and legacy systems. The skills sit across IT, procurement, and finance. If ERP isn't aligned, it dies on arrival."

"Exactly," Daniel said. "Readiness and phasing. Blockchain and AI for tax can't be isolated experiments. The benefit comes when tied into the wider enterprise, stitched into the systems already running the show."

Abhishek added, calm but firm. "And that's where so many fail. The challenge is alignment—finance, IT, procurement speaking the same language."

Maria observed them with pride and intrigue. Aldo's curiosity, Daniel's balance, Abhishek's realism—it felt like orchestration. For once, she saw what AlphaCorp could become.

Sophia kept her head down, pen moving briskly. She was cataloguing every phrase. What she didn't realise was the deeper, more profound truth: if strategy could be copied for instant success, there would be no market leaders. Delta Air proved it—its investment in technology and customer strategy put it ahead of its peers. Others tried to mimic it, but without culture, discipline, and integration, they had failed to beat Delta at its game.

Daniel let the comparison hang, then delivered the pivot. "Copying tactics is easy. Copying culture is impossible." He paused, letting the weight of it sink back into AlphaCorp's own journey. Then the slide shifted one final time: a single question, bold and sharp—

"What's next for AlphaCorp?"

As the glow of the digital ledger faded from the screen, Sophia tilted her head, voice laced with irony.

"All of this is... fascinating. But when we try to align twenty-one countries, twenty-one accounting teams, and three ERP systems, even the simplest workflow becomes a war zone."

Abhishek didn't flinch. His reply was almost inaudible, meant more for himself than the room.

"War zones don't scare me. It's the silent fractures you don't see that bring everything down."

Maria caught the words. And for the first time in hours, she felt a shiver from the past failures still living at her table.

The silence that followed was thoughtful, measured—the people in the room were ruminating on a roadmap question.

CHAPTER 22

The Tax Technology Roadmap

The War Room carried the air of finality. Screens cast sharp light against glass walls, charts and diagrams lay scattered on the table, each page representing months of diagnostics, interviews, and debate. Tonight, it would end with either conviction or collapse.

Maria entered last, her stride brisk, eyes unreadable. She scanned the team—Daniel Grayson, Sophia Chan, Aldo Maseko, and Abhishek Iyer—before letting her gaze settle on the glowing roadmap projected on the central screen.

"Enough circling," she said flatly. "Tonight, we leave with a decision. Please show me the roadmap. And show me the return."

The Roadmap Framed

Daniel clicked the remote. A structured sequence appeared: RPA, tax determination, compliance, and workflow. The chain glowed on the wall—less a list of tools, more a statement of intent.

"The Tax Orchestration Curve™ in this chart reveals a universal pattern in modern tax operations: volume is highest where complexity is lowest, and complexity peaks precisely where tax rules, data quality, and governance collide.

This framework shows why automation alone fails — and why orchestration across people, data, process, and technology is the only sustainable path forward."

Maria leaned back, eyes sharp. "All right. Let's stop admiring the machine. Let's see if it actually runs."

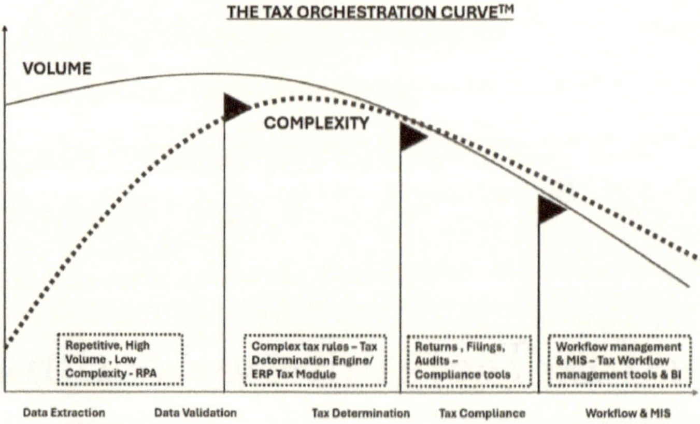

Daniel began his presentation with quiet pride. "Maria, this is what we propose for AlphaCorp."

Abhishek leaned forward. "How do you want us to read this chart?"

"We've mapped all the key tax activities that AlphaCorp's teams perform across countries on the X-axis," Daniel explained, pointing at the screen. "On the Y-axis, we've plotted both volume and complexity. The solid line represents volume and effort — highest in activities like data extraction, validation, and reconciliation, then tapering off as we move into tax determination, compliance, and MIS reporting."

He paused briefly before continuing, "The dotted line, on the other hand, tracks complexity. It peaks exactly where the solid line starts dipping — at determination, compliance, and reporting — while remaining lower for the data-heavy groundwork. That's the insight behind this roadmap: each layer of tax work demands a different class of technology."

Daniel's hand hovered over the graph as he concluded, "RPA handles the high-volume, low-complexity tasks. Tax determination and compliance engines, on the other hand, automate the thinking — the high-complexity, low-volume side of the spectrum. Together, they create balance between speed and intelligence."

Maria exchanged a look with Abhishek. The structure was elegant — a distillation of years of transformation learning. Daniel's team had seen patterns in AlphaCorp's operations that even AlphaCorp hadn't yet recognised.

Why This Roadmap

But Maria wasn't done yet. Her tone was measured, probing. "Why this order, Daniel? Why not flip the sequence?"

Daniel stood straighter. "Because the sequence protects us from collapse. RPA comes first—automated processing gives back thousands of wasted hours, freeing bandwidth for the team to focus on change. Without that relief, everything else suffocates. Tax determination next, because if the source data is wrong, automation accelerates the mistakes. Compliance follows—standardising filings, reducing country-to-country chaos. And finally, workflow—because governance only works once the core processes run consistently. If we tried workflow first, we'd be governing broken processes."

Maria leaned back slightly, eyes narrowing with precision. "But can't we skip RPA? If tax determination tools and compliance engines can integrate with our ERP systems, why does AlphaCorp need RPA for reconciliations? Why do we need all these reconciliations at all?" Her tone had the edge of a surgical blade.

Daniel didn't flinch. "A brilliant question, Maria. And in a world where an organisation runs on a single, integrated ERP—where most enterprise operations live inside one platform—you're absolutely right. A tightly integrated tax engine and compliance tool can eliminate the need for RPA in the early phase. But that's not AlphaCorp's reality. With our fragmented IT landscape, inconsistent data structures, and multiple ERPs, skipping RPA would drown us in noise. The sequence isn't cosmetic—it's risk containment."

Maria nodded, this time with clear, considered alignment.

Aldo nodded. "Think of it as foundation before scaffolding. Each layer prepares the ground for the next. The roadmap isn't a shopping list—it's architecture."

Maria's pen stilled. She agreed. But she wasn't finished.

Maria Turns Devil's Advocate

She turned to Abhishek first. "You've seen success and failure. At Hybrid, it worked. At Matrix, it collapsed. Why won't this collapse too? Aren't we just painting a neat picture while ignoring the mess beneath?"

Abhishek held her gaze. "At Hybrid, orchestration came first. At Matrix, it didn't exist—tools went live without alignment. Another difference—IT alignment at Hybrid was strong; they worked hand-in-hand with the business. At Matrix, cross-border policy inconsistency killed momentum. The risk here is the same: without governance, tools crumble. But with orchestration, it works."

Maria scribbled something, then shifted. "Aldo. Technology is your turf. Aren't we overestimating what vendors can deliver? You say 'content updates' for tax engines, but what if the vendor misses an update? What if integration fails? What if bots break silently and deadlines pass? Can AlphaCorp withstand that?"

Aldo didn't flinch. "That's exactly the risk. Tools don't self-heal. We need monitoring, fallback processes, and escalation triggers. The roadmap is scaffolding. Without discipline, it's brittle. With discipline, it scales."

Maria's gaze snapped to Sophia. "And you. You've painted the pain points well enough—but do you believe this fixes them? Or are you just repeating what consultants want us to hear?"

Sophia's smile was thin. Her words measured. "It fixes 70 percent of the recurring issues—attrition, ERP rigidity, reconciliation chaos. But if sponsorship falters, if leadership loses patience, these tools will rot like the last ERP module." Her eyes slid briefly away, pen stilled mid-note.

Maria let the silence hang. "So we admit it openly: vendor risk, governance risk, adoption risk, integration risk, leadership risk. And still you argue this blueprint is the right bet?"

Abhishek spoke first, firm. "Yes. Because the alternative is worse—staying trapped in today's inefficiencies. We bleed millions every year in wasted effort and penalties. This at least gives us a fighting chance."

Aldo added, "And it's sequenced to contain risk. Each step is tested before scaling. Failures caught and trained young."

Sophia's answer was calm, polished—too polished. "Yes, I believe it's the right path. With the right support." But inside, her calculation was different. The roadmap was her ticket—evidence she could carry elsewhere, or weaponise here.

Maria then moved on to what was really important to be able to sell the idea to the board, "What about the returns of all these investments? Why should we invest in these tools?"

Daniel was expecting this as the obvious next question from Maria. He was prepared with the answers, but they all decided to take a short coffee break before getting together to take the discussion forward.

CHAPTER 23

The ROI of Tax Technology

After their brief coffee break, the room was filled with the quiet hum of expectation as Daniel stepped forward, a remote in one hand. The lights dimmed slightly as the first slide glowed to life behind him—a bar chart. Short bars for bots. Towering ones for humans.

"Sometimes," he began, his voice steady, "transformation doesn't begin with a revolution—it begins with how we choose to fight the battles we're already in."

He glanced at the chart. "Right now, our tax teams are fighting a David-versus-Goliath battle every single month. Limited people. Fragmented systems. Nonstop deadlines. That's Goliath. And what are we using to fight back? Spreadsheets and emails."

He paused. "Tax technology tools are David's sling. These give us accuracy, speed, and focus. They let us aim."

He clicked again. A new slide appeared: Making the case for RPA.

"Across AlphaCorp's 21 countries, 1 to 2 tax professionals per country spend 4 to 5 full workdays a month just pulling, formatting, and reconciling tax data."

"That's a minimum of 10 person-days per country per month. Multiply that across jurisdictions, and we're looking at over 2,500 person-days annually. Add in ERP delays, scattered documentation, and handoffs? We cross 3,200 easily."

Maria sat motionless, mentally calculating.

Abhishek jumped in. "And that doesn't account for the time lost in clarifications, digging through versioned spreadsheets, or redoing work due to broken links and outdated templates."

Daniel nodded. "That's nearly nine full years of human effort—every single year—just to get tax data ready. At $65,000 per tax FTE annually, that's approximately $585,000 in lost revenue due to inefficiencies. Even if we reclaim only 60 percent, that's $350,000 saved—and even more importantly, capacity redirected to analysis, planning, and audit readiness."

He clicked again.

"Post-RPA, here's what the new workflow looks like:

- Bots extract data directly from ERP and procurement platforms during off-peak hours.
- Predefined logic catches missing fields and mismatches and sends them to workflow-defined stakeholders for resolution, with full logs.
- No more manual templates or dependency on region-specific files.
- Error rates drop. Speed rises. And tax teams finally focus on what truly matters."

Aldo nodded. "And we're not burdening ERP performance. Bots will operate silently during non-peak hours. Lightweight, stable, and invisible to business users."

Maria tapped her pen against the glass table.

Her voice, when it came, was measured.

"I've seen bots fail. Treasury. Reconciliations. A minor glitch cascaded into four systems and paralysed us for weeks. Savings look clean—until they collapse."

Sophia spoke next, smooth as glass.

"And that's assuming data consistency. In reality? Each country has quirks, exceptions, and undocumented workarounds. Bots don't heal bad data. If anything, they make the cracks sharper."

She leaned back, folding her arms—a reasonable concern on the surface—an escape hatch beneath.

Abhishek caught the undertone. He said nothing, but his thoughts burned. She's not wrong. But she isn't right either. At Matrix, 'bad data' became the shield everyone hid behind. It was the excuse that killed us, he thought.

Daniel stayed firm. "We pilot in one country. Run bots parallel to manual processes for months. Failures trigger alerts; humans fall back instantly. Deadlines never slip."

He clicked again. A chessboard filled the screen—half-cleared, a queen in the centre.

"We're not just moving faster. We're repositioning the board. Right now, we spend energy shoving pawns around. It's time to play the real game."

The room fell silent. Then Maria spoke, her tone cool and CFO-sharp. "Numbers are impressive. Promises sound safe. But I'll ask you this: when do I see net savings—savings that survive failure, penalties, and exceptions—in my financial statements? That's the only battle the Board will let me fight."

She set her pen down.

"Bring me that answer. Then we'll talk about the next move."

Daniel inclined his head. "Understood." He advanced the slide. "Then let's move to the million-dollar problem—tax determination."

The Million $ Problem: Making the Case for Tax Determination

A scatter graph filled the screen, dots climbing a steep curve.

"This is the foundation," Daniel said. "If tax is wrong at the source, everything downstream leans on a cracked wall. Invoices, returns, audits—they all tilt."

Maria arched an eyebrow. "So fix the wall. Patch ERP coding. Why buy another tool with its own cost and upkeep?"

Sophia jumped in before he could reply, her tone animated. "Because ERP is like twenty-one foundations, each slightly different. Patch one, the others shift. A tax determination engine stabilises the ground—updates automatically with law changes. Expand into five countries tomorrow? The rules are already there."

To Maria, it sounded logical. To Abhishek, it sounded like Sophia at her best: answering without ever taking responsibility for the messy parts.

Daniel added, "This isn't an ERP enhancement. It's a standard, future-proof calculation layer that avoids ripping ERP open every time a rule changes."

Maria crossed her arms, lips curling in a smirk. "Compelling. But does it pay like RPA?"

Daniel smiled faintly. "Let's follow the money."

A map of AlphaCorp's shared service centres appeared. "Coding is handled in India and China by junior finance staff, not tax experts. Turnover? Twenty-five percent a year. Within three years, the whole team changes. Every exit means retraining tax codes, workarounds, ERP quirks."

Maria frowned. "So we're investing in training we know will evaporate."

Sophia slid in, smooth as ever. "Exactly. And every departure resets the game. Retraining is Groundhog Day—expensive, repetitive, endless."

Abhishek stayed quiet, but his mind flickered back. Matrix was worse. Whole quarters are lost fixing errors by new hires repeating old mistakes. Training wasn't prevention—it was erosion.

Daniel kept the pace. "Errors from SSCs don't stay hidden. Country tax teams spend 8 to 10 percent of their time reviewing and revalidating. Eighty-one professionals. At $65,000 each, that's roughly half a million dollars a year correcting what should've been right at entry."

Maria tapped her pen twice. "Now we're in dollars."

Daniel nodded. "And penalties add teeth. Thirty-six per cent of our countries report VAT reconciliation issues. A quarter have faced audits in two years. Twelve percent paid fines tied to wrong determinations."

Maria exhaled. "So the cost isn't just internal time—it's audit exposure."

Sophia leaned in. "Exactly. And with a determination engine, updates are automatic."

Aldo finally spoke. "Speaking of IT—last year, we spent $200,000 just to force tax updates into legacy ERPs. That's duct-taping a sinking ship."

Maria's mouth twitched. "Expensive duct tape."

Daniel grinned. "With the engine, the duct tape goes away. Updates flow in without ripping systems open."

Maria steepled her fingers. "So put a price tag on it."

Daniel clicked.

"One-time implementation: $250,000. Annual license: $50,000. Compare that with updating twenty-one ERP systems separately—easily double the cost, and twice the lock-in."

Sophia chimed in, "And every ERP update becomes a mini-war: delays, overruns, escalations. The engine is cleaner, faster."

Maria's eyes narrowed. "And does this bring costs to zero? Or shift the pain?"

The air hung heavy. Aldo and Sophia traded a glance.

Daniel leaned in, voice calm.

"No, Maria. Not zero. But expect 60 to 70 percent reduction within two years with real, disciplined implementation and ongoing governance."

Maria tilted her head. "Why two years?"

Daniel didn't flinch. "Because the danger is over-customisation. The more we force quirks into the system, the more it becomes another rigid ERP. Success means discipline—keeping it clean, out-of-the-box, scalable. That takes time."

The screen shifted: before-and-after bars slashed nearly in half.

"Review effort down 60 percent. IT costs down 70 to 80 percent. Training is cut in half. Penalties halved."

He let the numbers hang.

"Or—we keep burning a million a year fixing errors, on vendor duct taping, and pay fines as a cost of doing business."

Maria drummed her fingers. Her voice was even, but her eyes were sharp. "Alright. That's reasonable. However, let me be clear—I want results that I can point to in the statements. Otherwise, this is just another PowerPoint."

Daniel inclined his head. "We wouldn't have it any other way."

Maria leaned back, signalling the close.

"Then move us on."

Daniel took a sip of water and faced the room again.

Closing the Loop with Tax Compliance Tools

"Getting tax right at the source is half the battle. But if we can't report it accurately, pay it on time, and retrieve it when an auditor knocks? Then we've lost the war."

He clicked. A slide lit up with survey data from AlphaCorp's 21 countries.

"Here's what we found:

Ten to twelve percent of our tax teams' time goes into filing returns, validating reports, and chasing payments.

Some countries have real-time, auto-filled returns—nightmare reconciliations every month.

Others still want paper submissions, which vanish into filing cabinets.

Deadlines slip, penalties follow.

And when staff leave? Half the records go with them."

He paused. "Across 21 countries, it's chaos. Inconsistency. Manual overload. Risk exposure."

Maria tilted her head. "Where's the real pain?"

Sophia leaned in, polished as always. "Some teams spend days chasing ERP mismatches. Others can't produce a three-year-old filing when auditors demand it. I've seen moments where credibility slipped because the evidence was scattered. We have had cases where we have failed to claim tax refunds from authorities because we were not able to respond to their queries in time."

Abhishek felt his stomach tighten. Matrix, again. The day the auditors requested VAT returns covering the previous two years. After three weeks of digging and four escalations, we still handed over fragments, he remembered. By then, our credibility was shredded.

Aldo cut in. "And let's be honest—there's no single source of truth. It's twenty-one shoeboxes of receipts. Try finding one faded slip when the tax authority wants it tomorrow."

Maria allowed herself the faintest smirk. "And auditors don't like shoeboxes."

Daniel nodded. "That's why we need a compliance platform—to unify, automate, close the loop."

He clicked again. Key features filled the wall: automated return prep, real-time reconciliation, central deadline tracking, secure archive, integration with RPA and the tax engine.

"Returns filed automatically, reconciliations flagged early, deadlines tracked with alerts, records archived securely, all integrated."

Maria's pen tapped twice. "And the business case?"

Daniel was ready. "Eighty-one tax professionals. Ten to twelve percent of their time goes into compliance tasks—that's 1,500 to 2,400 workdays a year. Six to ten FTEs, costing between $750,000 and a million annually. Cut that in half? We save $375,000 to $500,000 every year."

Maria raised her eyebrows. "That's not small change."

Sophia added quickly, "It's more than money—it's credibility. We've all felt the sting of an audit where we couldn't produce documents fast enough. With this, we reduce that risk dramatically."

Her tone was smooth, persuasive. Yet Abhishek caught the undertone—she was framing it as "we" while never once implying she owned the fix—another subtle sidestep.

Maria's pen hovered, then stilled. She looked around the table—first at Daniel, then at Sophia, then Abhishek and Aldo.

"So," she said slowly, "bots cut the grunt work. The determination engine fixes the foundation. And a compliance platform ties filings together."

Her eyes narrowed. "On paper, it sounds like we've built a machine that never sleeps."

She leaned back, voice dropping to CFO steel.

"But machines don't run themselves. Who makes sure the bot didn't miss a field? Who ensures the tax engine is updated correctly across twenty-one countries? Who catches the compliance system before it lets a filing slip?"

She tapped her pen once against the glass table.

"Technology may be the sling, the foundation, the shoebox we never lose. But none of it matters if no one is orchestrating the whole symphony. So tell me—who conducts? Who owns this end-to-end?"

The room went still.

Daniel clicked the remote. A new slide glowed to life: a simple looped circle with a single word at the centre—Workflow.

"The conductor," he said quietly and clicked on to the next slide.

Workflow Management–The Control Tower

A clean graphic appeared: concentric circles, a hub feeding every spoke.

"Maria, we've automated the 'what'—tax determination and compliance. Now we need to streamline the 'how.' Today, tasks move by email, spreadsheets, and late-night phone calls. It's brittle. Risky."

Maria folded her arms. "Sounds like chaos disguised as process."

"Exactly," Daniel said. "A workflow tool becomes our control tower. Every filing, approval, escalation—tracked and visible in one place."

Maria leaned forward. "And integration? I don't want a fourth silo pretending to be the fix."

Daniel shook his head. "It's seamless. It pulls from the compliance tool, assigns tasks, triggers alerts, and escalates if deadlines slip."

Maria's eyes narrowed. "And approvals? That's where things disappear."

"Every step logged," Daniel said. "From draft to sign-off. Nothing vanishes into inboxes. Full traceability."

Sophia spoke next, her tone smooth, almost too polished.

"And audits, Maria? No more last-minute hunts. Instead of combing shared drives, you get instant, audit-ready trails."

On the surface, reassurance. To Abhishek, it sounded like Sophia again—aligning with the winning side while neatly avoiding any mention of who enforces discipline when people ignore the tool.

Daniel clicked forward to the next slide:

What AlphaCorp Gains:

- Task Assignments: crystal-clear ownership.
- Standardised Workflows: consistency across borders.
- Built-in Collaboration: comments, approvals, fixes in-system.
- Central Storage: one place, no shoeboxes.

Aldo leaned in. "And IT effort?"

"Minimal," Daniel said. "Cloud-based. Doesn't strain ERP. We're not adding another beast to feed."

Maria glanced at the slide, then leaned back, frowning slightly. "Daniel, are we over-engineering this? Bots, a determination engine, compliance automation, now workflow. Are we building a Ferrari when we only need a bus? What happens if this collapses under its own weight?"

Daniel nodded. "Valid concern. But think of it like gears. Alone, each wheel spins. Together, they drive motion. The determination engine feeds compliance automation, which flows into the workflow. They're not four projects—they're one drivetrain."

He paused. "Take a simple example. Today, a country team spends ten days a month reconciling, coding, and filing. With these tools connected, that drops to two. Same output. Eight days freed for analysis, audits, planning . . . that's like engineering for survival."

Abhishek's chest tightened. Hybrid succeeded because we had a governance backbone. Matrix failed because no one owned the orchestra. Workflow is really the conductor.

Maria studied the slide one last time, then let her pen fall onto the table. "So—bots reduce grunt work. The engine fixes the foundation. Compliance ties filings together. And workflow ensures it all plays in rhythm."

Maria studied the final slide in silence. Then she set her pen down and looked at Daniel and Aldo.

"Alright," she said. "On paper, this holds. Bots, the engine, compliance, workflow—it's a solid architecture. The ROI stacks up, the pieces connect. But let's not fool ourselves. A machine doesn't run itself. Who's going to keep this alive?"

Aldo leaned in, voice steady. "That's the heart of it, Maria. We need more than tools—we need a team to run the orchestra. People who own governance end-to-end. Data standards. Change control. Escalations. If that's weak, the whole drivetrain seizes up."

Maria nodded slowly. "I've seen it before—great blueprints, wasted because no one set up the guardrails. Data went stale, processes drifted, and controls got bypassed. That's where failure starts."

Daniel folded his hands, his tone calm but deliberate. "Exactly. Technology is not a panacea. At one client, they installed a tax engine with a beautiful implementation—except that no one updated the governance model. Within eighteen months, half the rules were overridden manually, data reconciliations stopped, and by the next audit, the system had become just another black box. They saved nothing. In fact, they spent more."

He paused, then added, "That's why governance has to be the backbone."

Maria glanced at Aldo. "And you think we have the people to run this?"

Aldo met her gaze. "We have the core. But we'll need to strengthen it. A transformation of this scale demands architects, not just operators. People who can see the data flow, anticipate risks, and enforce standards. Otherwise, we're just buying a Ferrari without knowing how to drive."

Maria allowed herself a small smile at the metaphor. "So we don't just need the vehicle. We need the drivers, the pit crew, and the race strategy. A governance structure that ensures this doesn't end up as another failed experiment."

Daniel nodded. "Exactly. This isn't just tax technology. It's a tax transformation. And transformation is orchestration—people, process, governance, data, technology—all tuned together. Leave one out, and the music stops."

The room was quiet for a beat. Then Maria drew a deep breath, her decision clear.

"Alright. We've talked about efficiency. We've talked about architecture. We've talked about risk. Now we've talked governance. It's time to put this in front of the Board."

She leaned back, her voice calm but firm.

"We take the full roadmap—RPA, tax determination, compliance, workflow—framed as one story. And we make it clear: the technology is powerful, but only if AlphaCorp builds the right team and the right governance to sustain it. That's how we win."

Daniel inclined his head. "And that's how we convince them."

Aldo smiled faintly. "The Board won't just see tools. They'll see a system. A future. A tax function that's no longer reactive, but a control tower for the business."

Maria looked around the table, resolve sharpening.

"Then let's prepare. Next Tuesday, we take AlphaCorp's tax transformation roadmap to the Board. And this time, we're ready."

Aldo and Daniel exchanged a look of cautious satisfaction.

The architecture was strong, the numbers tight, the story compelling.

Abhishek sat back, silent but steady. He had spoken little today, but inside he felt the weight of Hybrid and Matrix pressing on him. This is where programs live or die, he thought. Governance isn't glamorous, but it's the reason Hybrid worked and Matrix collapsed. If the Board approves, the real test begins. He didn't crave the spotlight—what he wanted was for the orchestra to play in tune.

Across the table, Sophia closed her notebook with a soft snap. Her expression was serene, even faintly pleased. She had leaned in when Maria demanded clarity, nodded at the right moments, and never once tied herself to ownership. The deck was polished now, every slide a story. Mission accomplished, she thought. With this roadmap, she had everything she needed— for AlphaCorp, also for her future. Richard's words echoed in her mind: We build faster, smarter, somewhere else.

Maria rose, signalling the close.

"Let's get ready for Tuesday."

The room exhaled as one. The pitch was rehearsed, the roadmap sealed.

Sophia was the first to leave. Her heels clicked softly against the marble as the AlphaCorp Tower doors closed behind her. She had barely stepped onto the plaza when her phone buzzed in her hand. Unknown number. Again.

She didn't hesitate this time. She answered.

"Richard."

Her voice carried the faintest smile.

INTERLUDE: THE POISONED WELL

The café was half-empty, its windows fogged against the late London rain. Sophia slid into a corner booth, black woolen coat still damp from the drizzle. She placed her leather notebook on the table — the same one she had closed with such satisfaction inside AlphaCorp Tower only hours ago.

Richard arrived late, as always. No apology. Just the faint smell of cigar smoke clinging to his overcoat and a smirk that made Sophia feel both valued , , , and somehow expendable.

"Well," he said, easing into the seat opposite her, "how was my old kingdom today?"

Sophia didn't waste time. She opened her notebook, pages dense with shorthand notes and sketches from the final ROI session. "They've got the full deck now. RPA for grunt work, a tax engine for determination, compliance tools to tie returns, and workflow as the conductor. Maria's framing it as efficiency plus governance. The Board will like it."

Richard's eyes flicked over the notes, his smirk deepening. "Good. Very good. And that's exactly why we need to gut it before it grows legs."

Sophia raised an eyebrow. "How?"

He leaned back, savouring the moment. "I still have friends."

He tapped a finger on the page marked Tax Engine ROI. "I'll tell them about a global bank whose bots froze payroll and triggered a regulatory fine. I'll tell them about an FMCG giant that overspent twenty million on a tax engine that couldn't adapt to local quirks. And I'll remind them how many compliance tools end up as expensive document cabinets no one trusts. The trick," he added, lowering his voice, "is to make Maria's slides feel like déjà vu. Nothing terrifies a Board more than funding what already failed elsewhere."

Sophia listened, expression neutral, though a curl of satisfaction touched her lips.

"And if they press for evidence?"

Richard smiled wolfishly.

"Case studies are public. Names are forgotten. But the doubt will stick. I don't need proof, Sophia. I need narrative. By the time Maria walks into that room, half the Board will already be wondering if she's selling them another black box."

He leaned closer, voice turning razor-sharp.

"You've done your part. Mission accomplished. You gave me the pressure points. Now let me do what I do best — poison the well before they even sip from it."

Sophia closed her notebook, sliding it back into her bag. Her tone was smooth, detached.

"Then it's over to you."

Richard chuckled.

"No, my dear. It's just beginning. Maria thinks she has momentum. By Tuesday, she'll be fighting quicksand."

Outside, the rain thickened, streaking the glass. Inside, Richard lit a cigarette, his eyes gleaming with the quiet satisfaction of a man who knew the game was rigged long before the first move was played.

Sophia slipped her notebook back into her bag, her face composed. But inside, a thrill ran through her. So this was it—the endgame.

She pictured herself walking out of AlphaCorp for the last time, resignation letter crisp and final. Ahead lay something better: a seat of prestige, beside Richard, where decisions were bold and power was raw.

She had started dreaming of the good times already—rooms of influence, deals whispered over late dinners, her name attached to transformation on a global scale. And it hadn't even been as tricky as she had once imagined. One meeting, one polished deck, one well-placed phone call, and the foundation was shifting beneath AlphaCorp's feet.

Yet beneath the glow of anticipation, a sliver of unease remained. She didn't know Richard that well. His charm was edged with something more challenging, something colder. But Sophia pushed the thought aside. For now, the future looked bright.

She rose from the booth, coat still damp from the rain, and stepped out into the night. Her phone buzzed again, the same unknown number. This time, she smiled before answering.

CHAPTER 24

Taking It to the Boardroom – A Defining Moment for AlphaCorp

Tuesday morning, the AlphaCorp Boardroom gleamed with polished wood and glass, the skyline of Canary Wharf glittering beyond. For once, the tax transformation team felt a ripple of confidence.

Maria walked in first, portfolio in hand, the weight of weeks of preparation distilled into one story. Behind her, Daniel wheeled in the final deck, Aldo carried the technical backup files, and Abhishek trailed, quiet but proud. For him, this was redemption—Matrix behind him, Hybrid beside him, AlphaCorp ahead.

The directors were already gathering, exchanging greetings in low, easy tones. The scrape of chairs, the quiet thud of folders on polished wood, and the low hum of conversation filled the room. Maria moved from one to the next, shaking hands, smiling with practised warmth. She could feel Daniel's calm presence beside her, Aldo's quiet energy, Abhishek's contained excitement.

Then she reached him.

"Maria," said Edward Grant, rising from his chair with a smile that never reached his eyes. His grip was firm, calm, and professional. The pleasantries were there, but the warmth was not.

Maria froze inside. She knew Edward. Veteran of the Audit Committee. Old-guard finance. And Richard's long-time golf partner—the one director who had never hidden his loyalty.

The handshake lingered just a fraction too long. Edward's smile stayed polite, but his eyes flicked past her, already moving to the subsequent greeting.

Maria moved on, her smile intact, but a note of unease lodged itself under her ribs. *Odd. He was warmer last quarter. Why cold now?*

Then Sophia entered. Impeccable as ever—tailored suit, notebook in hand, composure that looked effortless. When she approached Edward, his demeanour transformed. His eyes brightened, his smile softened, and for a fleeting second, admiration flickered with something more than professional regard.

It was subtle, but unmistakable: the way his gaze lingered a beat too long, the way his posture shifted as though pulled toward her.

Maria noticed. She always noticed. And the unease sharpened.

Sophia offered Edward a brief, knowing smile before gliding to her seat, settling in as if she belonged at his side as much as at Maria's table.

Abhishek slid into his chair, catching the anticipatory hum in the room. Aldo whispered, "We've got this," and Maria nodded, forcing her focus forward. The team had earned this stage.

But Edward Grant's cool handshake—and the warmth, tinged with admiration, that he reserved for Sophia—echoed in Maria's mind like a warning bell only she could hear.

Meeting the Board

Maria opened with confidence, laying out AlphaCorp's tax transformation roadmap. Daniel guided the slides with crisp assurance. Aldo interjected with technical clarity. The architecture looked seamless: RPA to cut grunt work, a tax determination engine to fix the foundation, a compliance tool to tie filings, and workflow as the conductor.

The first few slides landed well. A few directors nodded. Maria felt a flicker of hope.

Then Edward leaned back, voice deceptively calm.

"Maria, forgive me, but haven't we tried this before?"

The room stilled. Even the hum of the air-conditioning seemed to hold its breath.

He tapped his Montblanc pen slowly against the table. *Click. Click.* "Treasury. Bots. A few years ago. That project failed spectacularly. We lost millions cleaning up the mess. Why should we believe this will be any different?"

Maria straightened. "That was the treasury. Different scope, different controls—"

Edward cut her off, his voice slicing through hers.

"Different scope, same promise. Efficiency. Automation. Fewer errors. And the result? Disaster."

A murmur rippled across the table.

Daniel leaned forward, his voice calm but carrying a weight of memory. "With respect, Edward, I've studied why Treasury failed. That project had no parallel runs and no fallback controls — the safeguards were missing from day one. Our design avoids those mistakes. We've built layered protections, because I've seen in other institutions what happens when you don't."

Aldo added quickly, "And bots today don't touch ERP core. They operate through APIs."

Edward waved a dismissive hand.

"So you say. But the last time I heard these promises, AlphaCorp paid the price. Shareholders don't forgive déjà vu."

The chill in his tone spread across the table.

Before Maria could recover, another director spoke—Helen Turner, head of the Compensation Committee.

"And if you *do* succeed?" she asked, her tone sharp, voice cutting like ice. "Automation replaces manual work. What happens to the people? What's the plan for redundancies? How do we manage layoffs?"

Daniel hesitated. Aldo leaned forward. "We're focused on redeployment. Tax professionals freed from grunt work can pivot to analysis, planning."

Helen shook her head. "That's theory. What's the *plan*? Numbers. Roles. A communications framework. Because the first question from the unions won't be about analysis, it'll be: Who loses their job?"

The words landed like a hammer. Maria's throat tightened. They hadn't prepared that slide.

Abhishek cleared his throat, voice steady but quiet. "We should map ownership before rollout—governance of data, of tasks, of exceptions. Without it—"

But Edward spoke over him. "This is AlphaCorp. Not a classroom. We need answers."

Abhishek's voice died in the hum of the air-conditioning.

Daniel jumped in too quickly. "Other clients—large retailers, global banks—they retrained staff, reskilled, redeployed—"

Edward's palm hit the table with a sharp crack. "We are not other clients, Daniel. This is AlphaCorp. What is *our* plan?"

Silence thickened. Maria tapped her pen once, twice, against the folder in front of her. For the first time in months, she had no answer.

Helen pressed further. "And the unions? In Europe alone, you're talking about headcount impacts. What's your strategy for collective bargaining? For reputational fallout?"

Maria tried to parry, but her words felt hollow even to her own ears. "We... we're still assessing options. Workforce impact modelling will come in the next phase—"

Helen's expression was icy. "So you don't have a plan."

Maria's cheeks burned. She felt like a defendant under cross-examination. Every careful slide they had built was being ripped apart, piece by piece, as if everyone already knew what was missing.

From the corner, Abhishek lowered his gaze.

Sophia, two seats down, remained silent, her notebook closed. But Maria caught it—the faint curve of her lips, the quiet satisfaction in her eyes.

Edward leaned forward, voice sharp as glass.

"This roadmap is incomplete. You've built a machine without a driver, and now you want us to hand you the keys."

He let the silence stretch before delivering the final blow. "Go back. Fix the holes. Come back when you have answers. Until then, this discussion is over."

The gavel wasn't literal, but it may as well have been. The meeting was dead.

Maria gathered her notes with mechanical precision, her face calm but her chest burning. *At least a month lost. Momentum shattered.* She rose, every step heavy, her fury contained but alive.

Behind her, Daniel closed his laptop with quiet frustration. Aldo stared at the table, jaw clenched. Abhishek walked out last, silent but watchful, his mind replaying the red flags. And Sophia? She closed her notebook softly, serene, her lips curved in the faintest smile.

Showdown: Maria vs. Sophia

Maria's office was silent when the team filed in. The blinds were half-drawn, her desk still scattered with papers from the Board pack. She didn't offer coffee or small talk. She didn't even sit.

"Let's debrief," she said tightly, her voice clipped but level.

Daniel began, offering technical defences — how he'd tried to salvage the RPA narrative, how Edward cut him off. Aldo added his observations, calm but pointed, about how the Board's pushback was less about numbers and more about politics.

Sophia, arms folded, spoke with an edge that made the air prickle. "Maria, the truth is the Board saw through the gaps. We weren't ready. We should have anticipated it."

Maria's pen tapped against the desk. Once. Twice.

Abhishek tried to soften it. "There were... angles we couldn't have known. The unions, the layoffs—"

Sophia cut him off, voice rising. "Everyone else knew. You could see it in their faces. This wasn't about angles. It was about preparation. We walked in overconfident and got slaughtered."

Maria's eyes flashed. She straightened slowly, her voice trembling with fury. "That's exactly what bothers me, Sophia. How come everyone else knew, and we were the only ones who didn't?" She slammed the pen down, the crack echoing off the glass. "I carried this transformation on my back for weeks. I defended every damn number. And you sit here in my office and tell me we deserved to be slaughtered?"

Her voice rose, breaking past its usual steel. "You think you can second-guess me, undermine me, after the worst Boardroom I've sat through in ten years?"

Her words came faster, sharper, her face flushed. "Don't you dare sit there smug, as if you had the answers tucked in your little notebook."

Her voice was now a shout, ragged at the edges. She was trembling, hands gripping the desk as though it were the only thing keeping her anchored.

For once, Sophia didn't shrink back. Richard's safety net burned bright in her mind, buoying her spine. She rose slowly, meeting Maria eye-to-eye.

"You don't intimidate me anymore," Sophia said evenly, her voice sharp. "You lost control out there. You're losing control in here. And if you keep shouting at me like this, I'll not take it anymore. Don't test me."

The words landed like a blade between them.

Maria froze, chest heaving, fury sparking against disbelief. Aldo shifted uncomfortably, Daniel looked down, and Abhishek's jaw tightened. The air was toxic, charged, electric.

Sophia snapped her notebook shut. "Good luck, Maria. You'll need it."

She turned, heels sharp against the floor, and walked out, leaving silence in her wake.

Maria collapsed into her chair, trembling, her face pale. Rage and humiliation coiled in her gut like a storm with no outlet. For the first time, she felt challenged, cornered.

Maria Breaks Down

Maria drove home in silence, her hands gripping the wheel tighter than necessary. London's lights blurred past, her anger still raw, trembling under her skin. By the time she stepped into her apartment, her jaw ached from holding it clenched.

Arjun looked up from the sofa, surprise flickering across his face. "You're home early."

Maria dropped her bag with more force than she meant to. "Don't ask."

He hesitated, then guided her to sit. "What happened?"

The words tumbled out in fragments—Edward's ambush, Helen's questions about layoffs, Sophia's smug retort and threat. Her voice rose, cracked, softened, rose again. By the time she finished, her hands were shaking, and her eyes burned with unshed tears.

Arjun listened quietly, arms folded. When he finally spoke, his voice was calm, too calm. "Maria, this all sounds as if it were staged. Edward has always been Richard's man. Helen is predictable in the workforce. This wasn't about numbers — it was politics. You walked into an ambush."

Maria shook her head, eyes weary.

Arjun leaned forward, his voice dropping to a firm register. "You're brilliant in the Boardroom, Maria. But you think the deck and the numbers are enough. They aren't. Someone lobbied before you walked in. You left space to be swayed. You were thorough, but not through."

Maria's stomach twisted. She had come home desperate for comfort, not a verdict. "Arjun, please. Not tonight."

But the words lingered like a wound—leadership failure. No alignment. She lay in bed later, staring at the ceiling, replaying Edward's cold handshake, Sophia's calm defiance, and Arjun's judgment.

Sleep came, but it was heavy, poisoned. Even in her dreams, Maria felt it—that gnawing truth: she had walked into the Board unarmed where it mattered most.

Abhishek's Vigil

Across the city, Abhishek sat at his kitchen table, long after his wife had gone to bed. A cold cup of coffee sat untouched beside his notebook, the pages filled with half-scribbled thoughts.

The Board meeting replayed in his head — Edward's ambush, the union's question, Maria's silence. He had wanted to speak, to steady her, to share what he knew. But he had held back, knowing his words would have been drowned in the noise.

He rubbed his temples. *This is what killed Matrix.* Everyone had focused on the technology, the rollout, the promises. No one had prepared for the people, the politics, the governance. No one had orchestrated the human side of change. And by the time the cracks showed, it was too late.

At Hybrid, it had been different. Not perfect — far from it — but there had been a rhythm, a conductor keeping teams aligned, even when the music was messy. That was why it worked - because the tools and the people moved in sync.

He looked down at his notes: one word circled again and again.

Orchestration.

Abhishek leaned back, closing his eyes. *Maria is strong, but she can't fight this alone. Someone has to hold the centre. Someone has to keep the music from falling apart.*

The thought didn't comfort him. It weighed on him. But it also clarified what he already knew: the next chapter of AlphaCorp's battle wasn't about technology. It was about leadership, vision, and the human spine that held both upright.

In the silence of his apartment, Abhishek whispered to himself, almost like a vow: *We won't repeat Matrix. Not here. Not again.*

CHAPTER 25

A Battle of Nerves

The morning after the Boardroom humiliation, Maria arrived at AlphaCorp Tower to an email stamped Confidential: Ethics Committee Acknowledgement.

Her stomach sank. She opened it.

The Committee has received a formal complaint lodged by Ms. Sophia Chan alleging unprofessional conduct during an internal meeting on Tuesday evening. The matter will be reviewed. You are advised not to take retaliatory action while the case is pending.

Maria's jaw clenched, the words burning into her—unprofessional conduct. Sophia had done it. She had gone nuclear.

The project floor was already alive when Maria walked in. Daniel was speaking in a low voice to Aldo, Abhishek was flipping through notes, and Sophia sat poised at the far end of the table. Immaculate. Unruffled. Her notebook was open, her pen resting neatly across the page.

She looked up, her expression the very picture of composure. "Morning."

Maria forced a nod and sat down. She couldn't touch her. Couldn't sideline her. Couldn't even freeze her out without feeding the complaint.

And Sophia knew it. Enjoyed it.

By noon, Maria was summoned upstairs. Isabel Hartmann's assistant ushered her into the CEO's office.

"Maria," Isabel began, not looking up from the window where the Thames curved grey beneath the skyline. Her tone was clipped, her German accent sharper when she was irritated. "I've received the complaint. The

Board has heard whispers. This is the last thing we need after yesterday's performance."

Maria drew a breath. "It was a heated moment. Sophia—"

Isabel cut across her. "No excuses. You are the CFO. You do not lose control. Not in front of your team. Not now. If the Committee escalates this, we may be forced into mediation. And Maria—" she turned, fixing her with a gaze as cold as the river below—"if this project stumbles again, you may not be the one presenting next time."

The words landed like a hammer.

Maria stiffened. "And what about Richard's influence? Edward's ambush wasn't spontaneous. Sophia is feeding him—"

"Proof," Isabel snapped. "Bring me proof. Until then, she stays. She is part of this project. And so are you. Which means I expect professionalism, not warfare. Am I clear?"

Maria swallowed her fury. "Crystal."

As she left Isabel's office, Maria's pulse was pounding. Her fury had nowhere to go. She had been dressed down as though she were the one under suspicion, not Sophia. By the time she stepped back into the lift, she had already steeled herself: No slips. Not again.

Back on Level 27, the war room had been stripped bare of gloss. Whiteboards scrawled with marker filled one wall. Post-its formed a jagged mosaic across another. In red, underlined twice: 30 days to the Board.

The air was heavy, taut. The squeak of markers, the shuffle of papers, even Sophia's light pen tapping sounded louder than it should.

Maria stood at the head of the table, every muscle rigid. Sophia sat three chairs down, notebook open, tapping her pen lightly — the rhythm almost taunting.

Daniel started. "Three gaps killed us last time: governance, workforce impact, unions. If we don't plug them, the Board will bury us."

Aldo added, "And Edward will be waiting. This time, the numbers and models must be accurate and precise. They'll want line of sight into EPS, redundancy reserves, everything."

Sophia tilted her head. Her voice was soft, but her words were knives. "Or we admit the Board was right. Maybe this roadmap isn't ready."

Maria's grip tightened on her pen until it hurt. She forced silence.

Abhishek leaned in, voice steady. He walked to the whiteboard, uncapped a marker, and drew a circle.

"This isn't a stack of tools. It's an orchestra. RPA, tax engine, compliance, workflow. Without a conductor, the instruments play noise. Governance is the conductor."

The room stilled. Daniel's brows lifted. Maria's pen stopped mid-tap. Aldo nodded slowly.

Sophia smirked faintly. "Nice metaphor. But governance doesn't stop unions from rioting."

Aldo's jaw tightened. For a split second, he saw again what had once drawn him to Sophia — her fire, her composure. He hated himself for it now. You're poison, he thought. And I almost believed you.

He cleared his throat. "Governance doesn't fix unions. But it forces us to prepare for them. Escalation paths. RACI models. Real accountability. Without that, technology will multiply error paths."

Daniel backed him. "I've seen programs succeed or collapse on exactly this. You can spend millions on tools, but without governance, the cracks always win."

Sophia leaned back, amused. "You talk like we have time to build a cathedral."

Maria cut in, sharp. "No cathedral. But a foundation. Abhishek is right — we don't sell tech in a month. We sell orchestration. That's our story."

For the first time since the disaster, alignment flickered in the room.

Sophia wrote something in her notebook, serene, untouchable.

The meeting dragged into the evening. One by one, the team filed out, drained. Maria lingered, collecting her papers, her mind already spinning toward tomorrow.

That was when she saw it.

On the table, sleek and buzzing, lay a phone. The lock screen lit up, flashing a name.

Richard.

Sophia's phone. Left behind.

Maria froze. Her pulse quickened. For a moment, she stared at it, her mind racing. One swipe and she'd know. Proof. Or nothing. But if she touched it, everything could blow up.

She forced herself to step back, her jaw clenched. She took a picture of it then and there.

For the first time in weeks, Maria felt the balance tilt, just slightly, back in her favour.

The battle wasn't over. It was only the beginning.

CHAPTER 26

The Smudged Roadmap

The investigation room was cold, deliberately so. Maria sat with her palms pressed flat against the table, her last card trembling in her hand. She slid her phone forward, the photograph glowing on the screen: Richard's name lit up as an incoming call on Sophia's phone.

"This," Maria said evenly, "was why I reacted the way I did."

The committee members exchanged looks, then one cleared his throat. "Not conclusive," he said flatly. The photo was logged, then pushed aside. Sophia, meanwhile, was praised for her composure. Maria felt the air thicken; her defence had been dismissed before it had even landed.

Two weeks later, the letter arrived:

"You are hereby requested to transition from your current position as Chief Financial Officer of AlphaCorp. The Board has decided to redeploy you to lead the Finance function in the Asia-Pacific market."

On paper, it was a realignment. In reality, it was exile—far from headquarters, far from the transformation she had bled for. Maria folded the letter with surgical precision, slid it into its envelope, and placed it on the corner of her desk. She wanted to scream, *This was my fight.* Instead, she swallowed the ache. Exile demanded composure.

Within a week, John Hutchings arrived. Tall, composed, with the easy charm of someone born for polished boardrooms, he shook hands with the Board as though he had always belonged there. Maria wondered if his contract had been signed before her hearing even ended.

John wasted no time. Within days, he summoned Aldo, Sophia, Abhishek, and Daniel to a closed-door meeting. One hour. That was all it took. Maria wasn't invited, of course. She only heard the outcome later, whispered over coffee in the executive lounge:

"The project has merit," John had said. "It wasn't sold rightly."

Months of Maria's work, reduced to a single sentence. The roadmap hadn't failed—*she* had.

Four weeks later, the Board reconvened. Maria, now a guest awaiting her transfer abroad, sat in the back row. John stood at the head of the table, flanked by Sophia and Daniel. The presentation slides were painfully familiar. RPA, tax determination, compliance, workflow management—the pillars Maria had fought for, now repackaged in John's diplomatic tone.

Approval came easily. It took John one hour to secure what she had battled for across months. Maria's chest tightened. The roadmap hadn't changed. Only the messenger had.

The restructuring followed immediately. Sophia was formally named Head of Tax Transformation, entrusted with leading the program. Abhishek was instructed to assist her. Their first exchange told him all he needed to know.

"We'll make this work, Abhishek," Sophia said, her tone clipped. "Just keep things in line with the way I want them. And don't bring me another Hybrid story—this isn't Hybrid."

Abhishek nodded, but inside he bristled. He had experience that Sophia lacked, but now found himself cast as her second-in-command, trapped between professionalism and resentment.

John maintained courtesy with Maria, always polite in public, even deferential, but there was steel beneath the smile. "Your new role in Asia-Pacific will give you a chance to shape strategy in a critical growth region," he told her one afternoon. His tone carried the finality of a man who had no intention of looking back.

People already treated her as if she were gone. She had once been AlphaCorp's anchor; now she was a nameplate to be moved across continents.

Before her departure, Maria asked Aldo and Abhishek to join her in a quiet corner office. Daniel, she noticed, had chosen not to attend. His polite excuse made sense—consultants survived by neutrality. *Better to sit this one out,* he must have thought. *This wasn't the hill to die on.*

Maria closed the door. "I need to know," she said, voice steady. "Do you believe this project can still succeed?"

Aldo leaned forward, fingers steepled. "The project isn't the problem. The alignment is. If Sophia and John run it like a checklist, we'll drown in bottlenecks."

Abhishek exhaled, his jaw tight. "I've seen it before. At Hybrid, orchestration saved us. At Matrix, the lack of it ruined us. Right now, AlphaCorp feels more like Matrix."

Maria studied them both. They were younger, less scarred, but carried the same unease she felt. Her time was over, but theirs wasn't.

"Then make sure," she said quietly, "that when the storm comes, you're not caught unprepared."

At the close of that meeting, Maria lingered as the room emptied. The final slide of the approved roadmap glowed in her mind—a plan she could recite in her sleep.

Her plan. Her fingerprints—erased, overwritten.

Maria stood, gathered her papers, and walked out in silence. The echo of her heels in the corridor sounded less like footsteps and more like a countdown—to her departure, and to the storm she knew was coming.

CHAPTER 27

From Blueprint to Reality – Kicking Off the Transformation with Project Governance

The boardroom victory was done. But as Sophia sat quietly with her notebook before the governance meeting, she knew this next phase would decide everything.

This wasn't just a project. It felt more like preparing for war—one fought with strategy, influence, and execution. In her mind, she saw a battlefield map:

- The Executive Steering Committee—her high command.
- Daniel's PMO—the generals in charge of deployment.
- Country tax leads—regional commanders.
- Technology and tax experts—the special forces, each with a critical mission.

Morale was fragile, already clouded by fear, politics, and pride.

She had seen how battles were lost in the preparation. Today, they were not kicking off a project. They were entering a war room to define how AlphaCorp would fight and win.

The executive meeting room buzzed with anticipation. John Hutchings presided at the head, but everyone knew Sophia was now in charge of tax transformation. Aldo leaned back, arms crossed, while Abhishek sat stiffly beside him, his role officially defined as Sophia's assistant. Daniel adjusted his glasses at the far end, neutrality etched into his posture.

They reviewed the final blueprint. With Board approval secured, the next challenge lay in execution: turning a polished roadmap into lived reality across 21 countries.

They had seen Matrix LLC collapse under poor governance and siloed execution. They remembered Hybrid LLC's success, where orchestration had pulled people, process, and data into alignment. Now, those lessons would be tested here.

Building the Right Governance Model – A Collective Decision

"We all agree," Sophia began, voice firm, "execution is where most large-scale projects fail. And this time, failure is not an option."

Aldo nodded, though his jaw was tight. "Agreed. Twenty-one countries, different laws, multiple stakeholders—without structure, we'll stall fast."

Daniel added, calm but clipped. "Assign decision rights early, or we'll be stuck in neutral. I suggest a multi-tiered governance model."

Abhishek leaned forward. "Let's not repeat the mistakes of LatAm—six months lost just fixing reporting gaps. We need clarity now."

Sophia glanced at him. "Noted, Abhishek. But let's keep our focus on what *will* work, not old war stories."

A flicker crossed his face, but he said nothing more.

Together, they mapped the governance:

- **Executive Steering Committee (ESC)**: John, Sophia, Aldo, Richard Langley, regional heads, legal, and external advisors. Strategic oversight, budget approvals, and high-level risk resolution.
- **Project Management Office (PMO)**: Daniel's team plus regional PMOs and functional leads. Craft plans, track risks, standardise tools.
- **Risk & Compliance Committee**: Monitor regulatory exposure and tax authority interaction.
- **Regional/Country Implementation Teams**: Adapt global templates to local contexts, escalate issues upward.
- **Workstreams/Functional Teams**: Deliver the specific components—technology, change management, training.

Addressing Internal Resistance – The Human Factor

But governance was only one battlefront. The real war lay with people. The project had already stirred factions. Some believed HQ was hijacking leadership roles while leaving the heavy lifting to country teams. Others dismissed the transformation as optics, another stunt to impress the Board.

At a tense alignment meeting with country tax leads, frustrations boiled over.

"We've led complex portfolios for years," said Omar, the Egypt tax lead. "Yet we're sidelined while others get PMO roles. It feels like decisions are made behind closed doors."

From Mexico, another voice: "If we don't manage this narrative, trade unions will. Once they see automation as job cuts, resistance won't be passive—it'll be organised."

Sophia listened, expression steady. But under the surface, she felt the cracks forming. This wasn't just about tools and workflows. It was about trust, inclusion, and power.

After the meeting, Aldo muttered to Abhishek, "It feels like Matrix all over again—processes, but no harmony."

Abhishek gave a tight smile. "Hybrid worked because people believed in the vision. Right now, no one does."

Sophia overheard but kept walking. Their words stung because they were true.

That evening, Richard invited Sophia to a private Mayfair club. He raised his glass, smiling thinly. "Congratulations. John tells me the Board was impressed. You've handled yourself well."

Sophia sat, guarded. "Maria's out. The project's moving. Isn't that what you wanted?"

Richard's smile deepened. "What *I* wanted? No, Sophia. This is bigger than me. The committee, John, the Board's decision—I merely nudged. The machinery was already in motion."

Sophia studied him, unsettled. For years, she had thought she was playing Richard's game. Now she saw he was just another instrument in an orchestra she didn't yet understand. As she stepped into the night air, a realisation settled in her chest: *This is bigger than Richard. And if I wasn't the conductor, then who was?*

CHAPTER 28

Failing to Plan or Planning to Fail

The Board's mandate was brutally clear: quick wins first. Visible results early. No excuses.

Careers were tethered to that sentence—John's credibility, Sophia's authority, Abhishek's reputation, Daniel's neutrality, and somewhere across the ocean, Maria's name still echoing in the halls she'd left behind.

The governance was inked. Now came the hard part: a plan that could survive contact with reality.

The Working Session

Daniel's PMO staged a briefing. The wall-length display showed a living draft. Roles were clear on paper, but tension had its own seating chart.

In London, John presided. Sophia sat forward, pen poised. Aldo leaned back, guarded. Abhishek took the seat to Sophia's right, notebook open but jaw tight. Daniel stood by the screen, the quiet centre of gravity. From Singapore, Maria was requested to join on video, her window small but unmistakable.

"A project plan," Daniel began, "isn't a task list. It's a battle map. It tells us what matters, when it matters, who fights which battles, and where defeat is most likely. Scope is our boundary. Define it now, or pay for it later."

On the screen, AlphaCorp's footprint lit up—21 countries, different tax regimes, uneven maturity, uneven trust.

Phasing, or Drowning

"Same playbook everywhere on Day One is fantasy," Daniel said. "We phase, or we fail."

- **Phase 1**: High-volume, high-exposure markets where value can show fast—United States, United Kingdom, India, China, France, Germany. Quick wins via RPA on repetitive work and compliance dashboards for real-time visibility.
- **Phase 2**: The following 5–7 mid-tier countries—less complex, still meaningful. Lessons from Phase 1 are the template.
- **Phase 3**: The rest—tailored rollouts once credibility is banked.

"Quick wins aren't finishing the race," Daniel added. "They buy us air cover to run it."

Abhishek nodded, jotting notes with clipped precision. Sophia's pen didn't move. *Momentum was everything,* she thought. *Discipline could come later—if later ever came.*

"On that note," Sophia interjected suddenly, "we should consider piloting in Spain. It's not on Phase 1, but the Board is watching Europe closely. A quick win there could boost optics."

Daniel frowned. "Spain wasn't in the high-volume, high-exposure list. It'll dilute resources."

Sophia's smile was bright, rehearsed. "Sometimes optics matter as much as outcomes."

John said nothing, only closed his folder a little tighter. Sophia glanced down, her hand trembling before steadying her pen. *Did I push too far?* She wondered, before forcing her face back into composure. *They don't see it yet.*

Scope Creep: Death by Good Intentions

"If there's one quiet killer," Daniel said, voice sharpening, "it's Scope Creep." The slide he flashed up was blunt: **Death by a Thousand Good Intentions.**

- **Custom reports, Country A**: "Harmless extra dashboards linked to VAT filings. Sounds reasonable. Costs six weeks. Phase 1 slips."
- **Non-tax add-ons, Country B**: "Since we're touching invoices, let's cleanse vendor masters. Logical. Not tax scope. Focus shattered."

"Scope creep arrives as something reasonable," he finished. "Then it drowns you. We stay on the critical path. Everything else waits—or dies."

Silence. Then Sophia wrote, finally: *Enforce discipline—even against good ideas.*

Aldo's glance found Abhishek: a silent *We'll see.* Abhishek's jaw tightened, pen tapping once against the table. *Matrix all over again,* he thought. *Too much politics, too little alignment.* He opened his mouth, then shut it again, choosing silence over a fight he knew he'd lose today.

Data: Fuel, Not Afterthought

The next slide appeared, headed **Data—The Fuel of Transformation.**

"Our diagnostics are clear," Daniel said. "Bad data into the best engine still yields garbage. The bigger danger is ownership confusion. Tax defines needs. Finance and Master Data owns governance. If Tax 'owns' upstream quality, we become janitors—forever fixing what others break."

"Which means," he added, "data governance is not in scope. It's a prerequisite. Rebuilding foundations after the top floors are poured collapses the building."

Maria's inner voice cut through her thoughts, but she chose not to speak. "I agree on principle. But practically, if we don't address minimum governance in Phase 1, we'll stall before we start. We need a bridge—stabilisation inside the program while we make the case for a standalone governance track."

Aldo added, "The Board won't approve a separate data governance program yet. Carve a contained workstream now, prove value, then escalate."

Daniel exhaled. "Fine. Phase 1 receives a Data Stabilisation workstream—minimal, targeted, and time-boxed. But it doesn't become a dumping ground."

Abhishek underlined a single word in his notes: *Ownership.*

Mindset: The Human Battlefield

The final slide got to the center of things: **Change Management — The Real Battle.**

"Let's be honest," Daniel said. "Automation reads as job loss. However, our diagnostics indicate that 60 to 70 percent of tax teams' time is spent on clerical tasks. Not advisory. Not audits. Spreadsheets. Reconciliations. Automation doesn't take real tax work away—it gives it back."

He let that land, then added the sting. "If someone defines their value by manual control over fragmented processes, they'll resist—quietly."

On the screen, two columns appeared:

- **Strategic Mindset** → embraces learning, moves into advisory, governance, and optimisation.
- **Average Mindset** → clings to manual tasks, fears irrelevance, and avoids upskilling.

Sophia circled one word: **Mindset.** Maria's expression on the screen hardened—she'd fought this war before. Aldo murmured, "The map is neat. The battlefield won't be."

Daniel looked at the room, eyes heavy. *It was like watching a train gather speed toward a bend too sharp.* The real war wasn't scope creep. There was silence in the wrong moments.

Plan to Paper

Daniel then walked them through the backbone, going through the slides:

- **As-Is Study**: transaction mapping, data hygiene scan, ERP landscape, time-and-effort baselining for RPA.

Sophia frowned, already calculating how much country teams would resist extra time studies. Abhishek let out a soft sigh—he had seen this battle before at Hybrid, and he knew how quickly fatigue could sink momentum.

- **Design (Phase 1)**: prioritise high-volume, rule-based processes; design cross-country compliance dashboards; sketch the Phase 2 blueprint.

Aldo scribbled a note in the margin of his pad: *Dashboards don't win wars.*

- **Build & Test**: develop RPA, validate in varied conditions, and integrity-check dashboards.

  Daniel's voice grew sharper, as though trying to will discipline into the process itself.

- **Training & UAT**: targeted enablement; real-data tests in local environments.
- **Go-Live (Phase 1)**: staggered, impact-first releases with hyper care; cutover playbooks.
- **Post-Go-Live**: feedback loops, tuning, and prep for Phase 2 scaling.

John closed his folder. "Good. Keep it tight." His tone was polished but cool. It left no doubt he'd be watching for cracks. He straightened his cufflinks slowly, signalling finality. His eyes lingered on the Spain slide longer than the rest—already imagining how it might look in the Board's quarterly update.

Abhishek leaned forward. "One more point—exception handling on RPA. We need design changes before going live in India."

Sophia's smile was thin. "We'll iron out minor technicalities later. Momentum first."

Abhishek's pen stopped. Aldo's jaw set. Daniel said nothing. Maria's image flickered.

What the Slides Don't Show

As the room emptied, the plan looked solid: structured, realistic, well-governed. But no one felt relief.

Aldo thought about unions in Italy and the politics of speed. *Another brilliant design about to be throttled by optics,* he thought grimly. *Politics crushes brilliance every time.*

Daniel lingered behind, gathering papers. He found John waiting near the door.

"The plan is strong," Daniel said quietly, breaking neutrality. "But the alignment isn't. If leadership keeps pulling in different directions—"

John cut him off with a thin smile. "Make it work, Daniel. Optics are reality."

Daniel said nothing, but the dread pressed harder. *The train was already accelerating.* He knew the plan's most significant risk wasn't in the slides—it was in the people steering them.

In Singapore, Maria had just got off her daily video call with Arjun and the kids before they went to bed. The hum of the city below Maria's hotel window felt like another world. On her nightstand, notes were stacked into a private ledger of warnings. She underlined one line she'd written earlier: *When the time comes, I'll remind them.*

Sophia lingered, pen resting on her closed notebook. *Discipline is in my grip,* she told herself. Then, as she rose to leave, a sharper thought cut through the doubt: *If optics are reality, I already master optics—and prove them all wrong.*

The scope wasn't a formality. It was survival. The following months would test discipline, nerve, and truth-telling.

And far sooner than anyone expected, the map would meet the battlefield.

CHAPTER 29

From Map to Territory

The boardroom silence after Daniel's "battle map" lasted less than a day. Noise flooded in—Teams pings stacking like warning lights, emails phrased like disclaimers, and calendar holds marked **"AS-IS: URGENT"** that no one accepted.

Grayson & Holt's AI had already scanned AlphaCorp months earlier, an X-ray of its corporate skeleton. It flagged missing master data attributes, broken processes, duplicate vendors, free-text tax codes, and dead interfaces. Useful, yes. But scans weren't surgery. Now they needed hands—people tracing every transaction, every approval, every ledger jump from invoice to return.

No one volunteered.

The First Pushbacks

New York – 8:30 AM

"This is a tax project," said Sam Jones, US CFO, voice flat. "If tax wants transformation, tax should map its own workflows. Controllers are already slammed."

Paris – 3:10 PM

"We can't design anything without an as-is," the French CIO shrugged. "But mapping isn't IT's job. We build systems; we don't document them."

Mumbai – 7:45 PM

"Finance owns the ledgers," the Indian tax manager retorted. "We'll define tax treatments. Please don't ask us to map purchase approvals or intercompany reconciliations. That's finance."

Across 21 countries, the same triangle formed: Finance pointed to Tax, Tax pointed back to Finance, and IT raised a red flag. Ownership fell through the cracks.

Daniel watched the escalation dashboard light up. He knew the truth: if you don't draw the city as it exists, you can't redesign the roads. Saying it didn't make anyone pick up a pen.

Sophia's Angle

Sophia sat in the London hub, three screens open: the AI diagnostic, the PMO tracker, and a deck titled *Data Readiness – Unvarnished.* Opportunity hummed beneath her skin.

"This," she thought, "is where Maria and Abhishek slip."

She began circulating AI extracts annotated with "governance gaps," CC'ing John, sometimes even Isabel's chief of staff. Italy's broken vendor masters. The Gulf's nonstandard tax codes. India's missing IDs. Each slide framed Finance as negligent, left Tax looking reactive, and made Maria's absence feel like neglect.

On a global call, she unsheathed the blade.

"If Finance had enforced basic data governance," she said, pen tapping, "we wouldn't be debating as-is. The AI told us months ago that we weren't ready for automation. Perhaps leadership underestimated the gap."

Abhishek felt the air thin. He'd signed off on the AI sweep—and argued it wasn't a substitute for real mapping. He opened his mouth, then closed it. Not here. Not like this.

Aldo's jaw set. Performance art, again.

The Meeting That Buckled

Daniel convened **AS-IS Ownership – Final** with the US, UK, India, and France.

"Let's be concrete," he said. "Who maps what?"

"Tax should map as-is," said US Finance. "We'll validate."

"No," India Tax shot back. "Finance maps processes. We'll supply treatments."

"Without a signed as-is, IT can't design," France IT added. "We're blocked."

Sophia stepped in, glossy and composed. "Compromise: a light-touch, country-led sprint. Finance captures process, Tax annotates events, and IT confirms system touchpoints. Two weeks."

It sounded neat. It wasn't math. Two weeks wouldn't even cover purchase-to-pay in one large market.

Abhishek unmuted, voice calm but firm. "We can't annotate tax events without reliable transaction lineage. The analysis must trace purchase and sales flows end-to-end with a commercial context. Without that, overlaying tax is like applying plaster without an X-ray."

Sophia's smile thinned. "The country accounting manuals already have all that detail. Why reinvent the wheel?"

"The manuals haven't been updated in years," Abhishek replied evenly. "Systems have changed. Processes have changed. Tax has changed. If we pivot off stale documents, we'll miss the real fractures."

The silence was heavy. Then Sophia pivoted lightly. "Fine. Let's start with the manuals, update as needed. The point stands—we need country teams engaged."

Daniel noted quietly: *Sophia glossed. Abhi rescued.*

Maria's Consequence

Singapore, 11:52 PM. Isabel Hartmann's name lit Maria's phone.

"How did we miss the depth of the governance gap?" Isabel asked. "I'm reading this isn't a three-week fix."

Maria stood, hand pressed to her desk. "We didn't miss it. We fenced it. Phase One includes a stabilisation workstream. A full governance track needs political air we don't yet have."

"This has snowballed," Isabel replied. "I want one answer: when do I see tangible improvements? These tax-finance debates are centre-stage now. I need them offstage."

"Weeks for visible controls. Quarters for systemic."

"Send me a one-pager tonight," Isabel snapped, then hung up.

Maria let the phone rest in her palm. Shouldn't John be answering this?

Aldo and Daniel Recalibrate

At his desk, Aldo opened a blank Notion page: **Field Guide: As-Is Mapping**. Four short Looms. A universal swimlane template. A lineage stencil. A "two-hour sprint" kit for controllers. A dashboard grading completeness by risk.

He pinged Daniel: *If they won't map because it's heavy, make it light. Pilot UK + India. Two weeks.*

Daniel built a new artefact: **AS-IS Charter – Who Maps What.**

Finance = processes and accounting.
Tax = events and treatments.
IT = system touchpoints.
48-hour escalation clock.

He hit **Post.** Neutrality had to give way to clarity.

The Night the Notice Landed

London, 10:07 PM. Abhishek's phone exploded.

INDIA INDIRECT TAX – URGENT

Audit summons. 30 days. Transaction-level reconciliation.

SSC India's chat lit up: mismatched intercompany journals, vendor credits in suspense, spreadsheets with no version control.

Abhishek dialled the India CFO and put him on speaker.

"We need clean ledgers," the CFO snapped.

"We need lineage first," Abhishek countered. "Invoice to ledger to declaration. If we jump straight to ledgers, errors will bury deeper."

"Give me something for officers on Monday."

"By morning," Abhishek promised, "you'll have a triage pack: top mismatch vendors, follow-up proof, draft response. And a sprint template to trace worst flows."

When the global sync opened, Sophia didn't wait.

"An audit in India," she said, voice neutral as ice. "Right when Abhishek's group is supposed to be leading the transformation. If compliance is failing, we're not ready for automation."

Maria's jaw clenched on camera. Aldo DM'd Daniel: *Deploy the charter. I'll ship the Field Guide directly to India.* Daniel replied: *Do.*

The Meeting Behind the Meeting

That evening, in a Mayfair hotel, Sophia sat across from Richard—two glasses of still water between them.

"It's gridlock," she said. "IT won't move without as-is. Finance says tax. Tax says finance. India's under audit. Maria's in Singapore. Daniel's posting charters."

Richard listened. "And your plan?"

"Impose discipline. Make CFOs own mapping. Hold Tax to document treatments. Frame IT as arbiter. And tell the board the truth: this is barely manageable."

Richard's mouth quirked. "Two things. One—ambiguity is leverage. Don't solve too fast. Two—never be first to call a fire a fire. Bring smoke and witnesses. Let John say 'fire'."

Sophia absorbed it. Ambiguity as leverage. Smoke and witnesses. She nodded once.

Optics Are Reality

Next morning, in AlphaCorp's pantry overlooking a wet London street, Sophia told John:

"The as-is is a mess. Finance disowns it. Tax disowns it. IT's frozen. India's under audit. Even day-to-day compliance feels like balancing on glass."

John stirred his espresso but didn't drink. "And your assessment?"

"We need enforcement. A visible line of ownership. Otherwise, optics worsen."

He smiled faintly. "Optics are reality, Sophia. Keep painting the picture."

She nodded. Fatigue flickered across her face, then vanished.

The Quiet Countermoves

Maria shipped Isabel a one-pager: **Stabilise Now, Govern Next.** 21 days to visible controls. A quarter to embed. Attached: draft memo to country CFOs—Finance owns process and accounting; Tax owns treatments; IT owns lineage. She listed Daniel as a co-author without asking.

Aldo published his Field Guide to the UK and India channels. Header: *Two weeks, not two months.* Within days, controllers clicked *Start.* One wrote: *First map done. I hate how simple this was.*

Daniel pinned the AS-IS Charter globally, escalation clock ticking. Comments disabled. Blocking issues only.

Abhishek delivered the India triage pack by sunrise: top 20 mismatches, officer response drafts, and document retrieval list. The CFO replied with a single line: *This reads like control. Thank you.*

The Line That Snapped

At noon, Sophia presented *Data Readiness – Unvarnished* to John, two board members, and the CEO's chief of staff. The slides were brutal—broken governance, reactive compliance, and allergic ownership.

Mid-presentation, alerts popped up: Field Guide adoption in the UK/IN. Charter pinned. India CFO: *Control.*

She didn't flinch. Ambiguity was leveraged; smoke and witnesses.

"Can we even keep the lights on?" one board member asked.

"We are keeping them on," Sophia said smoothly. "But dim."

She closed her laptop, staring at her reflection in the black screen. For a heartbeat, she saw a tired woman confusing power with proof. Then she blinked, and the glass was just glass.

Between London and Delhi, the train of AlphaCorp's transformation picked up speed. Charters pinned. Guides published. Audits summoned. Optics curated.

The map had finally met the territory.

CHAPTER 30

Transactions Mapped, Masters Prepped

"Before you build anything, you need to know what you're building on," Daniel said flatly, staring at the dashboard glowing red. "In tax, that means transaction mapping—lineage, end to end. And master data? That's the bedrock. Without it, every fix collapses."

The words hung in the air, but the reality at AlphaCorp was chaos. Controllers were refusing to touch manuals. Finance pointed at Tax, Tax pointed at Finance, and IT claimed they were blocked. Escalations poured in like monsoon rain—heavy, relentless, drowning out any sense of order.

Delays logged in PMO dashboards. Controllers refusing to touch manuals. Tax managers firing scope-creep emails. IT leaders claimed they were blocked. Every thread led back to the same question: who actually owns this?

By midweek, the backlash had gone public. Controllers across Germany, France, and India were openly mocking the plan in calls and emails.

"These manuals are fossils."

"They don't match current approvals."

"You want 2025 mapped with documents from 2018? Does London even understand what the ground realities are?"

On a tense regional call, a CFO in Latin America snapped back at London and followed up with a blunt note: *"This wasn't a meaningful as-is study. It's academic theatre."*

Screenshots of dashboards lit with red flags were forwarded up the chain. Every escalation carried the same refrain: 'not my ownership.' The hot potato of responsibility bounced until it finally landed back with John.

The Master Data Quagmire

The most challenging flashpoint arose with master data. On a stormy late-night call, tempers flared.

"You expect us to classify every SKU in the catalogue?" an Indian controller demanded.

A finance manager from France cut in, "We don't have customs expertise. This isn't our job."

Tax pushed back sharply: "Without codes, compliance collapses."

IT's voice followed, clipped: "And without codes, nothing automates."

The shared screen froze under the weight of an Excel file with 80,000 rows. Someone cursed as the laptop crashed. Even if they brute-forced the codes once, no one could answer the bigger question: *Who governs it tomorrow?*

John's Closed-Door Session

John called a quiet session first. No country CFOs yet. Just Sophia, Daniel, and Aldo. Abhishek wasn't on the invite.

The room was dim, blinds drawn against the London drizzle. John leaned forward, jacket off, tie loosened, irritation clear in his voice. "We already agreed who needs to do what—so why are we discussing this again? Is SteerCo not effective? Why must I intervene in every escalation? Where are the gaps? Who is leading this on the ground?"

Sophia spoke first, crisp and assured.

"Finance owns process flows. Start with the accounting manuals. IT maps system interactions in swimlanes. Tax annotates treatments. Country teams support updates. That's the only way we can move quickly."

Daniel stayed neutral. "It gives us structure. At least on paper." He glanced at John, then muttered almost to himself: "Escalations aren't governance—they're just noise."

Aldo added quietly, "As long as we frame it as swimlanes, not paragraphs. Manuals alone won't hold."

John cut him off. He pressed further, frustration evident. "If everyone is so clear about everything, why are there red flags all over? Every email from every team reads like a house on fire. Do any of you really know where the real challenges are? Why are teams deflecting? What can douse the fires immediately? Sophia, you are the tax transformation lead—what's your view on this?"

He didn't look up. He just wanted the fight off his desk.

Sophia leaned in, deflecting under pressure. "Finance leadership across countries doesn't want to review and update the manuals. They say they're obsolete. Tax cannot be built without a foundation, and IT is stuck until Finance and Tax provide the necessary mapping. Nothing is moving. Every email is a fire drill because Finance won't take ownership. John, if you ask me—the teams are deflecting, and unless you give Finance a clear nudge, this will not move."

Daniel added swiftly, "I feel your nudge would definitely go a long way, John. Teams need to address this in live workshops, working collaboratively. Otherwise, the ping-pong will never end. We may also think about delinking this exercise from the updating of the accounting manuals."

Aldo nodded in agreement. "I can ask IT teams across countries to join hands. I agree that a collaborative approach is necessary to succeed."

John looked at Sophia, his expression tightening. He wanted to ask why her every answer sounded like someone else's problem. The thought crossed his mind sharply: Sophia wasn't solving, she was offloading. For the first time, he wondered whether her leadership was part of the problem rather than the solution.

The Side Conversation

After John's session broke up, Aldo and Daniel lingered in the corridor with Abhishek. He had been silent through the sparring, but his notebook was filled with scribbles.

"This feels like déjà vu," he said quietly.

Daniel tilted his head. "Matrix?"

Abhishek nodded. "At Matrix, we let commercial teams own the code. It looked like a quick fix. But within a year, chaos: divergent codes, customs mismatches, VAT refunds blocked. When audits came, nothing reconciled."

He paused, then added, firmer now: "Hybrid was different. Painful at first, yes—we built a dedicated Master Data Governance team. But it became the backbone: clean lineage, consistent reporting, automation that didn't rot."

He tapped his pen against his notebook. "Master data isn't plumbing—it's DNA. If it mutates, everything mutates."

Aldo murmured, "So the choice is simple: rot disguised as speed, or pain disguised as governance."

Abhishek's gaze dropped. "And AlphaCorp just chose rot." He exhaled, then added more quietly, "I raised this before starting with stale accounting manuals, which was never best practice. Now it's unravelling exactly as predicted. And look at John—he stays above the clouds while the ground burns. Leadership has to bridge the gap between stratosphere and street level, or the whole structure cracks." He hesitated, then added, "And culture flows from the top. When leaders step back instead of stepping in, it sets the tone that no one cares. With Maria, it was different—her presence lifted the bar. With John, it feels like we're circling back to Richard's times."

Later that night in Singapore, Maria scrolled through the summary on her phone. The words blurred with fatigue, but one sentence cut through: 'Governance later.' She set the phone down and spoke aloud to the empty room, as if answering the chorus of escalations she'd read all day.

"They'll call this delivery. I'll call it a delay, disguised."

Aldo's words echoed in her head—rot disguised as speed.

CHAPTER 31

When Design Meets Discord

The workshop room felt less like a boardroom and more like a bunker. Whiteboards were scarred walls, smeared with half-erased swimlanes. A dozen Teams tiles flickered across the wall display, faces pixelating under weak Wi-Fi. Coffee cups and cables tangled across the table, as if the clutter itself were bracing for battle.

Daniel stood at the head, arms folded, surveying the room. His team sat behind him, five professionals with the restless focus of sprinters waiting for the gun. He tapped the marker against his palm once, twice, then smiled— just enough to say: *I've brought the cavalry.*

"Before we talk design," Daniel began, his voice steady, "you need to meet the people who'll carry it."

The Fusion Team

The five exchanged quick, knowing glances — the kind that pass between people who sense they aren't just stepping forward, but assembling. Something in the room shifted; the lights seemed sharper, the air charged, as if the future had quietly pulled up a chair.

Lina Alvarez moved first.

Petite, sharp-featured, hair cinched into a disciplined low bun, she carried both a lawyer's precision and a technologist's calm.

"I trained in law but ended up in APIs — application programming interfaces. My job? Turning legislation into logic."

Aldo's smile flickered, but behind it a thought clicked into place: She's the bridge. The kind of hybrid mind the next decade will be built on.

His eyebrow arched. "Finally, someone who can make tax code sound like... code."

Rajesh Malhotra stepped next — tall, immaculate, sleeves rolled with mathematical symmetry.

"Data and project management. If it doesn't reconcile, it doesn't exist."

Abhishek's eyes sharpened. There. Discipline. Structure. Someone who understands that data isn't a report — it's a foundation.

A silent nod passed between them, professional respect sparking like flint.

Chloe Martins followed, energy bright enough to cut through the fluorescent lighting.

Curls bounced freely, mustard blouse unapologetically bold.

"Started in indirect tax. Automated half my reconciliations before anyone noticed. That's when I realised I liked building bots more than doing the work myself."

Aldo felt a pulse of recognition — a generational signal. This is what the future looks like. People who automate themselves out of old lives.

Her confidence, her ease — it was the language of tomorrow spoken today.

David Kim stepped forward with measured calm.

Neatly parted hair, minimalist glasses, charcoal jacket — order wrapped around stillness.

"Controls aren't buttons," he said softly, tapping his notebook twice. "They're choices."

Abhishek absorbed the line, feeling its weight. Finally... someone who gets that risk isn't paperwork. It's behaviour.

Daniel gave the faintest smile, "He'll anchor the team when chaos comes."

Amara Singh was last.

Tall, composed, forest-green tunic blending tradition with modernity.

"Accounting degree, systems engineering brain," she said. "I design workflows like bridges — strong enough that no one falls through."

Aldo watched her closely. An engineer who speaks accounting... this is the architecture transformation has been starving for.

Her quiet conviction reminded him of blueprints — clean, strong, trustworthy.

Daniel looked across them — Lina's sharp logic, Rajesh's discipline, Chloe's creative defiance, David's precision, Amara's structural calm.

A rare team. A balanced team.

For a moment, he felt the strange certainty that he was witnessing the future — as a concept in the shape of five human beings standing before him.

"We do not treat our teams as commodities," Daniel said, pride threading quietly through his voice. "We are partners. The people who delivered recovery targets everyone else believed were impossible."

Chloe winked at him, bracelets chiming softly. "And living proof that tax careers don't have to stay inside old boxes."

At the far end of the table, Sophia sat immaculate and unmoving.

Sleek hair, perfect blouse, notebook positioned like ritual.

But the faint, aimless lines she drew betrayed the truth: she could feel the ground tilting — and the unsettling possibility that the future she once expected to lead had already begun arriving without her.

RPA: The 'Easy' Win

Daniel uncapped the marker and turned to the board. "We'll start with RPA. Quick wins. We earn momentum, then we take on the heavier lifts."

The room shifted forward, tension sharpening. Lina strode to the whiteboard and scribbled fast: *Reconciliations. Refunds. Intercompany. Exceptions. Journals. Returns.*

"Where do we actually bleed hours?" she asked.

Abhishek pointed immediately. "India VAT reconciliations—days lost. Brazil refunds—weeks of chasing. Europe intercompany—months of ping-pong. But bots only run if every step, every trigger, is mapped."

Sophia leaned back, arms folded. "We can prioritise now and refine later. Too much detail too early kills projects."

Rajesh didn't flinch. "Bots don't run on instinct. They run on triggers." He turned sharply to the screen. "Carlos—São Paulo—what actually kicks off a refund packet for you?"

Carlos hesitated, eyes darting. "If I'm honest? When my inbox feels too full."

The room broke into uneasy laughter. Aldo groaned, dragging a hand down his face. "That's not a trigger. That's a migraine."

Chloe leaned in. "Then make it a flag. Status flips to *Complete* once all docs are in a shared folder. That fires the bot."

Amara sketched a box beside her. "Checklist built into the workflow. Judgement comes first, automation second."

Sophia tapped her pen twice, lips pressed tight.

Abhishek spoke low, almost to himself, but the whole room heard. "Matrix thought the detail was overkill. It broke. Hybrid sweated it. It held."

The silence that followed was heavier than any argument.

Anchors in Question

The debate over RPA split into who would anchor design discussions at the country level.

Sophia came prepared with a list that was crisp and tidy. "Brazil—Carlos. India—Indu. France—Jean Paul. They've been around long enough; they know the flows."

Abhishek frowned. "Carlos is good, but he's not close to reconciliation anymore. And JP? He's been managing somehow. We need people who live the steps."

Two of Sophia's nominees backed out within a week. Another never joined the call. In contrast, Abhishek's choices—Priya in India, Gabriel in Brazil—showed up prepared, mapping processes in detail. Priya even sketched a refund flow live in the session, earning nods from IT.

Sophia still had her wins—JP proved unexpectedly decisive on French workflows—but the balance was shifting. The scoreboard wasn't on the whiteboards, but everyone could feel it. Wins and losses were being tallied, and trust was tilting.

Beyond Bots: Engines and Middleware

Once the dust on RPA settled, Daniel steered the conversation forward. "Phase 1 is bots. But the engines come next—tax determination and compliance tools."

Aldo took over, voice firm. "No more Frankenstein ERP customisations. We'll go off-the-shelf. The question is whether AlphaCorp can feed them the right data points."

Abhishek leaned in. "Which extends our as-is. Every condition has to be captured—jurisdiction, product, entity, treatment. If the source doesn't hold it, the engine spits out junk."

Aldo nodded. "That's why middleware matters. I'm not bending old ERPs into shapes they can't hold. We build a clean pipe—central signals in, tax engines do the rest."

Sophia finally spoke, her tone clipped. "Middleware is IT's concern. Tax needs to focus on treatments and positions."

The room stiffened. Abhishek exhaled slowly. "Treatments mean nothing if the system can't execute them."

Daniel's neutrality cracked. "Tech is the language of tax now. Ignoring it is ignoring reality."

Sophia looked back at her notes, but the page remained nearly blank.

Middleware vs. ERP: The Debate

Lina leaned forward. "ERP upgrades were an option. But the choice is off-the-shelf with middleware. Let's weigh it."

Aldo didn't hesitate. "Middleware keeps agility. One bridge to manage, not a dozen custom hacks across legacy ERPs. You adapt once, centrally."

Abhishek countered calmly. "But every bridge is also a seam. More moving parts mean more reconciliations. At Hybrid, middleware worked. At Matrix, too many layers fractured the system. Additionally, IT made the mistake of handing over governance of data mappings between the ERP and middleware to tax, which lacked the necessary hooks in the flow. The inevitable could not be avoided, eventually."

Lina circled *Reconciliations* on the board. "Then we automate the tie-outs. ERP to middleware, middleware to engine. Exceptions flagged automatically."

Abhishek considered it. "Bots that reconcile nightly. Clean logs. Human touch only where exceptions remain."

Aldo's eyes lit. "Exactly. Middleware as the bridge, bots as the guards. Lightweight, scalable, efficient."

Abhishek raised a caution. "But governed. Modular bots, version-controlled. Otherwise, they become another black box."

Daniel drew a triangle on the board: *ERP → Middleware → Tax Engine.* Beneath it, he wrote: *RPA Reconciliations.*

"This is the design," he said. "Data clean at the source, middleware as the pipe, engines driving the rules, and bots policing the seams. Agile. Efficient. And it reduces operational burden in the long run."

For once, there was no disagreement. The hum in the room wasn't a conflict but a quiet alignment.

Where Law Meets Ledger

The next morning, tension returned with fresh coffee—the fight this time concerned law versus accounting.

Elena circled a revenue line. "Accounting recognises here."

Abhishek marked another. "VAT triggers there."

"Then align VAT to accounting," Elena pressed.

"Law won't allow it," Abhishek shot back.

Sophia kept her eyes on her notes, silent.

Amara stepped in, quick strokes marking the board. "Two clocks. We built a handshake between them."

David spoke firmly. "And controls to prove the handshake."

Elena leaned back, weighing it. "If I see those controls in my dashboard, I can live with it."

Omar sighed, conceding. "If it's event-based, we can automate the proof."

Abhishek drew a bold line at the junction. "There. That's the handshake."

Aldo exhaled, half a smile tugging at him. "Ledger and law—finally bilingual. The middleware design will help us with this as well."

Sophia Under Fire

At the coffee stand, Abhishek caught Sophia staring out the window. "You're quiet," he said.

"I'm avoiding traps," she replied. "Commit too early, you get pinned with the fallout."

"Sometimes leadership is picking the right pins," Abhishek said evenly.

Sophia's eyes flicked to him, then away. She walked off without answering.

Sophia's Call to Richard

That night, long after the workshops had wound down, Sophia sat in her London flat staring at the city lights. The emails replayed in her head—country CFOs questioning her notes, Abhishek quietly undermining her in sessions, Aldo cutting through her arguments with ease.

Her hand hovered over her phone before she finally dialled. Richard picked up after the third ring, his voice as polished as ever.

"Richard. You said there'd be a place for me when you moved. A partner track. You promised." Her voice was clipped, the edge of desperation barely hidden.

There was a pause. Too long. When he spoke, his tone was slower. "Sophia, timing is... delicate. These moves don't happen overnight. We'll need to align the right opportunities."

She cut him off. "Delicate? I've stood by, I've carried your projects, I've done what you asked. And now, when I need you, you hesitate? Was it just words?"

Richard sighed softly, the practised patience of a man who had soothed many tempers before. "You know I value you. You know I'll do my best. But you must be patient."

Sophia's voice sharpened, cracking despite her effort to keep control. "Patient? While they tear me down in London workshops? While Abhishek plays saviour and Aldo plays oracle?"

Richard's tone stayed calm, almost paternal. "You're too sharp to be undone by them. Keep your composure, Sophia. Timing, remember?"

But beneath his words was something colder, a hesitation that didn't belong to him alone, as if he were speaking lines written elsewhere, careful not to stray. He knew, even if she didn't, that Sophia was no longer a queen on the board—just a pawn whose utility was running out.

When the call ended, nothing had changed. Richard had given her warmth, but no answers.

Sophia sat in the silence, fury tightening around her like a coil. She felt like an injured snake—cornered, waiting, venom building.

Momentum

Friday's session began with tired eyes and restless energy. The whiteboards were crowded, markers running dry, but the group pressed on.

Lina read from the board. "RPA candidates: Brazil refund packets. India invoice triage. Europe intercompany checks. GCC return workpapers."

Rajesh added crisply, "Each saves hours and has a backstop. No black boxes."

Chloe tapped her marker against the board. "And every trigger sits in the process—not in someone's inbox."

Omar exhaled, nodding at last. "The integration changes are feasible." His eyes shifted to Abhishek. "If your team owns the rule tables."

Abhishek nodded. "We'll own them—with version control and audit trail."

Aldo leaned back, satisfied. "From bandages to bone."

Daniel scanned the room—his young fusion team sharp with energy, AlphaCorp's leaders weary but, for once, aligned. It wasn't harmony, not yet. But the road was drawn, and this time, they looked ready to walk it.

"Phase 1 is where we learn to move together," Daniel said. "Phase 2 is where we decide who we are."

The words landed. No one argued. For now, Discord had been shaped into a direction.

CHAPTER 32

Between Resistance and Renaissance

"The past doesn't surrender quietly. It digs trenches and calls itself a process."

The whiteboards were wiped, the swimlanes captured, and the as-is finally mapped. On paper, the design was taking shape. But designs don't fail because of logic; they fail because of people, habits, and the invisible rules of process that refuse to change. Everyone in that room knew it — though no one said it aloud. The next battle wouldn't be about tax codes or system fields. It would be about whether AlphaCorp could abandon the shortcuts of decades and accept that, without process change, every new tool would buckle under old ways of working.

The Global CFOs Teams Call

The screen bloomed into a grid of faces: India, France, Mexico, Germany, Singapore. Some CFOs leaned forward, pen tapping against desk; others sat back with arms crossed, expressions locked in corporate neutrality. A dozen eyes flicked to Sophia as she shared her screen.

Her slide was a bulleted list — black text on white background, transactional and dry.

- Fixed asset transfers → route through AR/AP, not JVs.
- Discount vouchers → reduce sales, not booked as promos.

- Employee recoveries → tax invoices mandatory.
- AP/AR → item codes required.
- Credit notes → must reference original invoices.
- Petty cash → above threshold through PO.

Her voice was clipped, brisk, almost mechanical.

"These are legal requirements. They must be adopted immediately. Non-compliance is not an option."

The silence that followed wasn't agreement. It was pressure building.

India's CFO leaned forward, eyebrows raised. "So this is what we're here for? A list of transactions?"

The French CFO cut in, voice rising. "Why force AR/AP for fixed assets? JVs worked fine for decades. Auditors never challenged it."

Mexico's CFO gave a bitter laugh. "Tax invoices for mobile phone recoveries? Are you going to stand in front of two thousand employees and explain that absurdity?"

Sophia's jaw tightened. "These are legal requirements. They are not optional. If you refuse, you expose AlphaCorp to risk."

Her tone was sharp but shallow — the sound of someone mistaking authority for depth.

Maria's voice cut in like steel.

"No, Sophia. Quoting the law is not leadership. Leadership involves anticipating resistance, aligning stakeholders, and guiding them from 'Why should I?' to 'How do we.' You've done none of that."

Sophia blinked, thrown. "Maria, with respect—"

Maria didn't let her finish.

"You knew Finance would resist. You knew CFOs would fight for their reporting lines. You knew IT would push back on ERP changes. And still, you show up with nothing but a decree."

Sophia stiffened. "These are the requirements under law. The rules are clear. You don't get to pick and choose."

Then Maria's voice sliced across the chaos, calm and surgical.

"Has anything changed in tax laws across 21 countries requiring these changes? If not, how were we managing so far? Is this project about increasing bureaucracy in our processes? Because if that's the path you're on, Sophia, it will lead to chaos."

Sophia blinked, caught off guard.

Maria leaned in, every word a blade.

"This is all a huge surprise to all of us. Did you align with Finance before dropping this? Did you not think it was important to align with the respective finance teams and explain and understand their points of view? Did you propose a transition, or did you dump new rules like grenades?"

The CFOs went quiet — because Maria was voicing what they were all thinking.

The India CFO smirked; Mexico's CFO leaned closer, enjoying the bloodsport.

Sophia tried to recover. "It is my responsibility to enforce compliance."

Maria leaned forward, eyes narrowing.

"No, Sophia. You've made it our job to fix what you couldn't manage."

The mask cracked. Sophia's pen rolled off the desk, her hand fumbling just a moment too long to catch it. The sound echoed louder than it should have.

Maria delivered the blade.

"Transformation isn't about rules. It's about persuasion and partnership. If all you can do is throw law like a weapon, I am not sure where we are headed."

The silence was suffocating. Even John leaned forward now, eyes flicking between Maria and Sophia. The hierarchy of the moment was undeniable.

Sophia looked down, lips pressed tight, the fight draining out of her. For the first time, everyone could see it: the mask was broken.

Taxes & Accounting Misaligned

Abhishek cleared his throat. What followed was delivered in low, steady tones.

"We now need to move on to the next topic – that of discount vouchers. Discount vouchers are treated differently by financial accounting and for VAT reporting. For VAT purposes, these lead to a reduction in sales, whereas in financial accounting, they are treated as marketing expenses.

This voucher treatment isn't just a reporting preference — it's system impossibility. ERP cannot treat the same transaction in two ways. Either it's a P&L promotion or it's a sales deduction. If we don't align, tech will choke."

Sophia interjected, voice thin. "Then we choose Finance's treatment. Simpler, less disruption. We can't redesign everything for Tax."

Abhishek's reply was quiet but merciless.

"That's convenient. But it won't survive the audit. Vouchers are tied to receipts. If they're not deducted from sales, VAT returns fail. And the penalties will not be optional."

Daniel finally spoke, gesturing to his fusion Team. Lina, his process architect, shared a screen: two workflows, side by side.

"Option one: vouchers reduce sales — Tax safe, Finance worried. Option two: vouchers as promos — Finance comfortable, Tax exposed. Both cannot be true. The system breaks."

She zoomed in on a third option.

"Parallel reporting. Deduct vouchers in the tax engine, while Finance gets adjusted P&L through reconciled dashboards. One truth for compliance, one adjusted for Finance. Transparent. Governed."

Raj, the ex-Finance controller turned analyst, added:

"This is no different from suspense reclassifications. You can patch it month after month, or fix the mapping once. Middleware is patching. ERP is fixing. Choose."

John's voice was acid, finally cutting through.

"So the choice is between theatre and truth. Don't waste my time with theatre."

His contempt lingered like smoke, sharpening the stakes.

The IT Stalemate

The next eruption came from IT. "If you want every AP and AR transaction coded with item codes and tax codes, that means ERP reconfiguration. That's months of work. And once customised, we maintain it forever. Is that really what you want?"

Aldo raised his hand, measured. "They're right. Middleware scripts could replicate logic faster, without tearing ERP apart. Sometimes the smartest fix is scaffolding."

Sophia latched on. "Exactly. Middleware is enough. Let's not overcomplicate."

Raj piled on. "Who will identify which Journals go to the tax engine and which do not? What will happen every time that changes? AlphaCorp will need a middleware governance team apart from a master data governance team to maintain this."

Aldo exhaled, conceding softly — but not before one pushback. "I'm not against ERP fixes. But disruption today means delayed reporting tomorrow. If we rip too much, too fast, the business could stumble. That risk is real. That said," he looked at Daniel, "—delaying disruption can make it worse. I'll concede that."

The debate over middleware versus ERP had reached an impasse. Abhishek wanted structural fixes, Aldo balanced caution and sustainability, Sophia clung to the easy way out, and IT grumbled about scope creep.

Daniel leaned back, then gestured to Lina. "Go on."

Lina's calm voice filled the silence.

"Legacy systems always resist change. They're designed to protect the past. They usually do not enable the future. Finance will say reconfiguring ERP is too risky. IT will say it costs too much. Business will say: 'We've done it this way for decades, why change now?' And in the middle, Tax is left holding the non-compliance risk."

She clicked to a slide: two curves plotted across five years.

The first: middleware patches—low upfront cost, skyrocketing support costs.

The second: ERP reconfiguration—painful start, stable trajectory.

"If you choose middleware, you're not saving money—you're borrowing trouble. And it compounds every year. Every patch needs its own governance, testing, and reconciliation. By year three, your teams are working for the system, not the other way around."

Aldo frowned, still defensive. "But ripping into ERP creates disruption today. You can't ignore that."

Daniel stepped in, steady. "True. But disruption delayed is disruption multiplied. You can patch today and pay triple tomorrow, or fix today and lead tomorrow. Transformation isn't about what's comfortable—it's about what's sustainable."

Raj chimed in with the closer.

"Middleware is suspense accounting. ERP is clean mapping. Choose once, or reconcile forever."

Abhishek smiled faintly; the analogy landed where Sophia's commands never could.

Even John gave the slightest nod — the recognition of an argument well made.

Daniel leaned in. "That's why we build fusion teams. Because transformation isn't tax, it isn't finance. It isn't IT. It isn't operations. It's all of them—or it's nothing."

Budget Constraints

The German CFO finally broke the pause. "Fine. But how much more can we invest? We're already over budget. Why rip into ERP when middleware gets us over the line?"

Sophia pounced. "Exactly. We have to be pragmatic. Why change more than regulators demand?"

Raj leaned in, sharper now.

"With respect, this is where AlphaCorp contradicts itself. You run a strategy for the next three decades — expanding countries, factories, stores, signing leases, and acquiring brands. You assume permanence. Yet when it comes to investing in sustainable processes, suddenly it's all about short-term ceilings and budget fears. If you believe you'll be here tomorrow, invest like it. If you act like you're closing shop next year, then stop calling it strategy."

The French CFO bristled. "ROI still matters."

Daniel cut in, calm but cutting.

"ROI matters, yes. But short-termism kills it. If you believe in your business, invest with that conviction. Middleware is feared beyond its limited use cases. ERP reconfiguration is conviction. Which story do you want to tell auditors, regulators, and your own board?"

Abhishek sealed it.

"Constraints are real. But when you let them dictate, they become self-made bottlenecks. And bottlenecks choke strategy faster than any regulator can."

John finally stirred, his voice cold.

"Good. At least someone here remembers what strategy sounds like."

Alignment and Enlightenment

By the end of the call, decisions were made — grudging compromises hammered out despite Sophia's leadership, or the lack of it. Vouchers would be treated as sales deductions in the tax engine, with Finance given parallel P&L reports. Fixed assets would flow through AR/AP across entities, though intra-entity JVs were allowed for simplicity. Employee recoveries would be moved to monthly VAT invoices, consolidated and automated to mitigate the pain. The fusion Team had sketched the compromises, Aldo had helped balance IT's load, and Abhishek had kept the logic clean. Sophia had contributed little beyond repeating "non-negotiable" until the words lost all meaning.

As the last squares winked off the screen, the hollowness of her role sat exposed, and all the time spent dissecting Matrix's collapse and Hybrid's orchestration had meant nothing if the lessons couldn't be lived in practice. Leadership was not a slide deck, not a case note, not a tidy conclusion borrowed from someone else's battle. If notes and case studies could mass-produce leaders, business schools would be factories churning out CXOs by the dozen. But leadership wasn't memory — it was presence. And in this call, Sophia had none.

The war was now open, the sides drawn. Resistance had bared its teeth, and the cracks in AlphaCorp's foundations were no longer hidden.

And while Finance and Tax traded blows over process, the bots waited in silence — fragile lines of code about to take their first breaths. When they did, AlphaCorp would discover that machines don't fix human fractures. They expose them.

CHAPTER 33

Bots in the NICU (Neonatal Intensive Care Unit)

JFK International Airport – July 10

Rain slicked the tarmac as Abhishek stepped into a heavy New York evening that smelled of wet concrete and exhaust. Sophia walked a half step ahead, posture upright, laptop bag slung like an accessory rather than a burden. She looked every inch the leader, her eyes sweeping over the waiting staff as if she expected them to be ready for her arrival.

Not a single smile. The indifference in the reception mirrored the distance between her and Abhishek, though she let her tone turn warm when she finally spoke.

Sophia broke it with a half-smile. "Looks like the bots didn't wait for a ribbon-cutting. You'll see, this rollout will be smoother than people fear." It sounded encouraging, even generous, though he sensed it was a strategy more than comfort.

Abhishek didn't answer.

AlphaCorp Midtown Office – July 11, 9:00 AM

The 21st floor gleamed glass and steel, the skyline blurred by mist as if New York itself were holding back judgement.

Tom Welch, the Country CEO, rose with an open hand—warm, shrewd, willing to listen. Beside him sat Sam Jones, the CFO, arms crossed, eyes narrowed, fingers tapping a slow, sceptical rhythm.

Sophia placed her notebook neatly in front of her and leaned forward before Abhishek could settle. She decided to own the room.

Sam cleared his throat first. "Two members of the tax team left a couple of months ago. We haven't filled those roles. The team is stretched thin. We don't have much bandwidth to support your RPA work."

The point was simple: the project had arrived in New York expecting allies but would find only an exhausted, skeletal team.

Sophia absorbed it, her pen tapping once before she spoke. "Let's be practical—two resignations, no backfills—fine. But automation isn't magic. It needs the people who run the work today. Without them, bots replicate the mess."

Tom blinked, half-amused. Sam's arms stayed folded.

Sam replied with practised neutrality. "We've decided to hold off on hiring. If these bots truly work, we'll see." He carried scars from past programs—budgets blown, staff burnt out. Sophia's urgency sounded like déjà vu.

She recalibrated quickly. Her tone softened, coaxing. "Every hour you think you save today will cost double tomorrow if the design is rushed." Turning to Tom: "You've built this business on reliability. Let's not gamble it."

Tom nodded slightly, caught between her sharpness and Sam's caution.

Abhishek added carefully. "Every bot needs a clear trigger—like the NICU thermostat reading and adjusting for every newborn. Without those cues mapped with the people doing the work, automation falters—gasping at the wrong time or failing when it matters most. We'll build the map, but we need direct access."

Sam exhaled. "A few hours can be spared." His refusal was survival, not defiance.

Sophia didn't flinch. "Then we'll make those hours count."

The air grew heavier than the mist outside. Abhishek admired her control, even as unease coiled in his chest. Outwardly, she led. Inwardly, he knew she was playing with fire.

Tax Ops – Later That Morning

Sophia sought Julia, an old ally. Julia's laugh was tired. "Two exits. Everyone doubled up. But a consulting firm mapped end-to-end three months ago—SOPs, swimlanes. If we re-engage them, they'll hit the ground running."

Sophia blinked. A sliver of light. She turned to Abhishek with uncharacteristic warmth. "This could be our shortcut." The words sounded collegial, though he sensed the performance under the polish.

Abhishek's Hotel Room – Late Evening

He called Maria in Singapore. "Feels like someone's given her the whip," he said softly. "She's listening, but it isn't humility—it's camouflage. I'm not confident of this project—or my future here."

After the call, Abhishek sat in the quiet. Leaders bled, too. The realisation comforted him—and left him lonelier than before.

Six Weeks Later

Consultants returned, tightening as-is maps. Collaboration between Abhishek, the US team and consultants brought bots to life in four weeks.

Then the cracks showed. Bots stumbled—logic gaps, data rot. Attributes incomplete, defaults inconsistent. Sophia aligned with Sam to prioritise master data. Teams in India and China scrubbed fields night and day. People fell asleep at desks, woke with ink on their faces, and handed tasks across time zones like batons in an endless relay.

Abhishek pushed in a call: "Let's clean the master data for Phase 1 and 2 countries now. We won't relive this country by country."

Faces lifted, weary but resigned. "Feels like we're cleaning history, not data," one analyst muttered. The tired acceptance was proof he was right.

Gradually, dashboards steadied. Bots breathed—faintly.

The Glitch

A week later, bots misapplied tax in five states and reverted to outdated logic for intercompany transactions. The pilot wavered. The team pounced—diagnosing, patching, and rerunning late into the night. Stability returned, brittle but holding.

Abhishek studied the dashboard, which showed 4,000 transactions in two hours—speed intoxicating, but fragile.

Sophia's nod masked fear. To John, she spun it as her win. To herself, it was oxygen rationed at her bedside.

Daniel, in London, wasn't dazzled. Distance stripped away noise. The glitch confirmed what he'd long suspected: the leadership was fragile, Sophia's mask the most brittle of all.

Two Versions, Two Failures – The Call to Aldo

By the third stumble, Abhishek sighed, whiteboard bleeding with crossed logic. He dialled Aldo.

"The bot's deriving VAT from the invoice header, ignoring line-item," Abhishek said. "You don't have a hierarchy," Aldo replied. "The system latches onto the first 'location.'"

They dove in. ERP tables revealed inconsistencies; the whiteboard was filled with fixes.

"Hierarchy ensures the right signals are read," Aldo said. "Trace shows where the data came from. Controls catch the falter before it turns fatal."

Abhishek nodded. "Ledger and law—finally shaking hands." "Because they both showed up," Aldo replied.

Their rhythm steadied the room. For Abhishek, it was the first time he felt a true partner in the trenches.

Sophia watched from the back, jaw tight. Every fix they co-created felt like bricks laid without her.

Governance – August 28

Bots ran in parallel with manual processes, scripts humming alongside human effort. Exceptions dropped. Logs and checklists matched more often. One analyst whispered, "For once, it feels like they're keeping up." Thin laughter followed—the first sign of hope.

Abhishek exhaled, watching numbers climb: 14,000 transactions in eight hours. Proof demanded by the board was finally here.

Around the table, shoulders eased. Sophia smiled too, slower, measured. To Abhishek, she said, "Good work," warmth rehearsed.

But he knew better.

The bots were breathing—fragile, alive. Like infants in the NICU, each breath still demanded vigilance.

CHAPTER 34

Veni Vidi Vici

London—War Room, 07:40 a.m.

The dashboards glowed with hard-won numbers. After months of pilots and scepticism, the RPA rollout had crossed a milestone: bots running in the US, UK, India, China, and France, processing tens of thousands of transactions daily. Exceptions fell, reconciliations tightened, and for the first time in years, filings weren't sprinting toward midnight. It wasn't perfect—scripts crashed in Guangzhou, tax codes misfired in Marseille, a legacy ERP refused to talk to the bot in Pune—but fixes came faster than failures. Proof demanded by the board was finally here, country after country.

Analysts in Hyderabad whispered, "For once, it feels like we're keeping up."

Thin laughter followed—the fragile sound of relief.

Abhishek noted the throughput on his pad: Nearly 1.5 million transactions reconciled across AlphaCorp's global operations in a month with RPA humming at full capacity. Numbers no manual team could touch. He exhaled. This wasn't triumph—it was survival with a heartbeat. The bots were finally breathing. They had come, they had seen, and they had conquered—but in their wake, they left questions of what would remain standing after such conquest.

Human Fallout in the Shared Services Centres

In India, murmurs turned to noise. The bots had done their job—extracting, validating, and reconciling data—all now automated. However, in doing so, they had swept away layers of routine work that were once handled by dozens of team members in the shared services centre.

And now, those team members were informed that their roles were no longer needed.

Nikhil's Silence

Nikhil, a 26-year-old, had moved to Hyderabad from a small village in Telangana. This was his first white-collar job, and it was helping to pay for his sister's engineering education.

Now, he sat in a small HR room, staring at the paper across the table. The manager's words blurred: "role redundant... effective immediately."

His phone buzzed. A notification from an instant messaging group with friends lit up:

Friend: "Bro, you free tonight?"

Nikhil: "Not sure. Just got released. Need to update my LinkedIn."

Friend: "Shit. Already?"

Nikhil: "Yeah. Feels like my future just went blank."

He dropped the phone into his lap, the blinking cursor of his half-updated profile mocking him with silence.

Meenal's Question

In Pune, Meenal had worked nights to attend classes during the day, hoping to shift into data analytics eventually. She sat in a crowded cafeteria, her laptop open to an internal training portal.

A manager passed by, murmuring to another, "Upskilling won't save everyone."

Meenal caught the words, her stomach twisting. She typed a note to a colleague: *"Are we even wanted here anymore?"*

The reply came back fast: *"Not in this version of AlphaCorp."*

The food on her tray went untouched.

Liu Wen's Exit

In Guangzhou, Liu Wen quietly packed up her desk after 14 years. She handed in her ID and bowed politely as she left.

A younger colleague watching whispered, "Does loyalty matter anymore?"

IR 4.0

Sophia scrolled through her phone late that night, news apps buzzing with commentary. One op-ed headline caught her eye: *"From Loom to Algorithm: Are We Living Through a New Industrial Revolution?"*

She skimmed as pundits debated—comparing bots to steam engines, warning that livelihoods might vanish like artisans in the age of assembly lines.

Sophia closed her eyes, remembering a panel she once sat through in Frankfurt. The prophecy had arrived: AlphaCorp wasn't just automating—it was walking into Industrial Revolution 4.0, and she was trapped in its frontline storm.

Rajesh's Tragedy and Media Firestorm

Then came the news that turned unrest into fury. In Andhra Pradesh, one of the displaced employees, Rajesh, became the face of the fallout.

A father of two, he had risen from a farming background scarred by tragedy—his father had committed suicide years earlier after failing to repay debts.

Rajesh had taken the weight of his family on his shoulders, supporting his ill mother while working in AlphaCorp's shared services centre to build a different future for his children.

When the bots took his job, debt collectors closed in. Already stretched thin, harassed and cornered, Rajesh gave up. He ended his life.

Local media carried the story with the hyperbole typical of prime-time Indian news. Studio anchors thundered, waving printouts of Rajesh's debt notices at the camera.

"Is this the price of foreign efficiency? Is AlphaCorp responsible for another farmer's son dying under debt?" one host shouted, his voice rising above a flashing ticker: *'Corporate Greed or Corporate Murder?'*

Villagers wept on screen, sound bites looping endlessly. Talk shows staged fiery debates with union leaders, politicians, and activists shouting over each other.

Hashtags trended across India: **#AlphaCorpKillsDreams** and **#JusticeForRajesh.**

Around the world, reactions fractured the leadership team.

Aldo scribbled into his leather journal: *"Bots prove resilient. Humans do not. Optics failing. Reframe strategy."*

His calm face betrayed nothing, but doubt had entered his systems-first worldview.

Daniel slammed his tablet shut after watching a debate replay. "We had the story, and they let it slip into tragedy. This isn't about automation anymore. It's about control of the narrative."

Sophia scrolled endlessly through angry hashtags, each one landing like a bruise. One clip replayed a villager shouting, "Rajesh's children have no future now."

She closed her eyes, chest tightening, but said nothing in meetings. Alone in her hotel room, her silence felt like complicity. A faint sound from the hallway—a whispered name, maybe hers—made her snap upright. Paranoia wrapped around her like a second skin.

Maria, far from the war rooms now, heard updates through allies still inside. She closed her eyes and whispered, "Governance. I warned them. Without trust, every success curdles into failure. And this is worse—outsourcing doesn't just shift work, it shifts responsibility. Rajesh wasn't even on AlphaCorp's books. That loophole made him invisible, unprotected. Capitalism ring-fenced wealth and outsourced accountability. We built a system where the balance sheets are safeguarded, and the people carrying the weight are erased."

The leadership compounded the crisis. No one from AlphaCorp visited Rajesh's family. No statement was released. Silence became complicity. Unions marched in Hyderabad and Chennai. Local politicians seized the moment, accusing AlphaCorp of importing foreign efficiency at the cost of Indian lives. Social groups demanded compensation, investigations, and accountability.

Even employees who had once supported the transformation turned against it, whispering in canteens and corridors, "If they can erase him, they can erase any of us." In their minds, the bots had lived up to the title: they had come, seen, conquered—and left behind a trail of blood and destruction.

Formal Letter of Accusation

Then came the formal indictment, not shouted in studios but delivered in writing, sealed and deliberate.

Formal Letter (Excerpt)

Dated: 14 September, Hyderabad
To: Director – Human Resources, AlphaCorp India
CC: Regional CEO, Group CHRO
Subject: Request for Immediate Intervention in Tech-Driven Displacement of Labour

"AlphaCorp has implemented automation without transparency, leaving employees blindsided and humiliated."
"Thousands of livelihoods are being erased without consultation, social dialogue, or safety nets."
"We demand an immediate halt, an independent review, and direct engagement with worker representatives before further rollouts continue."

Signed,
Council of Union Leaders, Association of Service Providers

The accusations were crafted not just to question policy but to indict AlphaCorp's character, framing the company as reckless, opaque, and complicit in human suffering. The provider and its allies weren't merely resisting automation. They were orchestrating a counter-offensive—shaping stories, aligning with unions, and stoking political fires to force AlphaCorp onto the defensive.

In hushed conversations, a few senior managers whispered of unseen hands. The Indian vendor spoke with unusual confidence, hinting at support from 'friends in London.'

Richard, too, seemed to know more than he should, dropping casual remarks that Maria had never been truly safe on the board. Once, Sophia caught half a whispered call and a door closing too quickly. She thought she heard her own name, faint and muffled, before the line went dead. It left her unsettled, unsure whether it was real or imagined.

Boycott and Abhishek's Breakdown

The backlash didn't stop with angry headlines or formal letters. It seeped into the very fabric of AlphaCorp's operations, showing up as silence, cancelled meetings, and doors closed to the transformation teams.

In Hyderabad and Pune, shared service centres announced a quiet boycott. Transformation teams found that meeting invites were declined, access was denied, and workflows stalled. The message was unmistakable: *Rajesh's blood is on your bots.*

Abhishek's phone lit up with angry calls from ex-colleagues.

"This is your project, Abhi? You killed him."

"We thought you were one of us. Now you're the reason we bury one of ours."

The words struck harder than any headline. He sat frozen, the accusations ringing in his ears.

That night, he sat at the kitchen table, unable to touch his food. His wife placed a hand on his shoulder.

"It could have been us," he whispered. "Rajesh's children... they're no different from ours."

She answered softly, steadily: "Technology isn't the villain. But when leaders turn people into numbers, this is the cost."

He stared at the family photos on the wall, the line between provider and casualty now razor-thin. In that silence, he could feel what the new motto meant: victory for the machines, ruin for the men who once kept them fed.

And somewhere in London, Richard closed the news app on his phone, lips curving into the faintest smile. No one would ever prove how much of Rajesh's despair had been chance, and how much had been *helped along.* In his mind, the motto felt different: *They came, they saw, they conquered—and it was exactly as planned.*

CHAPTER 35

AlphaCorp in Crisis: Leaders Fall After Hyderabad Tragedy

The Rajesh tragedy hadn't just shaken AlphaCorp. It cracked its façade. Corridors once humming with chatter now carried only whispers. Coffee cups cooled untouched on desks, steam curling into silence. Spreadsheets glowed, but fingers hovered, motionless. Every glance asked the same question: Who will fall next?

Board Fallout

The London boardroom was a battlefield of stares, ties loosened, tempers fraying. Edward Grant, long-time Audit Committee Chair, broke the silence. He had admired Sophia's composure in the past, and now his gaze lingered on her empty chair. "The transformation was supposed to be progress. Instead, it has brought scandal and grief."

The debate split the room in factions, but within those, arguments ricocheted like gunfire.

Tom Becker slammed his fist onto the table, booming and blunt. "Shut it down—pause the whole program. We need to show contrition."

Mikhail shot back, his tone clipped, precise. "Pause and the markets will punish us. Do you want to see a five-point drop by morning? Technology doesn't wait for grief."

Raghav leaned forward, eyes flashing with urgency. "And what about people? Rajesh's face is everywhere. We ignore this, and every employee believes they're disposable."

Elena countered, voice smooth and cold as glass. "If we stop, we lose momentum. Competitors will eat us alive. Optics we can repair. Growth lost cannot be reclaimed."

Anwar tried to hold the line, voice steady, conciliatory. "There are middle paths—compensation, policy reviews, controlled restarts. We don't have to choose extremes."

The conversation turned toward Maria. Becker's voice softened, almost weary. "We erred in letting her go. She warned us. She would have steadied this storm. Bring her back—she alone has the maturity to lead this project to its close."

Edward's eyes narrowed, his tone icy with disdain. "Maria was never fit for leadership. She lacked alignment. We trusted her too long, and it cost us. John may not have been perfect, but Maria would have dragged us into paralysis. It was her idea to start this wretched project after all. Do not rewrite history now."

Raghav's retort cut sharp. "She was pushed aside because someone whispered in your ear. And now we are paying the price."

The room fractured further. The boardroom itself seemed to shrink as voices ricocheted off the wood-paneled walls. Heavy curtains dulled the rain outside, but inside the air grew hot, tense, smelling faintly of coffee gone cold and paper ink. Directors leaned forward, chairs scraping, papers tossed aside. Conversations overlapped, cutting each other off. Sarcastic laughter flared, muttered asides darted like knives. Edward sat back with a cold smile, fingertips steepled, while Raghav's pen snapped clean in two under the pressure of his grip. Elena's pearls caught the light as she shook her head in disdain, whispering to Jill with a roll of her eyes. Across the table, Becker crumpled a sheet of figures and hurled it aside. Edward and Mikhail exchanged the briefest of nods, subtle but unmistakable. It was no longer discussion—it was combat, every sentence a strike, every gesture a tell.

Finally, Anwar was once again the one to bring order to the room. He stalled the discussions, "Alright, let's talk solutions now, does anyone have any ideas or only fingers to point? We have gathered here with an agenda. Let us see it through."

Independent Investigation

Elena jabbed her pen in the air. "Rajesh's suicide has become one of the biggest negative publicity blows AlphaCorp has suffered globally. While the authorities are leading the legal aspects of it, we need to show the world we are serious about what, if anything, within AlphaCorp, contributed. We lead that investigation internally, we control the narrative."

Raghav nearly rose from his chair, his voice loud with conviction. "Control the narrative? If we run it ourselves, no one will believe it! Only an outside panel carries weight."

Mikhail slammed his notebook closed. His tone remained surgical, unflinching. "An outside panel drags out skeletons we don't want exposed."

Raghav leaned across the table, finger stabbing the air. "And covering them up will bury us alive!"

Anwar intervened again, voice deliberate, soothing. "Raghav, I think Elena and Mikhail have a point here. We should show we believe in our governance and infrastructure, and reinforce that belief to the outside world. It's how we present that will decide perception. And moreover, we are here to resolve things to everyone's benefit—not mould opinion."

Leadership Accountability

Mikhail's voice cut through, clipped and cold. "Investigations are fine. Optics require sacrifice. Isabel, John & Sophia must take responsibility. Isabel and John were at the helm—they should have known better. Sophia led the transformation project that has transformed us most of all. Their resignations will be symbolic."

Becker leaned in until his nose almost touched Edward's across the table, his voice thundering. "Or scapegoating. The rot goes deeper than three names on a press release."

Chairs screeched as both men half rose, voices colliding.

Elena muttered under her breath, disdain dripping. "This isn't a debate, it's a demolition."

The shouting rose and fell like storm waves. Papers fluttered to the floor, glasses rattled in their saucers. Even pauses were thick with tension, a room holding its breath only to erupt again. At one point, Jill's voice cracked into laughter that wasn't joy but fatigue. Across from her, Becker wiped his brow with a crumpled handkerchief, while Raghav's broken pen lay like a casualty on the table.

"Okay, we agree the leadership is accountable. But let us wait for the investigation report to say that." Anwar pressed.

Elena's answer was firm, dismissive. "We should not wait. The fall will be a masterstroke and revive confidence in the markets."

And finally the majority agreed.

Rajesh's Family

Anwar started on the next point. "I think we would all be unanimous on this one at least. In line with AlphaCorp's values, our employees are and will always be our greatest assets. I propose we offer generous support to Rajesh's family. Scholarships for his children until university. Healthcare support and a lump sum gratuity package. It's the least we can do."

Edward threw up his hands, voice sharp with frustration. "That sets a precedent—what about the next case? And the next? Are we writing blank cheques for tragedy?"

Anwar slammed his palm on the table so hard the water glasses trembled. "Maybe if we stopped creating tragedy, we wouldn't need to!"

"What do all of you have to say?" Anwar asked the room.

This time, the majority aligned with him. The action plan was agreed upon and noted.

Golden Handshake Scheme

Jill leaned forward, palms flat on the table, tone measured but urgent. "Since we have decided to continue the transformation journey, we must also agree on how to manage redundancies that are certain to arise from this project. HQ and country leaderships must ensure uniform communication adjusted for local contexts. From the financial side, we should roll out a golden handshake scheme across affected countries. This will send a signal we are serious about transformation—and about our people. A generous severance model shows compassion, buys time with unions."

Becker barked back, voice booming with disdain. "It also admits guilt without saying the words! Do you want tomorrow's headlines to scream 'AlphaCorp Confesses'?"

Elena snapped her folder shut, voice like ice. "These are two different things, Tom. Rajesh's suicide and the golden handshake scheme should be kept separate. This scheme will make us look human."

Papers scattered as Becker shoved them aside. "Human? Or weak?" he shot back.

Exhaustion finally thinned the voices. In the end, the compromise emerged, jagged and unsatisfying:

- Announce an independent investigation to demonstrate accountability.
- Refresh leadership optics—sacrifices must be made.
- Fund Rajesh's children's education, without admitting fault.
- Launch a 'Responsible Automation Policy' with severance, benefits, and re-skilling.

Edward's expression hardened, unreadable, but a flicker of calculation crossed his face. He had shaped enough of the decision to protect his ground. The compromise was now inevitable.

The Grilling

Next, the "accused" were called in. Isabel Hartmann, John, and Sophia entered, faces pale under the lights. The jury had already decided; now came the theatre.

Mikhail's tone was brutal, surgical. "You failed to anticipate. You failed to govern. You failed to act when the world looked to us."

Raghav leaned forward, voice harsh with finality. "Public confidence requires change at the top."

Elena gestured to John, her words sharp as steel. "You weren't even in the trenches. No attendance or oversight over steering committees where you were sponsor. Numbers, controls, filings—why didn't you see the storm coming? Delegation without oversight brought us here. Do you accept responsibility?"

John tried, voice faltering. He shuffled papers as though they might shield him. "The project leadership—if you look at the way—"

"Leadership?" Mikhail snapped, palm slamming down. "That is exactly what was missing here, John."

Raghav cut in, louder still. "Entire regions blindsided—China, India, France, US and the UK. You watched it happen, John. Watched and did nothing."

John opened his mouth again but Isabel jumped in, voice taut. "Processes were followed. Risk reviews were documented—"

"Processes?" Elena scoffed, tossing her pen. "Tell that to the regulators clawing at our door."

Raghav's voice rose again. "Implementation is leadership's duty, Isabel. Your processes delivered us chaos. How many more headlines should we bleed for?"

Jill raised a hand, eyes narrowing on Sophia. "And you—tell us, Sophia. Do you truly have the experience to manage a transformation of this scale? You pushed yourself forward, you whispered against Maria, and now you hide in silence."

Sophia raised her eyes briefly, lips parting as if to answer, but Becker barked across her. "Everything gone wrong, every outcome—it circles back to you and John."

Heat rose in her chest. She wanted to shout that she had been sidelined, that no one gave her the reins she was blamed for dropping. But the words stuck, strangled by the weight of the board's glare. Their eyes weren't searching for truth—they were searching for a culprit. She felt her throat tighten, resentment sparking against fear. They don't want answers, she thought bitterly. They want a body to bury. Her thoughts roared louder than her voice could. She wanted to scream at Mikhail, to tell Raghav they were wrong, to hurl back every accusation—but she stayed still. She did not have a choice.

Raghav leaned in, voice cutting like glass. "Negligence is not governance. And this, my friends, is sheer negligence."

The room boiled with overlapping voices—Becker accusing, Elena scoffing, Isabel protesting, Raghav demanding blood—until Mikhail tapped the gavel softly. The sound cracked like a shot, silencing them. Around the table, directors leaned back, arms crossed, their silence a wall.

The verdict landed like a hammer: resignations demanded, effective immediately. Officially: "leadership renewal." Unofficially: scapegoats.

Media Storm

By midday, AlphaCorp's share price slipped two points. On trading floors, analysts filled the airwaves: "Automation scandal wipes confidence. Leadership vacuum must be filled fast."

That evening, prime-time anchors sharpened their knives. Screens across London lit up with pundits. A union leader shouted, "AlphaCorp cannot wash its hands of blood with scholarships!" A government spokesperson countered, "Transformation is vital for competitiveness." Voices clashed, hashtags crawled across screens, and the company's logo flickered behind every angry face.

One anchor leaned toward the camera: "Is this innovation, or negligence in disguise? Tonight, AlphaCorp is on trial in the court of public opinion."

Employee Reactions

In Hyderabad, whispers spread through the cafeteria. Trays clattered, conversations cut short when managers passed. "If Rajesh could be erased, any of us can," someone muttered. Another replied, "Compensation for his kids, but what about the rest of us?"

In Pune, Meenal watched the press conference replay on her phone. Around her, colleagues shook their heads. "Responsible Automation," one scoffed, "a fancy name for making us disposable." Phones buzzed with hashtags, screens lighting up like protest banners in miniature.

In Guangzhou, Liu Wen's former team huddled near the elevators. "Fourteen years of loyalty and not a word from leadership," one whispered. "They clap for cameras, not for us."

The media storm had spilled into every corridor, every canteen, every late-night instant messaging group. Suspicion and fear moved faster than the bots ever had.

Sophia's Exit

When Sophia handed over her badge to HR, the gesture felt like a verdict stamped in plastic. The manager's voice was clipped: "The board has decided. Thank you for your service."

Colleagues passed her in the corridor, but none met her eyes. Conversations cut off as she approached. To them, she wasn't a peer anymore—she was part of the scandal, a name on headlines, a caution whispered in canteens.

By nightfall, news tickers rolled across London: AlphaCorp Leaders Forced Out After Tragedy. Hashtags raged unchecked: #JusticeForRajesh, #AlphaCorpKillsDreams. Screens in cafeterias replayed her photo beside John and Isabel, the faces of failure.

Sophia pushed through the revolving doors. The rain had not stopped. Glass steps gleamed slick. Her heels struck sharp against wet concrete, the echoes folding into the city's low hum. Each step felt heavier, as though suspicion itself trailed her into the night.

A black car idled at the curb. The window slid down.

"Need a ride?"

Richard's voice. Smooth. Too smooth.

Sophia froze. The man who had once been her ally—and who knows, maybe her executioner—waited, calm as if the entire scene had been rehearsed. The door swung open—patient, predatory.

She hovered on the threshold of betrayal or escape. In her mind the boardroom still echoed—accusations, jeers, the gavel's crack. The silence she had wielded inside now pushed her forward. Richard's presence felt less like coincidence and more like inevitability. The rain blurred everything else, leaving only the open door, patient and predatory. And then the night swallowed them both.

CHAPTER 36

The Return of Maria

The city looked like a constellation spilled across the earth. From the twenty-seventh floor of the serviced apartment at Marina Bay, Maria stood with her forehead to the glass, watching ribbons of headlights thread the bridges, cranes blinking red above ship skeletons, the water holding the night like a secret. Her suit jacket lay over the chair; her heels were under the desk like two tired animals; her phone on the table pulsed with quiet light—the last of Abhishek's updates from London.

He had become her night compass: what the board had said after the gavel fell, the markets twitching in after-hours, the lawyers shifting language into careful boxes, the hush around Sophia's exit hardening into something like myth. With each message, she felt the orbit tug her closer to AlphaCorp again.

She let the newest voice note play and closed her eyes. Abhishek's tone was tired but warm.

"It's chaos, Maria. Honest chaos. They're finally seeing the cost. People are scared. Some are hopeful. A few even said outright—we need you back. For once, someone is thinking straight in this company. Rest tonight. You'll need your strength."

She pressed the phone to her chest and breathed in, steadying. Rest. The word felt like a paper boat pushed into a fast river. She hadn't truly rested since London had last turned its back on her. Since the small humiliations—eye-rolls disguised as jokes, praise assigned to other mouths, the slow removal of her name from the emails that mattered. She had carried those cuts like cold coins in her pocket, clinking when she walked.

She turned away from the window and paced the apartment. On the dining table, her notebook lay open to a half-drawn map: People. Process. Data. Vision. Governance. The orchestral score she believed in more than any single tool. No one note saved a symphony; the saving was in the arrangement.

She imagined the War Room as a stage left in half-dark: flipcharts like abandoned backdrops, marker smell haunting the air; Aldo's restless intelligence moving through it like a cat; Daniel's measured voice holding the room when it frayed; Sophia's... absence. Absence could be a presence, too.

She picked up the phone and scrolled back through Abhishek's messages. John gone. Isabel gone. Sophia gone. Three names punctured the feed like missing teeth. The hole they left felt larger than the damage they had done.

Her thumb hovered over Arjun's name.

When his face appeared, the light from London fell across his cheekbones and the framed stick-figure drawings behind him. The children were asleep.

"You are still up? Is everything ok?" Arjun asked.

Maria's voice sounded younger than she felt. She didn't pretend indifference. "I think they'll call me back," she said. "The way Abhishek is... putting things."

Arjun nodded. "And if they do?"

"I go," she said. "I'm done with proof. I go to lead. To stop the bleeding and turn the air into something people can breathe in again."

"I'm proud of you," he said. "We have waited for this so long. But they'll want results, Maria. They'll want markets to stop screaming. They'll hand you a violin and expect an orchestra."

"I know." She didn't flinch. "And if I'm honest, I want that too. To remind people that work doesn't have to be a threat to your life. To your sleep. To your name."

They spoke briefly about smaller things—Ishan's sudden fascination with Roman generals, Saira's cupcakes, the neighbor's cat who had adopted their garden. The call ended with a look that felt like a promise: Come home.

At five next evening, the phone rang with a crisp tone.

“Ms. Mehta?” The voice was glass-clear. “This is AlphaCorp HQ. The Board has decided to convene in London before the weekend. We request your presence at Headquarters no later than Friday noon.”

Request. The word wore its own irony. Still, she felt no sting. Only relief.

“I’ll be there,” she said, and when she ended the call she let herself sit on the bed and breathe through the rush.

Changi Airport smelled of coffee and disinfectant. Maria moved through it, not noticing its spectacular spaces, pulling with two suitcases and a feeling she refused to name as hope. She reached the gate with twenty minutes to spare. It was only then that she opened her the messaging app on her phone.

Aldo’s name sat at the top. The message preview was small and cruel in its brevity.

Aldo Maseko: *Abhishek in an accident. Seriously injured.*

The world narrowed. For a second her mind refused the order of the words—as if they were the wrong notes in a familiar song—and then the sense slammed in.

She pressed call. The ring wheel spun; She boarded the plane and settled into her seat. The cabin announcement crackled. An air hostess leaned gently into her space.

“Ma’am, we’re about to take-off. Could you please switch off your phone?”

“I—just one more—” Her voice cracked. “I’m sorry.” Another failed call. Each refusal felt like a door closing.

“Ma’am,” the hostess said again, firmer. “Phone off, please.”

Maria stared at the screen, at Aldo’s name, at the message tattooed on her palm. She powered down the phone.

The click of the button felt like betrayal.

Maria and the plane pushed through the headwinds; the runway carried them to the sky. Singapore slid away in the oval frame of the window.

In the dark cabin she sat with her hands folded, the words circling in her chest: *Seriously injured.* The War Room without Abhishek—a chair empty where her ally had sat. Aldo with his jaw tight, Daniel smoothing fear with slides. The board table a cold shore where waves of demand would keep crashing. And no one would measure what she did against who was missing. Only outcomes.

A thought slid in, treacherous and true. *Sophia.* For months Maria had worn the shape of Sophia in her mind like a bruise. But now she felt a flicker: even a flawed constant can steady a ship. A ballast is not a compass, she argued. And yet ballast keeps ships from capsizing when the wind decides to speak in tongues. The shame of the thought made her gasp softly, but she could not push it away.

She let the engines pray for her, their dumb commitment to forward a borrowed steadiness. Across the aisle, a baby sighed, a man coughed, an attendant tucked a blanket higher. The human orchestra—messy, unarranged, still somehow music.

When dawn leaked into the cabin, Europe rose beneath them in fields and frost. Maria flexed her fingers, feeling the ache of the fist she had made of herself through the night, and let her hands open.

Sophia gone. Abhishek injured. Aldo and Daniel holding a center that isn't built to hold without the rest of the circle. She mapped it with the calm of a surgeon drawing an incision line. She would not land into a welcome. She would land into a test. A battlefield.

The seatbelt light chimed. Maria reached into the seat pocket for a pen and wrote on the back of a catalog: **First hour: listen. First day: stabilize. First week: show the arc.** A conductor does not begin by playing louder than the chaos. A conductor begins by naming the beat.

When the wheels kissed the runway, Maria waited the extra seconds, then powered on her phone. Messages cascaded in. She stared at her reflection layered over the new light and said without moving her lips:

This isn't a return. It's a battlefield.

Then she stood, smoothed the navy dress that made her feel both sharp and forgiving, and stepped into the aisle, steady as a shore.

CHAPTER 37

London: The Mantle

Homecoming

Maria's cab rolled past familiar streets, the London drizzle streaking the windows like lines on sheet music. When the door to her townhouse opened, the music broke into a crescendo. Arjun stood there, eyes wet, unable to hide his relief. The children tumbled over each other to reach her first—Saira with flour still dusting her hands, Ishan clutching a book on Roman generals. It wasn't just a homecoming; it was as if life itself had returned to their life.

They refused to let go. On a school day, no less, they had stayed home—by choice, by rebellion, by love. Maria laughed and cried in the same breath, kissing foreheads, holding faces between her palms. The house smelled of masala tea and freshly baked cupcakes. For a moment, the wars of AlphaCorp felt far away.

Meeting Abhishek

By afternoon, she was at St. Thomas' Hospital. Aldo had briefed her on the way: Abhishek had been leaving the AlphaCorp office when a speeding car struck him. The police had ruled it an accident, but Maria's chest tightened with each detail. His phone had been unlocked, mid-dial—her number on the screen.

Vaidehi rose from the waiting bench, her face pale but composed. Maria clasped her hands. "You're not alone in this. Whatever you need—logistics, childcare, prayers—it's yours."

Vaidehi's voice cracked. "He was calling you. He was trying to tell you something."

Maria could only nod, throat too tight to answer. She placed her hand on Abhishek's, the steady beeps of the monitor the only sign of battle being fought beneath closed lids. In that sterile room, the guilt pressed down like another weight on her chest. *If I had answered sooner... if I had been there.* The thought twisted like a blade. She pushed it down, but it stayed, burning. The unfinished call echoed in her mind, louder than the machines, like a voice trapped between worlds.

Back in the Boardroom

Thursday morning, AlphaCorp HQ. The Boardroom's polished oak gleamed under white lights. Maria entered with measured steps, every footfall echoing the memory of her last walk here six months ago—when the same board had voted her off. Back then she had left with her dignity intact but her heart in pieces. Today, she felt no pride in their reversal, only a steady satisfaction that time had tempered wounds and brought clarity.

Mikhail, Elena, and Jill rose as she approached. For a moment the formality cracked—their faces broke into genuine relief, as if they were welcoming not just a leader but a lifeline. Their eyes softened, glances exchanged across the table as if silently admitting regret for the choice they had once made. Jill leaned forward first, her tone unusually warm: "We heard about Singapore, Maria. About the way you steadied that office in the storm. Do you regret leaving?"

Maria shook her head lightly, pausing just long enough to let the question land. "Lessons learned," she said, her voice steadier than she felt. She let her eyes flick briefly to the polished table, then back up. "Singapore gave me distance—and clarity."

Mikhail followed, his brows furrowed yet his voice gentler than she remembered. "And Abhishek? We're concerned. He's been a pillar."

Maria let the silence stretch a moment before answering. "He is fighting. I've just come from the hospital. Until he is back, I'll carry what he cannot."

Even Elena, usually so sharp-edged, leaned closer with a softened tone: "And your family? Arjun, the children?"

Maria's voice softened. "They are the reason I can stand here. They remind me what leadership is meant to serve."

Inside, she felt the strange symmetry of it all—this same board that had once sent her packing was now reaching out with open hands. She wasn't proud; pride was too fragile, too brittle. What she felt was steadier, deeper: a quiet satisfaction that time had mended what anger could not, that wounds had scarred into lessons rather than festering as infections. For the first time in months, she allowed herself to breathe as if she belonged here again.

The questions seemed to settle the room, almost cleansing it. Then Elena's voice wavered slightly as she spoke. She drew a breath before the formality returned to her voice. "Maria, the last meeting changed everything. John, Sophia, and Isabel were asked to step aside. It was decisive, necessary, and it left the house unsettled. Today we call you back because the transformation demands resilience —it is about giving you the opportunity to stand at the center and prove what true leadership looks like. We need conviction, and we believe you can bring it. Are you prepared to take this responsibility and deliver against the odds?"

Maria let the words settle in the room. She straightened the notes in front of her, a small motion that steadied her hands before she lifted her eyes. For a heartbeat she saw the ghosts of that last meeting—the coldness, the verdict, the exile. Now they were offering her the mantle again as a test of her strength. She breathed once, steady, then inclined her head. "Yes, I am ready," she said, her voice carrying both acceptance and resolve. "I will bring order to this house. That I promise."

As she spoke, a subtle current of satisfaction moved beneath her calm. This time she was not being pushed or judged; she was choosing to return, and on her terms. The sting of exile had ripened into resolve, and she allowed herself a quiet sense of redemption—firm, measured, and entirely her own.

From the far end, Edward leaned back in his chair, his pen tapping in a slow, sarcastic rhythm. His eyes held hers, daring. "No Singapore this time, Maria. If you fail, there won't be a second exile." His tone was low, edged with warning, like steel beneath velvet.

The jab cut, but she didn't flinch. The satisfaction in her chest hardened into resolve. She met his gaze. Her voice was calm, professional, yet edged with quiet steel—tempered by exile and return. "I'm here, Edward. I'll let the results do the talking."

A hush rippled across the table. Some looked down, others exchanged glances—subtle acknowledgments that they saw the difference in her, that they recognized a steadier Maria than the one they had exiled months ago. Maria didn't gloat. She straightened her shoulders, letting that silence speak for her.

Taking the Lead

Later that day, Maria convened in the War Room with Aldo, Daniel, and the Grayson & Holt fusion team. Charts lined the walls, project dashboards lit the screen, and for the first time she saw the machinery in motion without Sophia's veiled interference.

Aldo gestured to the PMO lead. "We've stabilized reporting lines. Risks are mapped—data readiness, system cutover, audit exposure. Deliverables tracked against milestones. Without this structure, we'd be blind."

Maria studied the framework. It wasn't just data; it was choreography. Aldo's voice carried pragmatic energy, focused on structure and deliverables. Daniel, by contrast, radiated caution, weighing every risk. Maria felt the choice hovering between them: structure or hesitation, conviction or caution. "Good," she said quietly. "Otherwise I'd be patching together shards while the orchestra burned."

Daniel leaned forward. "The project has momentum. What it needs is a conductor. Someone to hold the baton."

Maria glanced at Aldo. "Names?"

Aldo shook his head. "None fit. Not in this window."

The silence stretched, until Maria broke it. "Then I'll take the mantle. At least until Abhishek is back on his feet."

Daniel's eyes flickered, half-surprised, half-resigned. He hesitated before adding, "We'll follow your lead, Maria. But you are still the CFO. This project isn't the only weight on your table—will you have the bandwidth it demands?"

Maria's jaw tightened. She knew the caution was well-meant, yet it felt like the safe hedging of a consultant. Urgency throbbed louder in her mind: the Board expected results. "I'll manage," she said firmly, setting his concern aside. *Consultants always try to play it safe,* she thought.

Sophia's Unease

Across the Thames, in a dim London flat, Sophia scrolled her phone. The headline froze her blood: *AlphaCorp Executive in Critical Condition After Accident.*

Her breath came shallow. Abhishek. She read the lines twice, three times. An accident, they called it. But something in her gut twisted.

She whispered into the empty room, but what surfaced wasn't a question—it was a memory. Rajesh's suicide flashed unbidden across her mind, the same eerie sense of something unfinished, unexplained. She let the silence hold it, leaving even herself unsure what she meant or what she feared. The silence gave her no answer, only the echo of her own fear. Yet even as dread seeped in, another thought surfaced—sharp, unbidden: *If it wasn't an accident, then someone is already playing the next move.*

Her hands trembled as she set the phone down, the room suddenly too small, the air too thin. For the first time in months, Sophia felt less like a spectator—and more like prey.

CHAPTER 38

The Shockwave

The War Room screens glowed with dashboards that should have inspired calm. Rows of green lights flickered across compliance trackers, bots whirring in the background like invisible clerks. Phase 1 had shaved hours off filings across countries, and tax teams were reporting their first month in memory without a late submission.

India was different. Automation there had been paused from the outset, a political compromise that left RPA running in parallel with employees in the shared service center. What looked like hesitation turned out to be a blessing in disguise. The overlap had created an extended UAT—real humans checking every bot-triggered output, validating exceptions, and surfacing gaps before they could break the system. It wasn't savings yet, but it was confidence. And Maria knew confidence was the rarer currency.

Yet even here, in the glow of stable dashboards, every metric carried Abhishek's absence like a watermark. Without him, there was no quiet glance of validation.

Daniel noticed. He had watched Maria shoulder the transformation with steely calm since Abhishek's sudden exit, but he also knew what wasn't being said. Maria was stretched—holding her CFO portfolio while trying to grasp the intricacies of tax tech infrastructure that weren't in her wheelhouse. He knew she wasn't wired for system-level detail. Not because she lacked intelligence—she was one of the sharpest leaders AlphaCorp had—but because success in this phase would depend on defining and delivering highly technical milestones. And she was carrying too much.

He wrestled with whether to speak up. He didn't want to undermine her, but silence felt worse. Finally, between sessions, he leaned in.

"Maria," he said, "this next phase—it's not about program management anymore. It's a different beast. Complex configurations, country-specific logic, real-time tax triggers. We need people who breathe this stuff."

Maria nodded slowly. She had been thinking the same. Aldo had once told her, *It takes humility to lead what you don't fully understand.* She had never forgotten it. Her strength wasn't in scripting logic or configuring engines. Her strength was orchestration—pulling threads together, aligning people, holding the tension of competing priorities.

Daniel continued gently. "Maria, your gift isn't in schemas or OCR engines. It's in how you see the whole board. But lately you're in the weeds—firefighting, not steering. That's not good for you, and it's not good for AlphaCorp."

Maria exhaled. She didn't rebut. He was right.

That's when the answer began to take shape, less as an idea and more as a necessity. A Centre of Excellence. People who could anchor the transformation beyond her bandwidth and beyond Abhishek's absence. She would pick the sharpest instruments she could—and then the phone buzzed.

Aldo had laid out the shockwave the day before: the UAE's einvoicing draft law, the UK's VAT reporting reforms, Europe's digital push. The Board hadn't brought her back just to stabilize. They had sent her to war.

But when the summons come, the general doesn't always get to choose the armoury.

She had her first choice ready: Susan Khoury. Calm and precise, widely respected. With over eighteen years in the business, she had written AlphaCorp's original VAT playbook during its GCC expansion, navigated multiple audits, and carried both credibility and discipline. If anyone could anchor indirect tax requirements across jurisdictions, it was Susan. Susan was a weapon Maria trusted.

The second name arrived by email. It was from Mikhail, and his subject line was *Candidate for Transformation Office.* Attached was a CV. Matthew Jenkins. A finance manager from one of AlphaCorp's smaller European entities. Techsavvy, known for ERP rollouts, but little tax depth. Impatient, unstructured, often missing nuance. And yet his appointment wasn't debated—it was dictated. The message beneath the message was simple: *You will fight this war with the weapons we hand you.*

She read the CV twice, her unease rising. She imagined him under the Board's fluorescent lights, fumbling through a question on tax engine cutovers, Edward's pen tapping in disdain. This wasn't a hill she could die on—not with the Board's eyes on her and the next review less than a month away. Leadership, she reminded herself, is sometimes choosing how to deploy the kit you don't choose.

Later that week, she called Daniel and Aldo into a working session.

"I've made my picks," she said. "Susan on tax functional. Matthew on program management. Before we go public, I want alignment."

Daniel's brow tightened at the second name. "Matthew Jenkins," he repeated carefully. His tone was consultantneutral, signalling caution. "What's the play here?"

Maria met his eyes. "Strong endorsement," she said. "His ERP exposure could help on the connective tissue. With support, it can work."

Aldo leaned back, tapping his pen. "Unconventional," he said lightly. "But sometimes you inherit a legacy stack and still have to ship on time. We'll build guardrails."

Daniel sighed but nodded. "Then we get surgical. Susan documents and *owns* every rule, condition, edge case—by country, by product, by workflow. No ambiguity. Matthew translates those into structured requirements, shepherds them through project plans, tech coordination, UAT, and cutover. He's the integrator. But one wrong project call from him could collapse momentum."

Maria agreed. "Then we set tight interfaces. Clear lanes. This is the team that will hold the weight we can't carry alone." She heard her own words and understood their subtext: *This is the army I have, not the army I would have chosen.*

That night, Maria sat by the window in her townhouse office, Susan's file open on one side, Matthew's on the other. The faces looked back like kit laid out on a barracks floor—one blade she trusted; one tool she would have to learn to handle. The Board's review date was circled in red on her calendar. Less than a month.

She whispered into her cold tea: "One step at a time." But the doubt lingered—soft, persistent. Would this enforced legacy mix deliver, or would it unravel everything just when the mandates hit? Her mind drifted to Abhishek's phone, still lit up with her number on the screen when the accident happened. The unfinished call echoed in her thoughts, a reminder that clarity often comes too late. She tightened her grip on the teacup, the date of the Board review staring back at her in red ink.

Sophia

Across town, Sophia scrolled her phone in a quiet café. The headline still burned: *AlphaCorp Executive in Critical Condition After Accident.* Abhishek's name beneath it felt unreal. She thought of his calm in meetings, his quiet nods, the way he had seen through her evasions without saying a word.

Her phone buzzed. Richard's office. A meeting request.

She went, expecting an interview. A chance at redemption.

Richard's office was grander than she imagined—leather, glass, power softened into taste. He leaned back, a polished smile on his lips. "Sophia, I want you to lead tax transformation here. A greenfield mandate. No baggage."

Sophia didn't answer immediately. She let him talk, listening carefully as he described the culture of his firm, its appetite for bold moves, and its impatience with bureaucracy. He spoke of lean hierarchies, direct access to decisionmakers, and a disdain for red tape. The company rewarded those who delivered outcomes, he said, not those who clung to process.

She pressed further, asking about resources, reporting lines, and how transformation initiatives had fared in the past. Richard leaned forward, his voice smooth, assuring her of boardlevel sponsorship, crossfunctional support, and the promise of a clean slate. He painted a picture of a company hungry for disruption, eager to move fast and break away from legacy. "We don't do process theatre here," he added pointedly. "No endless sign-offs or bureaucratic stalls like you've seen elsewhere. Results matter more than rituals."

Only then, after weighing his words, she felt a flicker of mistrust. Richard's polished narrative was seamless—too seamless. His easy confidence, his careful phrasing, even the way he described board support . . . it all sounded rehearsed, like lines from a script he'd spoken before. Sophia's instincts pricked. She had survived in corporate corridors by reading what was unsaid as much as what was spoken. Something here didn't sit right.

She tilted her head slightly and finally dropped her question, cool and deliberate: "And Richard...have you heard about Abhishek's accident?"

For a heartbeat, Richard's pen paused midscratch, the faintest hitch before he set it down. His eyes flickered—just for an instant—toward the window, as if searching for cover. When they returned to her, the smile was back, smooth as glass, but his voice carried a faint tightness, a thin edge under the polish. "This role will be about building from scratch. You'll define the blueprint, shape the governance, pick the tools." His voice flowed past the question as if it had never been asked.

Sophia's blood chilled. She hadn't imagined the conspiracy ran this deep—or that she was now inside it. Unwittingly. Actively. And her instincts caught that flicker, that thin edge in his voice. He knew more than he let on, and in that moment she was certain his silence carried weight. It was the kind of omission that screamed louder than any admission.

When she left his office, the London drizzle clung colder to her skin. She no longer felt like a survivor circling the edges. She felt, indeed, like prey.

CHAPTER 39

Phase 2 Rollouts

The new Tax Centre of Excellence had begun to take shape.

Susan and Matthew were settling into their roles with varying degrees of confidence and friction. Susan was already becoming the pulse of the indirect tax workstream. People gravitated toward her instinctively, and her practical grasp of tax intricacies made her an early magnet for trust across regions.

Matthew, meanwhile, was still finding his rhythm. His calendar was complete, his emails responsive, but the noise around him hadn't settled. Maria noticed that he was listening more and interrupting less. It wasn't perfect, but it was a step in the right direction.

Still, the business and IT teams preferred to engage with Susan. Matthew often found himself on the sidelines—sometimes unintentionally, sometimes by design. A few early missteps didn't help. He walked into meetings unprepared, usually restarting discussions from the beginning, and frequently dominated conversations without inviting input. Susan tried to stay patient, but the restraint cracked on multiple occasions. Their exchanges grew terse. Eventually, Matthew escalated the friction to Maria, positioning himself as the one being sidelined.

Maria read between the lines. She knew Matthew wasn't wrong to feel excluded. But she also knew trust wasn't inherited—it was earned, minute by minute, meeting by meeting.

Over the next few months, challenges that AlphaCorp had faced in Phase 1 were finally resolved with generous golden handshake schemes and unions "understanding" the need for the automation.

Phase 2 had officially kicked off.

The UK was the first market chosen to roll out AlphaCorp's new tax determination engine and compliance reporting tool. The country offered a mature tax regime, decent data hygiene, and a finance team that, while opinionated, had bought into the vision early.

Maria stayed out of the day-to-day but watched from the edges, scanning updates and escalation reports like a strategist surveying her battlefield.

Daniel, now embedded with his team of consultants, led the discovery workshops with the UK tax and finance groups. These sessions were intense. During the first three weeks, the whiteboards were filled with transaction types, exception scenarios, and data flows.

"Before we build anything," Daniel told the room on day one, "we need to understand everything. Granularly. Not just what you do but why. Not just how the system works, but where it doesn't."

But not everyone shared Daniel's patience for depth.

Matthew, in particular, struggled with the pace and perceived complexity of the material. He often sat through the first hour of a workshop, then quietly excused himself, leaving Susan and Daniel to carry the weight of the discussion. Lately, he had started deputing a junior manager to sit in for him, framing it as "empowerment," though the subtext was hard to miss.

It wasn't just absence. Matthew's absences had an air of dismissal, as if the entire exercise could be bypassed with a few clean diagrams and innovative interfaces. Matthew's tone in meetings suggested that he viewed these deep dives as overkill—unnecessary intellectual indulgence when "common sense" would do.

But tax, as everyone in that room knew, rarely bowed to common sense.

His oversimplification frustrated the others. Susan struggled to mask her irritation when Matthew reappeared and challenged conclusions he hadn't had a chance to understand.

"He's acting like he was hired to lead, not to learn," one consultant murmured to another after a session. The sentiment wasn't uncommon.

Susan remained tactful but even started redirecting technical discussions away from Matthew. It wasn't spite—it was survival. There was simply no room for shortcuts in a landscape this layered.

Maria, observing from a distance, began connecting the dots. Leadership wasn't about showing up—it was about showing up right. And somewhere, Matthew had started to believe his role was about entitlement, not engagement.

Still, she withheld judgment. The story wasn't finished yet.

By the end of the third week, the group had something resembling consensus—a detailed process map, current-state architecture overlays, and a long list of gaps that would inform the design phase.

The team consolidated their findings into an 'as-is' mapping document, clearly outlining transaction flows, system touchpoints, manual interventions, and tax treatment inconsistencies. The document was a mirror that reflected years of improvisation and wasn't always pretty.

Without pause, the team pivoted to drafting the broad Business Requirement Document (BRD)—a foundational input for the design-and-build phase that would give tangible shape to AlphaCorp's tax technology and compliance solution.

To avoid designing in a vacuum, feedback was proactively sought from tax and finance leads in other major regions—France, the UAE, South Africa, and India—to ensure the Business Requirements Document (BRD) addressed the UK's landscape and global complexities.

What emerged was sobering.

There would be significant work required on multiple fronts:

- On data: cleansing, enrichment, and structuring across fragmented sources.
- On processes: realignment of flows, ownership, and exception handling.
- On technology: integrating legacy systems with new layers that could flex to evolving rules.

And layered above it all was something more challenging to quantify—mindset. The ability to accept change as a necessity, the willingness to let go of control and let automation in, and the humility to acknowledge that even long-standing practices might no longer be fit for the purpose.

One particular workshop on tax code design laid bare the fault lines.

It was supposed to be technical. Instead, it became theological—what is the true purpose of a tax code? Speed? Simplicity? Auditability?

Susan advocated for a future-ready model: a structured, comprehensive tax code framework to handle nuanced transactions across jurisdictions. It would cover everything from domestic standard-rated and zero-rated supplies to complex imports, intercompany flows, and special exemptions. Each code would carry embedded logic that enabled precision in both calculation and reporting.

"This isn't just about calculation," she explained, pointing to the whiteboard. "It's about clarity. When reviewers see a tax report, they should instantly understand the underlying treatment, without picking up the phone or digging into the GL."

To her, tax codes were the DNA of the entire engine. If you started with weak strands, the whole system would become chaotic.

Matthew, however, pushed back.

"We're overcomplicating it," he said. "Why not keep a lean list—10, maybe 15 codes max? We get up and running faster. We evolve from there."

It wasn't the first time Matthew had argued for simplification. But to Susan, this wasn't simplification—it was short-termism masquerading as pragmatism.

Worse still, the IT team had their agenda. They wanted to migrate the existing code as-is, arguing it would save time, reduce risk, and ease system mapping. To them, change was a threat to stability.

The room was tense. Diagrams turned into debates. Voices were raised, only to be reeled back in.

Then Daniel stepped in—calm, crisp, and firm.

"If we carry the same problems into a new system, we'll just automate dysfunction," he said. "Let's not digitise our mistakes."

He backed Susan's design, pointing out how the proposed code structure could reduce manual overrides, simplify reconciliations, and future-proof the compliance architecture for multi-country rollout.

It took several whiteboard sessions, examples, and pushback before the tide turned. Eventually, the group agreed that comprehensive tax codes would be built from the ground up. There would be no more lifting and shifting of legacy mess.

It was a small but critical win.

That evening, long after the whiteboards had been wiped clean and the last Teams call had ended, Susan and Daniel found themselves walking back from the office cafeteria, coffee in hand. There was silence between them until Susan finally broke it.

"Well," she said, half-laughing, "that tax code session was... something."

Daniel nodded. "You held your ground. Rightly so."

Susan exhaled. "It wasn't about being right, you know. It was about setting the foundation. If we messed that up, everything downstream would collapse like a house of cards."

He took a sip, then added, "But what gets to me is Matthew."

Daniel glanced sideways.

"I don't get how someone can sit through half a session, skip the part where the real debates happen, and still expect to influence direction," Susan continued, low but sharp. "He simplifies everything to the point of ignorance. And honestly, I'm starting to worry."

Daniel stayed quiet, letting Susan finish.

"This isn't just about one piece of the puzzle. We're discussing a comprehensive tax transformation and automation roadmap. If Matthew doesn't have the depth—or worse, doesn't think he needs it—how will he lead that part? And if he doesn't, how am I supposed to deliver on our mandates? We're already covering more ground than we should."

Daniel nodded slowly. "You're right. But you also know Maria's view—this is a team. Everyone supports each other."

Susan shook her head. "Support, yes. But substitute? No. That's not what Maria meant. She didn't mean one of us would have to consistently carry someone else's responsibilities to keep the project on track."

They paused at the elevator bank. The corridor was quiet; the day's buzz was now reduced to flickering lights and the occasional keyboard click.

Daniel finally said, "You've flagged it. To me, at least. Let's see how things play out in the later phases. Patterns tend to repeat—or break—when the pressure rises."

Susan gave a slow nod, the weight still lingering in her posture.

As the elevator doors opened, neither said another word.

But both knew—this wasn't the last conversation they'd be having about Matthew.

Later that week, Maria was in her corner office—screens off, lights dimmed, notebook open in front of her, half-scribbled diagrams and crossed-out thoughts covering the page. A soft knock at the door broke her focus.

"Got a minute?" Daniel asked, stepping in.

"For you, always," she replied, gesturing to the chair across from her.

Daniel sat and leaned back, arms crossed, thoughtfully, "We need to talk," he said.

Maria closed her notebook and gave him her full attention.

"It's about Matthew?"

Daniel nodded.

"I had a long walk-and-talk with Susan after the tax code session," he said. "She's holding it together, but the strain is showing. And I agree with her. Matthew is becoming a liability — he shows intent, but he's missing depth. And worse, he doesn't seem to realise that matters."

Maria sighed. "I've seen it too."

Daniel raised an eyebrow, surprised at her candour.

"He walks out of critical workshops, hands things off midstream, challenges conclusions he wasn't around to shape," she continued. "At first, I chalked it up to transition fatigue, but now it's starting to feel structural."

"But you haven't acted yet," Daniel said gently.

Maria nodded. "Because I can't—not yet."

She leaned forward, voice lower now. "We're just past the starting line, Daniel. If I flag dysfunction now, the whole project risks being labelled unstable. We'll lose air cover from the board, and every escalation will be seen as a weakness. This team needs to look like it's working before it is."

Daniel said nothing, letting the weight of her words hang.

"I told them this is a team," Maria continued. "That they have to support each other. But I just... I need a bit more time. Enough to let things settle—or break on their terms."

Daniel nodded. "Understood. But don't wait too long. We'll have bigger fires if it cracks at the wrong moment."

Maria offered a faint smile. "Thanks, Daniel. Keep me posted. Discreetly."

After Daniel left, Maria stayed in her office long past sunset. Outside, city lights flickered to life, casting fractured reflections on the glass. The silence suited her—it gave her space to think, to connect the dots that others hadn't yet noticed.

She thought of Susan, sharp and composed, now juggling the demands of the tax transformation with her ongoing responsibilities for indirect taxes. She had built trust slowly, methodically. Listened first, then contributed. She knew which doors to knock on and which required a softer nudge.

She had taken the time to understand the landscape before navigating it—the people, the systems, the unwritten rules. She hadn't assumed trust— she had earned it.

And then there was Matthew.

Maria had given him the benefit of the doubt. More than once. But as she sat there now, she couldn't ignore the truth staring back at her. He hadn't done what a true transformation leader should do upon joining:

- No immersion in tax processes.
- No real grasp of the systems or data constraints.
- No visible effort to understand the political or human context of the team.
- No curiosity about legacy pain points or why certain things had failed.

He hadn't jumped into the boat with a map. He hadn't even checked the tide.

He should have spent his first weeks listening, shadowing workshops, asking questions, observing dynamics, and mapping out the interplays between tax, technology, people, and data. He should've built trust across stakeholders, understood what success looked like for each of them, and only then started shaping the future state.

But he hadn't seen it.

Or maybe, worse, he didn't know he needed to.

Maria closed her eyes briefly, letting the weight of that possibility settle.

The question now wasn't just about Matthew's competence. It was about consequences. How long could Susan continue stretching to keep things afloat? How long before their mandates started slipping under the burden of carrying someone else's?

And if that happened—if her strongest players burned out or pulled back—what would be left of the transformation?

She opened her notebook one last time that night and jotted three bullet points beneath the empty org box she'd circled earlier:

- Observe closely in the design phase
- Contingency for leadership gap
- Quiet escalation strategy?

She paused, then added one final note, underlined twice:

Do not let silence become complicity.

She closed the book.

Intercut: Sophia & Richard

Across London, Sophia sat in Richard's glass office. He walked her through his firm's transformation blueprint—sleek slides, crisp governance charts, promises of board-level sponsorship. *"We don't do process theatre here,"* he said. *"Results matter more than rituals."*

She listened, but unease gnawed at her. The office hummed with the faint buzz of recessed lights, the air too perfectly conditioned, the slides so polished they felt sterile—like a set staged for persuasion rather than truth. His pitch was polished, too polished. She recalled the flicker in his eyes when she asked about Abhishek. Something unsaid, heavy in its omission.

That night, Sophia scrolled the financial headlines on her phone: AlphaCorp launches UK transformation pilot amid compliance overhaul. Maria's name threaded through the article, the CFO turned field general. Sophia exhaled slowly. Maria was fighting with legacy weapons. Richard was offering her a clean slate. Whether that made her a survivor or prey, she couldn't yet tell.

Maria closed her notebook. Across town, Sophia closed her phone. Two women, two wars, heading toward collision.

CHAPTER 40

New Currents, New Contours

The Mandate Wave

The dust from Phase 2 hadn't even settled when the storm rolled in. The ink on AlphaCorp's Business Requirements Document was still drying when Maria's phone lit up with headlines: the UAE and UK governments were moving forward with e-invoicing mandates, and AlphaCorp's name was already surfacing as a Phase 1 candidate.

By lunchtime the finance chat groups were buzzing, inboxes overflowing with bulletins. Saudi Arabia, Egypt, and India were scaling their einvoicing programs. France and Oman were planning their own mandates. What had once been dismissed as experiment was now a tidal wave.

Maria's Dismissal

Maria skimmed the notifications on her tablet, jaw tightening. She muttered, short and sharp: "Another IT-led exercise. Let the systems team handle it."

Her eyes flicked to the calendar. A red circle glared back—the next Board review. Edward's pen tap echoed in her mind like a metronome. She had just shepherded the team through brutal workshops and the never-ending BRD cycle. They were ready to build. In her mind, einvoicing was a distraction, another compliance fire drill.

What she didn't yet see was that it wasn't a detour. It was the highway—and it had just merged into her lane.

She rubbed her temples. Leadership wasn't just steering the ship—it was recognising when the sea itself had changed.

Daniel's Signal

Meanwhile, Daniel saw something very different. Alone in his office, mandate specs scattered across his desk, he read like a man staring at coordinates to buried treasure. This wasn't XML templates and API endpoints. This was data enrichment, transactional transparency, and a chance to rewrite AlphaCorp's spine.

The lamp at his elbow hummed faintly. He scribbled in the margin: *Don't digitise dysfunction.* Then underlined: *Design for scale, not survival.*

He leaned back, recalling too many boardrooms where ERP vendors peddled country kits and einvoicing providers sold one-off connectors. The same blueprint dressed in new covers, the same cycle of short-term fixes. Fragmentation wasn't failure—it was the business model in the industry and replicated successfully every time a new country announced its real-time reporting mandate.

"If we play their game, we lose," he murmured.

Nathan Alistair's words flickered in his memory. Years ago, in Nathan's cult book, he had underlined: *Mandates can chain you, or launch you. The difference is whether you design for survival or for scale.* The thought steadied him. Nathan had been right.

Susan's Alarm

While Daniel mapped futures, Susan walked back from a meeting clutching her coffee. A notification pinged: *UK and UAE announce einvoicing mandates.* She stopped mid-corridor, scanning the article. Cleaner master data. Real-time controls. Automated reconciliations. For a second, hope flickered.

Then Matthew's voice carried from a huddle nearby: "I'll lead the charge. We'll fast-track it." Laughter followed, pens scribbling in notebooks as though it were settled. Susan's cup rattled against its lid.

She cornered Aldo later by the elevators. "If Matthew owns this," she whispered, "we'll get a compliant shell and a broken engine."

Aldo frowned. "You think he'll cut corners?"

“You’ve seen the countries that already rolled this out,” she shot back. “Data not matching the portals. Tax returns bouncing. IT shrugging and saying, ‘not our job.’ Shared services blaming tax. Fresh grads too green to even know what broke. And everyone pretending it’s fine.”

Her voice dropped. “If that lands on my desk, I’m finished.”

Aldo’s jaw tightened. “I’ve lived that post-mortem. You’re right to worry.”

The elevator arrived, doors sliding open with a chime. Neither moved. Silence said enough.

Maria and Daniel’s Exchange

Maria summoned Daniel into her office. Papers and mandate briefs were scattered across her desk, the board date circled in red ink. Outside, the city lights blinked through the blinds; inside, the silence stretched taut with expectation. She tapped the cover page of the UK einvoicing mandate, then the UAE directive beside it, her pen tracing underlined clauses.

“Spell it out for me,” she said. “We’ve written a BRD, defined transaction flows, reconciled codes. That work covers our internal tax tools. How does einvoicing alter the design we’ve mapped, the data model we’ve been building, the reporting spine we’ve promised the Board?”

Daniel leaned forward, lowering his voice. “Maria, we have a choice. We can run it in parallel, tick the box. Or—we can use this as ignition. Rethink compliance, finance, tax—end to end. Survive the mandate, or reshape the business.”

Maria arched an eyebrow. “Ignition? Ignition for what exactly?” She leaned back, the glint of a consultant’s pitch all too familiar. She thought: *Trophy patients. If they succeed, it’s their medal. If they fail—well, the patient was already too far gone.*

She hesitated, then asked aloud, carefully: “Ignition sounds like cost, and aspiration. But ignition for what exactly, Daniel? Explain.”

Daniel’s tone sharpened. “Think beyond tax. Think supply chain reconciled in real time. Finance teams freed from firefighting. Audit risks evaporating because the data is right at the source. This isn’t about compliance—it’s about control.”

Maria’s eyes narrowed. “Aspirational. Who leads it?”

"I have someone in mind," Daniel said. "From our firm. Senior Partner. Runs global tax and ERP transformations. Led programs across the UK, GCC, Southeast Asia."

Maria folded her arms. "Name?"

"Nathan Alistair. He doesn't just implement. He reimagines. I want him to present directly to you and the Board."

Maria's scepticism lingered. "Another consultant with a slideshow?"

Daniel shook his head. "Nathan doesn't just comply; he capitalises."

Introducing Nathan Alistair

Nathan Alistair wasn't new to inflexion points.

He had walked into VAT launches in the Gulf, einvoicing mandates in India, tax overhauls in Africa. But what set him apart wasn't this, his broad experience, the logos on his résumé—it was how he treated mandates as missions.

As a senior partner at Grayson & Holt, Nathan led the digitalization of indirect tax for some of the most complex multinationals. He understood tax wasn't a back-office function—it was the bloodstream of every transaction.

His approach was surgical and strategic: automate what can be automated, connect what is fragmented, and continuously align tax with the business.

Maria Pushes Back

Maria hesitated when Daniel shared Nathan's credentials and proposed a direct presentation to the Board.

"No," she said bluntly. "Not yet."

She flipped through Nathan's CV—it was impressive, but she had seen enough glossy credentials with little substance.

"If you want me to consider him seriously, I'll meet him first. In person. I don't send strangers into boardrooms."

Daniel nodded. "Fair."

At the door, he paused. "If Nathan lives up to half of what I've seen... you might consider making him more than a presenter."

Maria looked up. "What do you mean?"

"Maybe he's your transformation lead. And maybe it's time Matthew found a more suitable role—somewhere his 'oversight' can't derail momentum."

Maria said nothing. But she didn't shut it down either.

The Blueprint Begins

While all of this was still cooking, Daniel had already given Nathan a heads-up.

"Send me your thoughts," he'd said. Later that night, Daniel opened the file Nathan had sent. It wasn't a deck. It was a vision:

- A unified global einvoicing strategy with only deltas customised.
- Intelligence at the source, cutting compliance costs by three-quarters.
- AP/AR reconciliations collapsing into real time.
- A lean, AI-enabled tax team focused on strategy, not clerical work.
- Global invoice flows coded for scalability.

It was bold. Disruptive. The future. And precisely what AlphaCorp needed.

Nathan's meeting with Maria went better than expected. She wasn't just impressed—she was energised. His clarity cut through, his lived experience grounding every claim. He commanded both the strategic and technical layers.

"This isn't a consultant," she thought. "This is a leader."

By the time their conversation ended, Maria had made up her mind. She would take Nathan to the Board.

Gathering Storms

That night, the evening news flashed across London screens. A breaking alert: *In the Abhishek Iyer case, the AlphaCorp tax executive remains in a coma, struggling for his life. Police sources now confirm this does not appear to be an accident, but an attempt on his life. Investigations are ongoing. The police have recovered the car and ID'd the driver. The search is on to nab the driver.*

Sophia watched from her apartment, the blue light of the TV flickering against the walls. The silence was heavy in the room, broken only by the anchor's voice. Her hands trembled; the words hollowed her to the bone.

Across town, Maria and Arjun sat frozen on their sofa, disbelief passing between them. Who could possibly want to harm Abhishek—a man so simple, so straightforward, barely a year into this city? Maria's throat tightened. Leadership was hard enough under scrutiny—how could she protect her people when danger was coming from the shadows? Shock flowed around them in their safe refuge.

In Mayfair, Richard sat at a bar, nursing a drink. Laughter rippled from nearby tables but barely touched him. When the bulletin flashed on the screen above the counter, he froze. A streak of sweat trickled down his forehead despite the chill of his glass. He raised it to his lips, but his hand shook. For the first time in years, Richard looked less like a strategist and more like a man cornered.

What some saw as burden, others saw as blueprint. And in the shadows of London, the story of Abhishek turned from accident to conspiracy, pulling every thread tighter toward collision.

CHAPTER 41

The Inflexion

Shadows at the Table

The boardroom stretched long and polished, its glass walls catching the pale London winter light. The atmosphere was already taut, as though the air itself knew what was coming.

Maria sat at the centre, flanked by Daniel and Nathan. Aldo was a few chairs down, notebook open but untouched. Around them, the directors had gathered: Jill with her usual fountain pen poised like a scalpel, Elena leaning back, calculating, Anwar with his gentle eyes, Raghav restless, and Edward—steely, once her fiercest critic—sitting unusually quiet. At the head of the table was Mikhail, the Chair, his reputation built on one-line judgments that could dismantle careers.

It was Anwar who broke the silence. "Maria," he said softly, "before we begin—have you visited Abhishek? How is his family holding up?"

The words sank into the room like a stone into water.

Maria's throat tightened. "I was at the hospital yesterday. He's still in a coma. His wife and daughter are with him—AlphaCorp is supporting them fully." She paused, steadying herself. "The doctors... they say it's touch and go."

A hush followed. For a moment, strategy, numbers, mandates—all of it felt irrelevant.

Mikhail tapped his pen once, reclaiming the rhythm of the room. "We must watch it closely and help the family in all ways possible. For now let's proceed with our agenda for the day."

Nathan's Opening

Nathan rose with an ease that came from decades of boardrooms. His voice was calm, deliberate.

"I know AlphaCorp is deep into a major transformation. You've delivered early wins with RPA. You've managed e-invoicing in fourteen jurisdictions."

He let that settle before leaning in. "So why am I here? To bring another layer of strategic alignment into this ambitious transformation program."

Jill raised an eyebrow. "We've done e-invoicing before. Many times. Why treat this as different?"

Nathan nodded, as though inviting the challenge. "Because for the first time, many of your jurisdictions—like the UK, France, Oman, UAE—are all moving together and in the same direction. This isn't about just another e-invoicing rollout. It's convergence. And convergence, if handled right, is ignition."

Mikhail's pen stilled. "Ignition is a grand word. Prove it."

The Pattern

Nathan clicked a remote. A heat map lit the screen: fourteen countries in green, seven in grey.

"You've already implemented e-invoicing in fourteen markets. But across those, you're juggling twenty-one separate vendor agreements. Some with the same providers, doing the same work, sold to you multiple times."

Maria felt her pen hesitate against the page. She had signed off on many of those contracts.

Nathan's tone sharpened. "Data mapping. API builds. Test cycles. Redundant every time. Millions wasted. And yet—across countries, seventy to eighty percent of the fields are identical. Seller. Buyer. Tax rate. Invoice line item. Amount. Treatment. Reporting."

He let the silence grow.

"We created our fragmentation. And we paid for it."

Elena leaned forward. "You're saying the uniqueness of each country is exaggerated?"

"I'm saying it's been monetised," Nathan replied.

At the far end of the table, Edward shifted in his chair, his pen tapping faster than usual. Maria noticed the flicker of unease across his face. He rarely let emotion show—but something about him today gave away his slipping composure. He was visibly rattled.

The Trap

Mikhail shifted in his chair, breaking the silence. "If the fields are so similar, why have we let this sprawl continue?"

Jill sighed, almost defensive. "Because every project team was told their country was unique. That was the design brief."

Aldo leaned in, his voice firm. "The design was legacy, fragmented from the start. Nathan is right. We've been building on sand."

Surprise flickered across a few faces. The Board members looked down, as though ashamed by what AlphaCorp had accepted as normal.

Nathan clicked again. A new diagram appeared—layers of middleware, each box wedged between ERP and tax authority.

"Here's the deeper risk. In nearly all of these rollouts, you've let middleware vendors 'absorb the pain'. They did. But they also took ownership of your compliance logic. Your enrichment rules. Even parts of your master data."

He turned to face the table. "Today, some of your VAT registrations, place-of-supply rules, product classifications—live outside your systems. Maintained by vendors. Invisible to you."

Raghav muttered, "That's a governance nightmare."

Nathan's voice cut clean. "And now you can't decouple. Pain absorbed. Ownership lost."

Edward cleared his throat. Maria braced, expecting the familiar barb. Instead, his tone surprised her—measured, almost receptive. "We saw this already. That audit two years ago. Local authority asked for logs. Vendor had collapsed. No trail. We paid."

His pen tapped again, too fast. Maria caught the tremor in his hand before he folded them together on the table.

The Hard Truth

Click. A news-style headline splashed onto the screen: *"AlphaCorp Penalised – $4.3M Due to Unreconciled e-Invoicing Records."*

Nathan didn't soften the blow. "This wasn't a systems glitch. It was governance failure, born of fragmentation and dependency. You've seen the cost. You've felt the exposure."

Mikhail leaned forward, pen between his fingers. "How will your design prevent this from happening again, Nathan? Show us how it changes the game."

Nathan met his gaze steadily. "Would you deploy different ERPs across your markets and rely on local vendors and teams to manage each one? That is what's happening with e-invoicing today. My design unifies it. Global e-invoicing rollouts are far closer to ERP backbone than to local compliance quirks. To be clear—e-invoicing isn't even compliance. Its customer is the tax authority, no more and no less than your books of account."

The room had stilled.

Mikhail broke the silence, eyes fixed on Nathan. "Heavy words, Mr. Alistair. *Governance failure* is not a term we use lightly. Have you seen this elsewhere, or is AlphaCorp your trial ground?"

Elena leaned in, sharp. "Yes. Tell us, Nathan—have you truly turned around companies of our scale, or are you trying to create your trophy patient here?"

Nathan stood firm. "I've worked with groups across the GCC, India, Africa. The pattern is always the same—fragmentation dressed as uniqueness and necessity, middleware sold as salvation. And I've dismantled it before."

Aldo supported him, his tone steady. "What Nathan says is true. I've warned for years that our design was legacy and brittle. This isn't theory—it's lived experience."

The Board shifted uneasily, some members exchanging looks. The pride of AlphaCorp was colliding with a truth they could no longer ignore.

Debate and Decisions

Mikhail glanced around the table. "You've told us how this model prevents another failure. But what does it mean for our bottom line? We are already stretched."

There was a murmur of agreement from a few directors before Jill leaned forward. "Yes, let's talk numbers. What about the cost? We're bleeding already."

"Unifying the design eliminates 75 percent of compliance costs," Nathan shot back without hesitation. "Shared service overhead drops by half. Reconciliations collapse into real time. Efficiency funds itself."

Elena frowned. "And the timing? Our people are exhausted."

Aldo leaned in. "If we delay, we are building duplicate infra for the same needs. Every country you add locks you deeper into the wrong model. Better one decisive change now than a decade of patches."

Daniel added, measured: "Integrate mandates now, and your tax engine becomes stronger. Delay, and you'll be layering fixes on fixes."

Edward's pen tapped once. "Better one decisive cut," he said quietly, "than death by a thousand."

Maria felt the shift. The old battlefield lines had blurred.

Maria's Moment

Mikhail's eyes settled on Maria. His voice was low, decisive. "Then who leads this? You are already struggling with the team."

The room seemed to tilt toward her. Fingers drummed on polished wood, chairs creaked, the weight of expectation thick in the air.

Maria drew a breath. "Nathan. With Aldo on systems. And I take accountability here, at the Board."

A silence followed, weighty. The directors exchanged brief glances; even Jill set her pen down.

Mikhail studied Nathan, then Maria. The pen stopped moving. "Then let's be clear: this is not another compliance patch. It is the spine of your transformation." His voice cut the air. He paused, eyes sweeping the table. "Approved."

One by one, the board members nodded. Even Edward, though his clasped hands betrayed tension.

Daniel exhaled quietly, shoulders loosening. Nathan closed his laptop with deliberate calm. Maria didn't smile, but a flicker of fire passed through her eyes—the spark of someone who had earned the room, if only for tonight.

Morning After

The next morning, Maria sat at the breakfast table, steam rising from her coffee. Arjun folded his paper to the finance section, but she was fixed on the front page.

"Driver in AlphaCorp Executive Attack Apprehended – Investigations Hint at Conspiracy."

Her fingers pressed against the newsprint. The man who had left Abhishek in a coma had finally been caught in the countryside. But the article hinted at more: startling revelations, threads tugging toward something deeper.

Maria read the article thrice, as if each re-read might reveal something new. But the article was unforgiving. The boardroom battle was won. But the war outside was only beginning.

CHAPTER 42

Running with/ from the Verdict

The Arrests

London woke to scandal. Screens replayed Edward Grant shoved into a van, Richard Hawthorne in cuffs at Heathrow. **FORMER EXECUTIVES ARRESTED, TO FACE TRIAL** blazed across tickers. Beneath it: **Driver Nabbed in Attack on Executive; Police Probe Conspiracy.** Abhishek's absence lingered like a shadow—*critical condition, coma continues.*

Maria entered AlphaCorp with IR on one line and Legal on the other. "No speculation, only facts. Continuity of operations," she said, hanging up as cameras outside hunted her face.

Trials and Theatre

Edward and Richard faced hearings, their names echoing through the courtroom as the jury settled in. The driver shuffled to the witness box, eyes down, voice unsteady. "Mr. Hawthorne hired me," he said, lifting trembling hands as if clutching the envelope he once received. "He gave me the map, the schedule. Said it had to look like an accident. Not to kill him."

Gasps swept the gallery. Richard's lawyer shot to his feet. "Objection!" The judge waved him down. Cross-examination followed, sharp as blades.

The prosecutor leaned forward. "So, Mr. Hawthorne instructed you directly?"

Richard's face drained. His voice cracked across the hush. "I only passed what I was told. Edward—Edward orchestrated it!"

The gallery erupted, whispers spilling like smoke. Jurors exchanged glances; one scribbled furiously. The judge's gavel hammered order. "Silence! This is not a theatre."

Edward slammed a fist on the table, his lawyer gripping his arm. Flashes popped from the press benches. The clerk rose: "Next hearing date—four weeks from today."

As guards led them out, jackets rumpled and shoulders bent, Edward stared straight ahead, Richard at the floor. Cameras fired as the doors shut behind them, leaving the air thick with sweat and scandal.

At AlphaCorp: monitors lit with the same footage, muted. Employees froze mid-stride in corridors, watching jurors file out as if they too were part of the verdict.

Outside, the press swarmed the courthouse. Reporters shoved microphones, live feeds flickered, and market tickers bled red: AlphaCorp stock sliding further.

Maria's Balancing Act

In a week the AlphaCorp stock had nosedived to historical lows. On the analyst call, Maria kept her voice steady. "Yes, two former executives are on trial. But AlphaCorp is not those men. The teams who build the future are still here."

She carried the weight into every meeting. Evidence and not mere speeches: status updates, progress briefs, redeployment plans. Courtroom drama outside; corporate defense inside.

Floorwalking in a Trial's Shadow

"People first," Nathan would say. "Tools and strategies come later. Without trust, nothing endures."

His first days were unhurried. Floor to floor. Desk to desk. One morning he joined the tax team's coffee break, sipped the bitter vending-machine cappuccino, and pulled a face. "Does anyone actually like this?" Laughter cracked the tension.

He asked about birthdays, commutes, school runs. "No workflows today," he grinned. "Just survival tips."

Across the room, Matthew Jenkins muttered, "Waste of time."

On Day Four, Nathan walked into Susan's office. A stack of flagged issues from the UK rollout towered on her desk.

"These are good," he said, flipping through them. "You've got a sharp eye."

Susan folded her arms. "Or just a tired one. Every time I fix one blind spot, another pops up. Feels endless."

Nathan smiled. "Let's not call them blind spots. Let's call them... legacy surprises."

Susan chuckled. "Legacy surprises. That's generous. But I'll take it."

Her eyes flicked to Abhishek's empty chair. "I hear him in my head all the time."

Nathan nodded. "Then let's work like he can hear us."

Matthew frowned, scribbled something, but stayed quiet. Nathan never contradicted him outright, never endorsed his flimsy points either. He'd redirect gently: "That's one lens. Let's explore another."

By month's end, collaboration felt less forced, resistance softened, and trust took root.

Arms around AlphaCorp

Daniel slid the onboarding dossier across the table.

"Light bedtime reading?" Nathan quipped.

"Diagnostics, maps, post-mortems. The whole autopsy," Daniel said.

That night Nathan muttered over the file. "Here's the crack. Here's the patch."

He didn't redo the as-is. "They already bled enough for that," he told Daniel. Instead, he traced behaviour to blueprint: "Who decided this? Why did it stick?"

Meanwhile, integration pressed on. Nathan handpicked a lean team—sharp AlphaCorp talent and Grayson & Holt fusion Team. "You're translators," he told them. "Turn compliance nuance into design."

Susan tapped a pencil against a flagged rule. "This one breaks without supplier categories."

"Good catch. Build it in," Nathan replied. "Keep surprises legacy, not future."

Listening tours added layers: finance in Egypt, tax managers in London, IT in Bangalore. Each answer built a map truer than any PowerPoint.

By Day 30, he had heard enough.

In a quiet meeting with Maria, he said, "We've got the design. Lean, scalable, tailored. But success won't come from the tool. It'll come from the temperature. Right now, lukewarm."

Maria tapped her pen. "Lukewarm doesn't win markets or unions. So what's the plan?"

"Ownership. Rituals. Check-ins. Everyone knows what they own. Just new rhythms should do the trick."

She studied him. "You really think rhythm can carry this through trials, protests, falling stock?"

"I think rhythm is the only thing that can."

She nodded. "I see why Daniel fought for you."

Later, Maria checked in with Susan. Susan admitted, "For the first time, someone else is steering and it's not swerving. I can focus on tax logic instead of fixing everything else."

Maria closed her eyes briefly. The tools were taking shape. Now the people were too.

Sophia's Dread

Across town, Sophia sat with courtroom reports scattered across her desk, words swimming like chains. She had watched Richard crumble, Edward deny, the driver testify. Each headline felt like a verdict on her too.

She whispered, "Rajesh in India... was that really suicide? Or were Edward and Richard behind that as well?" The thought chilled her. If they could be tied to Abhishek's accident, what else had they orchestrated?

Her pulse quickened. She hadn't touched any of it, but she knew the trail: That was enough to stain her forever. Enough to ruin her career—and maybe her freedom—in the UK.

"I never trusted Richard," she muttered. "Not then. Not now. Not ever."

Her resignation letter was already sent. On the bed, a suitcase lay open, clothes spilling like a confession. It was time.

She zipped the suitcase. Passport ready. Laptop glowing with one-way searches. "Not Paris, not even Dubai... somewhere else where no one would look."

At the window her reflection stared back, pale and tight-lipped. London glittered beyond, but it no longer belonged to her. She snapped the blinds shut, yanked the suitcase upright. Wheels rattled like a verdict.

She typed: *countries without UK extradition treaties.* Russia. China. Maldives. Names whispered like code words. Her finger hovered over *Book Flight.*

CHAPTER 43

The Altitudes of Leadership

Running Past the Glass

Sophia's suitcase wouldn't shut. Clothes kept springing up like denials. She pressed her knee into it, zipped, and stared at the blinking cursor on her laptop. *Countries without UK extradition treaties.* Tabs everywhere—Russia. China. Maldives. The names looked like exit wounds.

She yanked the plug. The room went quiet except for her breath and the little, traitorous creak of the flat when the wind shoved the window.

Why? Abhishek's voice rose from the hospital bed she refused to picture. Then Rajesh—softer, yet more damning—*Why did you do this, Sophia?*

"I didn't," she whispered. "I only... shared what everyone shared." The lie tasted metallic, bitter as blood.

The walls seemed to press closer, the air thick with shadows that weren't there. The handle under her palm stayed cold and immovable, as if the flat itself wanted to trap her inside. She yanked once, twice—the metal groaned. For a second she thought it would never turn.

Her heels buckled as she stumbled toward the lift, breath tearing out in gasps. The mirrored doors warped her reflection into something skeletal, eyes wide, hair disheveled. She pressed the button again and again, the light flickering like a warning.

When the doors finally slid open, she nearly fell inside, clutching the suitcase like a lifeline. The corridor hummed with a low, dreadful whisper that seemed to follow her down. Memories muscled in—the first

AlphaCorp ID photo, the cafeteria chicken wraps, the conference room where she said "We can fix this" and meant it.

The lift opened and the lobby spilled into view—bright, noisy, alive with people carrying parcels and chatting. For a moment relief washed over her; Her chest loosened.

Then she saw them—policemen striding toward the entrance, uniforms sharp against the glass. Her breath hitched again, relief collapsing into dread.

They're here for you.

Her first instinct screamed: *Run.* Every muscle begged for flight. But the Sophia inside—the one that had survived boardrooms and betrayals—forced her to halt. She drew in a ragged breath, straightened her back, and walked with a nervous ease toward the door. Eyes front. Not a sprint, not a saunter. Just another person with a suitcase and perfect posture. One step, then another. Her throat burned, but she forced her breath into rhythm.

She passed the first car, heart hammering. An officer glanced up—then laughed at something on his phone. Not her. Not yet.

Another pair moved toward the doors. She slid by, spine rigid, rehearsing innocence with every step. *Keep walking. Keep walking.* Her palms left damp crescents on the suitcase handle. Only when the glass doors slid shut behind her did she allow the faintest tremor to leave her lips.

Another hundred meters. The sound of her own pulse eased its grip. She waved at a black cab.

"Heathrow," she said, voice steady by force.

She risked a glance through the rear window. The policemen were still at the doors, laughing with each other. Relief slid in—thin, brittle. Her eyes darted to the mirrors as if they might follow anyway.

The taxi indicator clicked. The car crept with traffic. She pressed herself into the seat, whispering a prayer. Inside her, the two voices still fought: the panicked Sophia that wanted to fling the door open and run, and the colder Sophia that forced her to sit, still and composed, watching the city slide past.

As AlphaCorp's glass walls loomed and then slipped by, she kept her eyes forward, refusing to let either voice win. The camera of the world, if there was one, panned through the glass.

Inside those same walls, another story was unfolding—one not of flight but of focus, as Nathan leaned over a monitor and caught the first faint crack in the build.

Cracks Beneath the Surface

Inside AlphaCorp, the real work had begun—configuration sprints, test cycles, integration checks. And with that came the first waves of resistance.

It started small—the issue was easy to overlook in the noise of test cycles.

A standard cross-border service transaction script returned identical tax treatment for Egypt and KSA. At first glance, this seemed neat—too neat.

Nathan, reviewing the results in a passing glance, paused. "That doesn't look right," he murmured.

He called Susan over.

"This output," Nathan said, pointing at the test report, "shows both countries applying the same VAT logic. But the treatment of digital cross-border services differs, doesn't it?"

Susan scanned it. "Yes—KSA zero-rates this under specific conditions. Egypt applies the standard rate unless certain exemptions apply."

"So why is the engine giving the same result?" Nathan asked, already sensing the root of the problem.

Aldo, watching from across the table, frowned. "The base configuration was likely cloned across both countries early in the build and wasn't fully localised. It was an easy miss."

Nathan nodded. "And a dangerous one."

He didn't panic. He called a brief huddle with the configuration lead from Grayson and Holt, as well as the test manager.

"This isn't a tax defect," he clarified. "This is a configuration inheritance issue. Somewhere in the build process, jurisdictional divergence got flattened. We need to revalidate all copied logic."

The team jumped into action. Within 24 hours, they traced it back to a duplicated rule tree—a shortcut copied across jurisdictions. It was meant for efficiency, but the localisation step had been skipped.

Nathan leaned in, voice steady but firm. "Don't just fix it. Write down the why. Show the variance, show the rationale. Otherwise, three months from now someone will ask and we'll have nothing but memory."

Susan scribbled notes, Aldo nodded. The huddle buzzed with precision, the mistake already being reshaped into method.

"We're building a tool, yes" he said. "But we're also building auditability, traceability, and trust. If someone asks us why KSA treats this differently than Egypt, our answer should start with: 'Because the law says so—and here's how the engine reflects that.'"

By the end of the week, the engine logic had been corrected, retested, and approved.

More importantly, Nathan's team added a new layer to their test exit checklist: jurisdictional variance confirmation—a protocol to ensure similar-looking transactions were intentionally configured to behave differently where required.

Maria, upon hearing about it, smiled quietly. "He doesn't just catch errors," she said to Daniel. "He prevents their cousins."

Frameworks and Acceptance

Later that day, Aldo leaned over Susan's desk, phone face down. "You saw what Nathan did with that Egypt–KSA glitch?"

Susan nodded. "He didn't just patch it—he built a framework around it. Jurisdictional variance check. Simple but solid."

Aldo grinned, almost disbelieving. "And the way he made the team own it—it was great."

Susan tapped her pen, half-smiling. "That's consultants for you. They take something small, give it a shape, call it a framework, a matrix, a checklist—suddenly it looks like a doctrine."

"But it works," Aldo admitted. "And maybe that's what we needed—clarity dressed as method."

Susan leaned back. "Acceptance comes when the work holds up. Today—it did."

Maria passed by the open doorway, catching their words. She didn't interrupt—just let the corner of her mouth lift. Acceptance, finally, was happening in real time.

Strengthening the Weakest Link

Two weeks into testing, a deeper challenge emerged—the shared services team in China, responsible for invoice validation, was overwhelmed.

In Guangzhou, the new tax determination logic demanded data fields no one had trained them to capture. At one desk, Li Mei shook her head, re-entering the same invoice for the third time. "It keeps rejecting," she muttered. Two rows over, Chen Wei sighed, eyes on a red error log. "I don't even know what half these fields mean."

Errors piled up. Re-tests failed. Morale dipped. The shared services floor buzzed with frustration, the hum of overworked screens and weary voices carrying across the room.

The project leads were frustrated. Some whispered about rolling back that design part "just for go-live." Nathan disagreed.

"We don't change the design to match the weakest link," he said firmly. "We strengthen the link."

He flew to Guangzhou.

Nathan conducted a round of hands-on, simplified, human training sessions. He pulled up a chair beside Li Mei. "Show me where it fails," he said softly. She clicked through the invoice, the screen flashing red again. Nathan jotted a note. "Not you—this is on design."

At the next desk, Chen Wei rubbed his eyes. "I've entered this three times. It never clears." Nathan leaned closer, guiding him through the missing fields. "Watch. Here and here—this is what the engine expects. Not obvious, right? That's on us."

He walked the floor, listening, fixing, mapping every friction point with their words rather than slides. By the second afternoon Li Mei managed to clear an invoice without an error message. She blinked at the green tick, then let out a laugh she hadn't heard from herself in weeks. Chen Wei lifted his head and grinned, half in disbelief. "It went through?"

Nathan nodded, leaning on the desk. "Exactly as it should. And it'll keep doing that once the bot is in place."

The tension on the floor shifted. What had been sighs and mutters turned into cautious relief, small smiles spreading like the first breeze after a storm.

Then he made a bold call.

"This isn't a tax problem," he told Maria in a late-night call. "It's a process design gap. The field team was never part of the original workshops. We're correcting that now."

Maria listened, and for the first time in weeks his voice carried something lighter—like relief had seeped in between the words. She smiled into the receiver. "You sound different," she said.

"I heard them laugh today," Nathan replied. "Li Mei, Chen Wei, the processors. That's the sound I'm chasing."

Within a week, Nathan had retrained the team and helped build a validation bot—a lightweight automation layer that pre-flags missing or malformed fields before submission. The error rate dropped by 63%.

The China team sent a thank-you email, but what touched Nathan more was the subject line: "We finally feel like part of the project."

He didn't share it. He just smiled and archived it in a private folder called *People Wins*.

Building Belief

Three months in, the air within AlphaCorp had changed. Meetings lost the line *We hope this works.* A different sentence took root: *We know it will work.*

Ownership showed up with its sleeves rolled. In Nigeria, the finance controller stress-tested withholding. In Mexico, a business head rewrote supplier contracts to lock in e-invoicing data integrity. In Kenya, compliance calendars fed straight into the workflow tool like arteries.

Daniel watched the dashboard glow. "We've rolled out tools before," he told Maria. "This time, we've rolled out trust." He paused, then added with a wry smile, "That's the altitude of leadership, isn't it? Strategic when required, guiding from above when needed, and down in the trenches in Guangzhou when it mattered. Effective leadership personified."

Maria met his eyes, the faintest smile breaking through. "Yes," she said quietly. "And exactly what AlphaCorp needs right now."

She exhaled. "Belief scales faster than software." She glanced around the table and noticed it—the absence of dread. The ghostly pauses that once haunted every meeting were gone. Voices carried steadier now, conviction filling spaces that had once been hollow. And somewhere in the hum of conversation Maria caught it—the sound of laughter. The same sound Nathan had described from Guangzhou, now echoing in their own halls.

CHAPTER 44

The Great Escape

Heathrow

The queue at Terminal 3 moved in uneven pulses. Families with strollers, couples clutching duty-free bags, lone travelers gripping boarding passes as if they were talismans.

Sophia tried to blend in. Her passport was slick in her hand, damp with sweat. She rehearsed the words in her head: *Shanghai. Business meetings. A few weeks.*

The immigration officer scanned her document. The machine beeped once, then again—lower, longer. His eyes flicked to the monitor. He didn't look up right away. A pause, no longer than a heartbeat, was enough to snap her stomach into a knot.

He pressed a button under the counter. Two plainclothes officers appeared at her side.

"Ms. Chan?" one asked.

Her mouth opened, but no sound came. The suitcase slid from her grip and toppled with a dull crack on the polished floor. Passengers turned their heads. Some curious. Some indifferent.

"This way, please."

She didn't resist. Her heels echoed against the tiled floor as they walked her out of the queue, past the duty-free shelves of perfume and chocolate, into a corridor where the noise of the terminal receded into a hush of humming lights.

The Room

The interrogation room smelled faintly of stale coffee and cleaning fluid. A single strip light hummed overhead. On the table sat a folder thick with printed emails and transcripts.

Detective Harris—broad-shouldered, his rumpled face softened by eyes that seemed permanently patient—slid the folder toward her. "We've been through Richard Hawthorne's apartment. We found these."

Sophia stared at the stack of paper. Her name glowed in the headers like a curse. **Sophia Chan — AlphaCorp.**

Her throat tightened. "I didn't... I only passed information that was public."

Harris raised an eyebrow. "Public? Tax configurations? Draft board minutes? Internal audit notes?" He leaned forward. "Ms. Chan, help me understand why Richard Hawthorne had your emails marked *priority*."

Her fingers twitched in her lap. She tried to find the old Sophia—the boardroom tactician, the one who could stretch ambiguity into armor. But the room was too bright, the paper too heavy, the silence too sharp.

Her voice cracked. "Richard said he needed leverage. Against Maria. Against AlphaCorp. He said... he said they had ruined him."

The other officer, who had been listening silently to the conversation so far, asked Sophia quietly, "And you agreed to help?" Sophia looked at him. Officer Patel's shoulders sloped with a kind of honest fatigue, his once-crisp collar softened at the edges, the fine lines around his eyes deepened by long nights on the job. Looking at him in that moment felt unexpectedly human—like someone who had no interest in catching her out, only in understanding what had gone wrong.

Sophia's lips trembled. "He promised... opportunities. That he'd take me with him. I didn't think—" Her breath hitched. "I never thought anyone would get hurt."

The Slip

Harris tapped the folder with one finger. "Who else knew?"

She shook her head. "Just Richard."

"You're sure?"

Sophia swallowed. The old instinct—to distance, to evade—rose reflexively. "Well... Richard did hint someone else was calling the shots. But he never—"

She froze.

The officers exchanged a glance. Patel scribbled something on his pad. Harris's voice softened, almost gentle. "Edward who?"

Sophia shut her eyes, realizing too late she had opened another door.

The Spiral

For the next hour, she veered between denial and confession—blaming Richard, minimizing her role, then admitting she knew the data was sensitive. Every sentence bound her tighter.

The detectives let her speak, recording everything. Each slip gave them new names, new threads, new leads.

When she finally sagged into silence, Harris closed the folder. "You understand what happens next, Ms. Chan?"

She nodded numbly. The chair felt like an anchor, pinning her in place.

Patel switched off the recorder. The red light died. "This doesn't end with you. It starts here."

Sophia stared at her reflection in the interrogation glass, eyes swollen, lips trembling. For the first time, she saw herself as others might: as the weakest link in a chain of betrayals.

AlphaCorp Reels

Back at AlphaCorp, the news of Sophia's arrest spread like static across the building. The leadership team gathered in a closed-door session, the atmosphere thick with disbelief.

Maria stood at the head of the table, the file of preliminary updates clenched in her hand. "She was taken at Heathrow. Interrogation has already begun." Her voice was steady, but her eyes betrayed the weight of betrayal.

Susan exhaled, shaking her head. "How deep did this go? What exactly did she give Hawthorne?"

Aldo leaned forward, brows knitted. "If it included system configurations, draft workflows, or supplier data... that could compromise AlphaCorp's project and our position in multiple jurisdictions."

Maria nodded. "We've initiated an internal review. IT security is mapping every email, every attachment that left her account. We'll cross-check with what was found in Hawthorne's apartment once the police share their evidence."

Susan's voice tightened. "This isn't just a compliance breach. This could erode trust with regulators. We need to be ready for questions we don't want to answer."

Aldo added, "And we need to understand whether any of the design work—our frameworks, our differentiators and strategy—are now in someone else's hands. That's corporate theft, a sabotage waiting to happen."

Susan's eyes flicked away for a moment. "I trusted her," she admitted quietly. "It makes you question who else might be capable of the same."

Aldo sighed. "She was sharp. I never thought she'd be the crack in the wall."

Maria let the silence settle for a beat, then said quietly, "The damage is technical. And it's reputational. We will account for every leak. And we will prove—to the Board, to regulators, to ourselves—that AlphaCorp's foundation is stronger than one person's betrayal."

Nathan finally spoke, his tone calm but edged with conviction. "Sophia thought she was passing files. What she really did was much more grave."

No one disagreed. The room held a grim resolve. The betrayal was real, but so was the determination to contain it.

The Turn

The leadership team convened again — Maria, Daniel, Nathan, Aldo, and Susan — this time to review progress. They leaned over dashboards and reports in a huddle that felt markedly different: less tense, more focused.

Screens glowed across the table, casting pale light on tired faces. Daniel leaned forward first, tapping a graph. "Look at this run. Rock steady. I haven't seen results this consistent in years."

Susan drummed her pen against the file in front of her. "Consistency is good. But controls—governance—must keep pace. Speed without guardrails is just a crash waiting to happen."

Aldo let out a low chuckle, gesturing to the architecture diagram. "Crash? Not with this build. The system's holding up, and the teams are adapting faster than I imagined."

Nathan tilted his screen toward them, lines of green checks filling the dashboard. "Performance is holding. We keep this cadence, and we'll clear the phase."

Maria's gaze swept across the table. For the first time in months, she didn't see doubt—she saw alignment. The thought hit her quietly: Sophia's betrayal had nearly broken them, but the fracture had forced them to recommit. What sat before her now was earned unity.

By the end of the month, the build and test phase was complete. Test outcomes were consistent, field users were engaged, and the architecture was working and understood.

Nathan had overseen a build & test phase. He had built and tested belief.

The following weeks marked a new rhythm at AlphaCorp — less firefighting, more focused execution.

Maria flipped through her notes, then looked at Nathan. "The tools are stabilised, aren't they? Tax engine, compliance, einvoicing?"

Nathan nodded. "Stabilised and tested. What comes next is rhythm."

Aldo leaned back, a grin tugging at his mouth. "Rhythm? You make it sound like an assembly line."

Maria smiled faintly. "That's exactly what it feels like—the assembly-line era of transformation."

Susan pointed to the rollout plan. "Each jurisdiction is a chapter. We've got the playbook. The architecture's modular, the training's working. The confidence is finally contagious."

Nathan's voice was steady. "I don't chase perfection. I chase repeatability—with accountability."

The cadence played out in real time: onboarding, localisation workshops, configuration, parallel testing, golive support. Around the table, they no longer spoke of deadlines like burdens. They spoke of steps in a rhythm they all owned.

Everywhere the tools landed, they took root.

Daniel closed his laptop with a rare smile. "We've rolled out tech before," he told Maria. "But this is the first time we've rolled out belief."

By the end of the eighth month after Nathan had joined, 14 countries were live. The transformation that once felt overwhelming was now in full flow— because the tools worked, because the people had embraced them.

Things at AlphaCorp were busier than ever. This time it was different though. The frantic chases for missing filings were missing. The midnight scrambles over broken spreadsheets were gone. No one was panicking about reconciliations that didn't match. Instead, there was forward motion—controlled, purposeful, electric.

Across the city, rain slicked the windows of a quiet London hospital. Fluorescent lights buzzed in the corridor as a nurse pushed a cart past closed doors. She slowed outside a curtained bed, glanced at the chart, and hesitated. The name glared up at her: **Iyer, A.** She tucked the file under her arm. One word was scrawled across the page: **Status: Withheld.**

She drew the curtain half an inch, lingered a moment, then walked on, wheels squeaking against linoleum.

Back at AlphaCorp, screens flickered with their variable rhythms, connected to information flows. The boardroom silences that once felt like ghosts in waiting were gone now, replaced by a rhythm of voices with conviction. Where dread had lingered, belief had taken its seat. Sophia's absence was still felt, a hollow chair in the story of AlphaCorp, but it no longer haunted the rhythm. The work moved forward, her shadow fading against the brighter cadence of conviction. And in team calls from Lagos to Mexico City, bursts of laughter slipped through the lines—proof that stability had finally taken root across the fourteen live countries.

CHAPTER 45

House of Cards

Scotland Yard — The Briefing Room

Rain bled down the tall windows, each drop smearing London's gray into watercolor. Inside, the projector hummed to life. The first slide glowed against the wall: wire transfers, offshore shells, red lines looping across Cyprus, Mauritius, Hong Kong.

The room was closed. Detective Harris and Detective Patel led the session, joined by Caroline Morton, a Crown Prosecution Service lawyer with a severe coiffure and sharp glasses perched on her nose, and two Financial Conduct Authority regulators—James Whitaker, tall and gaunt, and Priya Desai, younger but already weary-eyed. No company executives were present—Maria and her team would only see the findings later.

Harris folded his arms. "Edward Grant wasn't just a contractor. He was bleeding AlphaCorp dry."

Patel clicked to the next slide: invoices stacked in neat columns. A red box highlighted the line item *"Overtime Manpower — Pune SSC."* "Every time a system broke, a new invoice appeared. Extra staff. Extra hours. Edward billed AlphaCorp to fix the mess he created. He had stakes in manpower contracts across the globe. Automation would cut those profits in half. He couldn't bend Maria, so he found another way."

The mood tightened. Caroline tapped her pen, lips pressed thin. James rubbed his eyes, exhaling sharply. Priya leaned forward, whispering, "How did this go unseen for so long?"

Patel's knuckles whitened on the lectern. Even Harris, usually stoic, clenched his jaw. The hush thickened, broken only by the hum of the projector and Caroline's murmur: "This will be open-and-shut when it hits the court."

The Lever — Richard and Sophia

The next slide lit up Richard Hawthorne's portrait. His corporate grin jarred against the damning quotes beside it.

Harris leaned in. "Richard was the perfect lever—already bitter, already compromised."

Caroline adjusted her glasses. "And Sophia?"

Her name appeared next: email extracts, draft board minutes, audit notes. Priya's lips pressed tight. "She thought she was pulling strings. She never saw she was being played."

Patel brought up the next set of photos: an East London flat turned command post. Laptops crowded the tables, cables coiled across the carpet. Screens mirrored AlphaCorp's workflows. A man pointed a laser pen at a diagram on the wall. Beside it, a sticky note read: *'If they test here, break here.'*

James muttered, "They weren't watching. They were rehearsing the failures."

Patel's eyes hardened. "Exactly. Edward's black team pre-empted every move, stage by stage."

The silence was heavy. Caroline scribbled faster, Priya stared down, James pinched the bridge of his nose. Harris finally broke it: "This project didn't stumble. It was stalked."

The Strikes — India and China

The next images showed shouting crowds outside AlphaCorp's SSC in Pune. Placards. Megaphones. Regulators leaned closer.

On screen, CCTV footage: union leader Shailendra Tripathi in the cafeteria, phone to his ear, glancing at the clock—3:02 p.m.—two fingers raised. Dozens of workers stood in unison, spreadsheets frozen mid-line.

Caroline shook her head. "That's not protest. That's choreography."

Harris let the footage loop. "Tripathi wasn't defending jobs. He was executing Edward's cue. India, China—it was the same playbook."

"Engineered chaos," James spat.

Priya looked up from her notes. "And every disruption kept AlphaCorp bleeding into Edward's contracts."

The Death of Rajesh

Caroline cleared her throat as Harris clicked forward. A smiling photo of Rajesh filled the wall. The mood in the room shifted.

Caroline's voice softened. "We need to talk about Rajesh Mehta."

James slid a folder across. Inside: a termination list, Rajesh's name circled. A union ledger beside it, Tripathi's scrawl: *'Debt-ridden. Easy push.'*

Priya's voice trembled. "So he wasn't just unlucky. He was chosen."

Patel's tone was flat, furious. "Targeted. His dismissal orchestrated with India HC head Shefali Gupta, timed to make transformation look ruthless. Edward picked him because he was vulnerable. And when Rajesh broke—Edward called it transformation."

The silence was suffocating. Caroline froze, pen mid-air. James shook his head. Priya whispered, "That's abetment... murder without a weapon."

Caroline exhaled hard. "Edward turned vulnerability into a weapon. That makes him a predator."

James struck the table with his palm. "If unions and HR colluded, this is systemic rot."

Harris's jaw was stone. "Rajesh's death wasn't collateral. It was a calculated move in Edward's war. He isn't just corrupt—he's a cold-blooded murderer."

The Lone Wolf — Abhishek

The slide shifted: a wrecked car, glass glittering across asphalt. Medical reports stamped *Status: Withheld.*

"With Sophia compromised and Rajesh gone, Abhishek Iyer was the last obstacle," Harris said, voice rough. "Edward didn't need him dead. He needed him delayed."

Patel clenched her fists. "The accident was engineered. Timing precise. It spiraled further than Edward planned."

Caroline's pen clattered onto the table. "First Rajesh, now Abhishek—was there no value to human life?"

James's face reddened. "Two men, both fathers, treated as disposable roadblocks."

Priya's eyes brimmed. "Rajesh's kids are barely in school. Abhishek's youngest isn't even five."

Harris's voice was iron. "Edward didn't just attack a project. He hunted its people. He shattered families."

The table sank into grim agreement—Caroline shaking her head, James muttering that this case already spoke louder than any argument, Priya wiping her eyes. In their minds the verdict was written: Edward and Richard were the worst kind of criminals. The case would be fair, but their judgment was already passed.

Caroline straightened. "The CPS will move quickly. We have enough to authorise charges."

James nodded. "First stop, Magistrates' Court."

Priya's voice was steady now. "Then the Crown Court, with a jury who'll see what we've seen today."

Chairs scraped back. Folders closed. The air was heavy, charged with grim resolve. This was the pursuit of justice.

The Courtroom

Weeks later, the oak panels of the Crown Court rose like sentinels. The trial unfolded like theatre. Witnesses stepped into the box, some steady, some trembling. Exhibits flickered across screens. Defence barristers prowled, objected, needled the investigators. The judge, his heavy robes draped on his shoulders, cut through the noise: "Weigh what you see, not what you feel."

Edward sat in the dock, silver hair combed back, a curl of disdain at his lips. Richard twitched beside him, arrogance drained. Sophia sat apart, mascara streaked, hands clenched as if in prayer.

The prosecution paraded testimony—Harris and Patel under oath, Whitaker and Desai tracing the money, experts showing how the black team rehearsed AlphaCorp's collapse. The defence strained to cast Sophia as naïve, Richard as careless. But the documents spoke louder.

Closing speeches came. The prosecutor's voice rang: "Edward Grant profited from decay. Richard Hawthorne enabled him. Sophia Chan armed him."

The judge gave careful directions. The jury retired. Hours stretched. In the gallery, whispers died to silence as jurors filed back. One exchanged a glance with another before the foreman rose. Edward leaned forward, a whisper dying on his tongue.

"We find the defendants guilty."

The gavel cracked like thunder, and the verdicts were read:

- **Edward Grant** — conspiracy, fraud, abetment to manslaughter, racketeering. *Thirty-five years' imprisonment.*
- **Richard Hawthorne** — conspiracy, breach of duty, fraud. *Twenty years' imprisonment.*
- **Sophia Chan** — aiding, abetting, espionage. *Twelve years' imprisonment.*

Edward's jaw stiffened, but he blinked—the first crack of fear. Richard sagged, shoulders hunched, boardroom swagger gone. He covered his face with one hand, as though hiding his senescence; the sentence had aged him years. Sophia turned, mascara streaked, eyes darting across the gallery as if Maria might meet her gaze. Maria did not. Sophia's lips moved soundlessly—*I didn't mean to*—before the guards lifted her to her feet and led her away. The press gallery erupted in a rustle of pens and clicking cameras, reporters whispering into recorders, already broadcasting AlphaCorp's reckoning to the world. By morning, headlines screamed across financial dailies, AlphaCorp's stock jolted on the exchange, and regulators issued terse statements promising deeper scrutiny.

Maria's Relief

The cold London air slapped Maria as she stepped onto the courthouse steps. Reporters shouted, flashbulbs burst, but the noise blurred into static. She looked up at the sky, at the rain pulling back, admitting a brittle shard of sun. For the first time in months, she felt she could breathe easy.

The faces of Rajesh and Abhishek lingered. Two men gone, two families broken, children left with questions no verdict could answer. Maria drew a breath, shoulders squaring. Justice had been served, but the cost would never be repaid. In that moment, she vowed AlphaCorp's transformation would honor them—it would never erase the pain, but it could assure that no life, no family, would ever again be collateral in the name of company progress.

CHAPTER 46

A Clear Sky

AlphaCorp Boardroom — One Week After the Verdict

Sunlight streamed through the glass, warm and steady, as if London itself had decided to offer a truce. The board table gleamed under the recessed lights; nameplates made a perfect arc, before faces that looked older than they had a month ago—and lighter.

Mikhail cleared his throat. "We've taken the hit. We've learned what we had to learn the hard way. Governance tightens. Controls reset. But let's be clear—" he glanced around the table, landing on Maria— "the worst is behind us."

A murmur of assent moved around the room. Maria felt her shoulders loosen a fraction. Across from her, Nathan sat with his hands folded, ready, unhurried. Daniel leaned back, the hint of a smile sitting comfortably on his face, like a man who had finally put down a heavy bag. Aldo twirled a pen and smirked at nothing in particular—eyes alive with the mischief of a new idea. Susan's notes were already in a neat grid, a line drawn down the center—Left: risks. Right: mitigations.

Jill spoke next. "We will institute quarterly deep dives on tax control monitoring as standard operating rhythm." A beat. "And we will stop outsourcing our conscience."

Dry laughter rippled. It wasn't cynical—it was relief.

Mikhail turned a page. "One more thing." He set the paper flat and looked at each person, one by one. "We proceed with the annual townhall. To celebrate the people who carried us—to honor the ones we lost and the ones who stood. AlphaCorp will not hide."

Silence, then the soft percussion of knuckles on wood—board members tapping in agreement. It was almost a clap.

Nathan spoke without theatrics. "Give me three minutes at the townhall to thank the floor teams."

"You'll have five," Mikhail said. "Take them."

Daniel tipped his chin toward Maria. "If this is the last board I sit through at AlphaCorp, I'll go happy." He exhaled, a satisfied draw. "We turned a house of cards into a foundation."

Maria smiled. "You're really hanging your boots?"

"Maybe not today," he said. "But soon. And with no unfinished business."

Aldo leaned across, conspiratorial. "Before he vanishes, can I pitch something indecent? Tax technology, but not like the vendors do it. Human-first, data-forward. Think of it as—" he drew a tiny rectangle on his pad— "the **Orchestra**. One score, many instruments. API-native, audit-persistent, plug-and-play."

Susan snorted, delighted. "You had the name ready."

"Had it since Guangzhou," Aldo said. "I was just waiting for permission to dream out loud." He angled at Maria. "Friends-and-family discount for AlphaCorp."

Maria raised an eyebrow. "I'll take equity instead."

Laughter, this time unguarded.

Mikhail closed the folder. "Maria, you'll lead the townhall. We'll stand behind you. Say what needs saying."

She nodded, feeling the shape of the words already forming. "I will."

The Floor — What Changed and Who Changed

In the days that followed, the building felt different. Desks were the same, but conversations had changed; the fear had drained out of them.

Nathan kept his promise to walk the floor. "We're not here to replace humans," he'd told the teams from the start. "We're here to restore them to roles that matter." He didn't say it for effect; he said it like a rule that would be enforced.

He started with a map —an actual wall map that showed where time had been returned to people: purchasing clerks no longer copy-pasting line items, tax reviewers no longer re-keying approvals at midnight, SSC analysts no longer reconciling phantom mismatches. Each pin on the map wasn't just hours saved; it was a person's evening back.

One night-shift SSC analyst stopped Nathan by the elevator. "Sir, last year I missed my daughter's school play because of month-end. This time, I didn't. Thank you."

Nathan only nodded, but Maria heard about it the next morning, and it stayed with her longer than any KPI.

"We must invest the time we've returned?" Nathan nudged HR and the functional heads.

That's how the Master Data Management Team was born.

Ganesh Pillai, steady as ever, stood over a whiteboard sketching the taxonomy of a product hierarchy like a cartographer. Next to him, a few familiar faces from tax processing and invoice review—people who used to live inside spreadsheets—leaned in, asking the kind of questions that made Nathan's eyebrows lift.

Maria stopped by with two paper cups of tea. "Promotion by stealth, Mr. Pillai?"

Ganesh looked sheepish. "I thought I was on my way out," he confessed. "Turns out I was just getting started."

"You weren't on your way out," Maria said. "You were on your way *up*."

They were handed manuals and immersed in the logic. Configuration walkthroughs, sandbox drills, post-mortems that showed how one bad master-data field could choke an entire return. They memorized rules; they understood cause and effect. The team began to treat master data like an instrument that had to be tuned, not a bin that had to be filled.

Across the hall, glass panels stenciled with a new sign: **Data Analytics CoE — North Wing**.

Inside, a first-week ritual had formed. A domain expert would pair with a data analyst to walk a dataset like a crime scene—to admire the numbers, and to ask them questions.

Farzana, a former tax compliance associate with an eye for patterns, shifted a dashboard filter. "Stop looking at the month view," she told the analysts. "Refunds don't brag in months. They whisper in days."

The lead analyst frowned, then followed. The scatter tightened. Three jurisdictions lit up with odd refund velocity.

"Pricing will need a nudge," Farzana said softly. "If we catch it now, it's an email, two months down, it will be an escalation."

Later the analyst admitted to Maria in the corridor, half-amused, half-awed, "We've been looking at this data for months. We didn't know what to look for."

Walls were now perforated at AlphaCorp. People started speaking in shared dialect—tax asking for feature flags, analytics using the words 'tax point' without flinching, procurement asking to see the HS code dictionary before a vendor onboarding. The work got intelligible.

Audit, Evolved

Internal Audit had always kept a respectful distance from tax—like visiting a temple where you removed your shoes and stayed near the door. When Nathan proposed a dedicated **Tax Internal Audit Team**, the first reaction was honest skepticism.

"Tax audits are... precise," IA's head said, weighing the word *precise* like a scalpel.

Nathan nodded. "Which is why we borrow tax brains and teach them audit muscle." He slid a sketch across the table: a risk-based audit plan mapped to country footprint, sensitivity scores, and each tax authority's appetite for surprise. "We're extending your reach."

To IA's credit, they leaned in. They trained the new team in audit planning and documentation. They co-authored an assurance template that actually read like English. They committed to sponsor risk tracking at the committee level.

By the end of the quarter, the tax auditors logged three early warnings:

- A mismatch between invoice issue dates and tax point logic in a Central European market.
- An outdated exemption list still haunting a medical procurement catalog.
- An overstatement of VAT credit—subtle, systemic—triggered by a mapping edge case inside the return.

None were critical yet. All could have become so.

The Audit Committee's report added a new line item:

Tax Control Monitoring — Internal Insights

For the first time in years, it was written by AlphaCorp's own.

A short note from the regulator circulated that week too: *"Initial confidence restored. Monitoring ongoing."* The markets steadied by Friday's close.

Nathan and Daniel took their coffee to the windowsill just outside the meeting.

"We've not just fixed how tax works," Nathan said, watching the cranes shoulder the sky. "We've fixed how it's kept in check."

Daniel let the cup warm his hands. A satisfied smile. "Now that is what sustainability looks like."

Four Voices

On a slow Friday evening, they found themselves together in a project room that had survived three leadership teams and two paint colors. Someone had taped a printout above the whiteboard: *Outcome > Optics.*

Susan closed her laptop. "For the first time, tax doesn't feel like a back office. We're in the heartbeat."

Aldo chuckled. "Careful. That's how startups happen."

"Speaking of which," Maria said, glancing at him.

Aldo lifted his hands. "Only a gentleman's rumor. But yes, I think I finally know what I'm building next. Orchestra isn't vapor anymore. The prototype goes into demo next year." He grinned. "And for the record, Orchestra will not replace people. It will make them unignorable."

Nathan arched an eyebrow. "Make sure your investors understand that sentence."

"They will," Aldo said. "I'll make them sit in on a tax close."

Daniel watched them with the fondness of a teacher letting the class run. "If I disappear after the townhall, assume I'm somewhere quiet, fishing for bad metaphors." He looked at Maria. "You've got this."

Maria met his gaze. "I won't let it slip." She felt the line before she spoke it, the promise annealing into resolve. "Not after what it cost."

They were quiet for a breath. In that silence sat two names, unspoken and present.

Preparing for the Townhall

On Sunday, Maria sat at her dining table with a mug of ginger tea and a blank slide. The cursor blinked like a metronome. She typed the title:

AlphaCorp Annual Leadership Summit — 25 October 2025.

Her fingers hovered, then moved.

AlphaCorp's tax transformation wasn't built overnight. But when it started working, it didn't stop.

She read it once, then again, and felt the chord resonate. She added one more line beneath it:

We didn't roll out tools. We rolled out trust.

She saved the deck and shut the laptop. The room was quiet . . . quiet that was charged with potential.

Outside, the city lights stitched together into a patient constellation. Tomorrow, she would stand in front of AlphaCorp — with a proud invitation.

CHAPTER 47

Extinction of Tax as We Knew It

The morning sun spilled across London like a benediction. The Thames caught the light and scattered it in a thousand fragments. The glitter was shattering but beautiful: a reminder to AlphaCorp that rebirth had come at a cost—and was worth every scar.

Inside the headquarters, the summit hall throbbed with expectancy. Executives, analysts, and partners leaned into conversations, laughter tumbling out of them like people outdoors, free after a long winter. No one said it aloud, but every heartbeat carried the same thought: *We made it.*

Maria Mehta stood backstage, hands lightly pressed to the podium edge, eyes closed. The murmur of the hall was a tide she allowed to wash over her. In the quiet of her mind, other voices flickered—Rajesh's warm laughter, Abhishek's quiet certainty, Nathan's unshakeable steadiness, Susan's meticulous notes, Daniel's low warnings that had steered her through fog. Even Sophia's silhouette drifted past her memory as part of the mosaic that had brought them all here.

And in the farthest corner of her mind, darker shadows lingered. Richard's cold ambition. Edward's arrogance and greed. Their downfall was complete, their convictions etched into the legal record. Yet the specter of what *might* have been—if they had won—remained a silent warning.

The spotlight struck. The room rose to its feet in unison. The air had changed.

Maria stepped forward, her heels striking the stage with a rhythm that silenced the hall.

Her first words were not loud, but they carried like a prayer. "Seventeen months ago, we stood at the edge of collapse. Our data was broken. Our trust fractured. Our people divided."

She let the silence breathe. Faces leaned closer.

"Today," her voice rose, strong, unshaken, "we are not the same company. We are not even the same people. We chose transformation before it chose us. We chose courage over comfort, design over drift, belief over fear. That choice has given birth to something extraordinary."

She gestured gently to the room. "Tax was our beginning—but it became our blueprint. The discipline of compliance became the architecture of trust. The rigor of reconciliation became the rhythm of every shared service. What started as a burden became our backbone."

Her throat caught, but she steadied herself. "Some of us are not here to see this day. Rajesh—your sacrifice still echoes. Abhishek—you showed us what orchestration meant. We carry you with love and pride, with us."

A ripple moved through the audience. Heads bowed. Eyes glistened.

Maria lifted her chin, the steel in her gaze softened by gratitude. "And to those who stand among us—Nathan, who built not just systems but belief. Susan, who taught us that precision is not the enemy of humanity. Aldo, whose vision will light futures we haven't yet imagined. And yes, Daniel, who reminded us that leadership is not volume, but gravity. We honour you all."

The applause swelled, but Maria raised her hand and the hall hushed again.

"This, my friends, is the extinction of tax as we knew it. Not an ending, but a dawn. We have proven that technology without humanity is hollow, and that humanity without structure falters. But together—vision, governance, data, leadership—we have written a new language for business itself."

She stepped closer to the edge of the stage, her tone gathering momentum. "We've reduced our tax operational costs by nearly a third. We've built an infrastructure that makes global compliance virtually effortless. Our procure-to-pay and order-to-cash processes—once fragmented and painful—are now faster, cleaner, and more consistent than ever. Shared services run with a rhythm that feels almost orchestral. Finance closes in days, not weeks. And these results came not from making people redundant, only their roles."

She paused, eyes shining as she looked across the hall. "Jobs weren't lost. They were reborn. Compliance officers became auditors. Report preparers became risk analysts. Tax leads became business partners. Each of you proved that transformation is not a threat—it is an opportunity to redefine purpose."

The energy in the room rose like a tide. Maria let it build, then continued. "Tomorrow's tax leaders will not just manage rules—they will shape them. They will leverage technology to comply but also to propel businesses forward. The transformation we've achieved here at AlphaCorp isn't the end—it's the foundation. Nathan and the team have already crafted plans for an AI-enabled Finance and Tax function that will see further efficiencies of fifty to sixty percent. Imagine that—freeing resources not to do more of the same, but to innovate, to lead, to create."

Her voice trembled now, but she did not hide it. "AlphaCorp, you are no longer survivors. You are pioneers. And the world is watching. Our story does not end. It just begins here. The best is yet to come."

For a heartbeat, silence. Then—an eruption. Applause thundered against the glass walls, people on their feet, some with tears, others with fists raised high.

Maria stepped back, a single tear sliding unchecked down her cheek. She let it fall. For once, she did not hide. The hall's ovation became one unbroken roar. And as Maria turned her face toward the light, the future waited, wide open.

# ACKNOWLEDGEMENTS

No journey is ever undertaken alone. The creation of this book—and the experiences and insights that shaped it—would not have been possible without the guidance, inspiration, and support of the incredible individuals I have been fortunate to meet along the way.

This book would not have been possible without the patient acceptance and support of my wife Jyotika and my children Ananya and Viaan who tolerated my incessant disappearances in the evenings and on weekends writing this book in my home office over the past year.

I wish to extend my heartfelt gratitude to the leaders and mentors who have significantly influenced my professional and personal growth. I also wish to acknowledge my brilliant colleagues, peers, and friends with whom I have had the privilege to work throughout my career. Each of you has contributed to my learning and growth, and for that, I am deeply grateful.

My sincere appreciation to my editor, Ann Klefstad, whose thoughtful comments, incisive questions, and careful editorial guidance strengthened this manuscript and helped refine its voice. Your craft and clarity were invaluable in shaping the final form of this book.

I would also like to thank Thomas Baker, Editor, International Tax Review (ITR) for taking time to endorse the ideas in Extinction of Tax as We Know It.

Lastly, to the beta readers of this book, who have engaged with me on this journey - your perspectives, feedback, and encouragement have enriched this work immeasurably: Satish Karnam, Justin Whitehouse, Rashmi Kapoor, Sampada Borkar, Rohit Johnson, Dakshita Mishra, Kamran Tork, Ritesh Shah and Richard Davis.

This book is as much a reflection of my experiences as it is a tribute to all those who have walked alongside me on this path.

With heartfelt gratitude,
Nitin Agarwal

ABOUT THE AUTHOR

Nitin Agarwal is a Chartered Accountant from the Institute of Chartered Accountants of India, an INSEAD alumnus and ADIT-qualified transformation leader with roots in India's enchanting northeastern state-Assam. Now based in Dubai, he is known for simplifying complexity through narrative. A keen observer and learner, he has successfully led large, multifaceted transformation programs across regions.

www.ingramcontent.com/pod-product-compliance
Lightning Source LLC
Chambersburg PA
CBHW031336230926
51848CB00002B/265

* 9 7 8 9 3 3 4 4 2 8 7 4 2 *